Religious Architecture in the Czech Republic in the Light of Geophysical Prospection and Archaeological Excavation

Vladimír Hašek
Josef Unger

BAR International Series 2128
2010

Published in 2016 by
BAR Publishing, Oxford

BAR International Series 2128

Religious Architecture in the Czech Republic in the Light of Geophysical Prospection and Archaeological Excavation

ISBN 978 1 4073 0669 8

© The authors individually and the Publisher 2010

The authors' moral rights under the 1988 UK Copyright,
Designs and Patents Act are hereby expressly asserted.

All rights reserved. No part of this work may be copied, reproduced, stored,
sold, distributed, scanned, saved in any form of digital format or transmitted
in any form digitally, without the written permission of the Publisher.

BAR Publishing is the trading name of British Archaeological Reports (Oxford) Ltd.
British Archaeological Reports was first incorporated in 1974 to publish the BAR
Series, International and British. In 1992 Hadrian Books Ltd became part of the BAR
group. This volume was originally published by Archaeopress in conjunction with
British Archaeological Reports (Oxford) Ltd / Hadrian Books Ltd, the Series principal
publisher, in 2010. This present volume is published by BAR Publishing, 2016.

Printed in England

BAR titles are available from:

	BAR Publishing
	122 Banbury Rd, Oxford, OX2 7BP, UK
EMAIL	info@barpublishing.com
PHONE	+44 (0)1865 310431
FAX	+44 (0)1865 316916
	www.barpublishing.com

TABLE OF CONTENTS

1. INTRODUCTION 1

2. BASIC CHARACTERISTIC FEATURES OF RELIGIOUS BUILDINGS FROM THE 9TH UNTIL THE 18TH CENTURY IN BOHEMIA AND MORAVIA 3

    2.1. Burial Rite in Religious Architecture 6

3. GEOPHYSICAL RESEARCH 7

    3.1. Historical Survey of Applying Geophysical Methods in Prospection of Religious Buildings 7

    3.2. Methodology of the Field Works 9

    3.3. Other Non-destructive Methods of Prospection 12

4. DISCUSSION OF PRACTICAL RESULTS AND OBSERVATIONS 13

    4.1. Church Buildings from the 11th to 12th Century 13

    4.2. Church Buildings from the 13 to 15th Century 16

        4.2.1. Village Parish Churches 16

        4.2.2. City Parish Churches 29

        4.2.3. Monasteries 41

            4.2.3.1 The Benedictines 42

            4.2.3.2 The Cistercians 45

            4.2.3.3. Premonstratensians 53

            4.2.3.4. Augustinians 60

    4.3. Church Buildings from the 16th – 18th Century 65

        4.3.1. Village Parish Churches and Chapels 65

    4.4. Jewish Monuments Connected With Religion 78

5. CONCLUSION 87

REFERENCES 88

LIST OF PHOTOS

Photo 1. Veveří by Veverská Bítýška: The Late Romanesque Chapel of Assumption of the Virgin, view from the northeast 7

Photo 2. Brno – Královo Pole: The veduta of the Carthusian monastery area with a picture of the Chapel of St. Vitus 9

Photo 3. Terrain measuring by the DEMP method. Multifrequency conductometer GEM-3 of the firm GEOPHEX (USA) 11

Photo 4. Preparation of the apparatus RAMAC/GPR X3M GEOSCIENCE MALA´ for terrain measuring outside of the sacral building 11

Photo 5. Radar measuring in the church interior by the apparatus RAMAC/GPR X 3M GEOSCIENCE MALA´ (Sweden) 12

Photo 6. Proving pedological holes – rig LSS-25 12

Photo 7. Camera research of the tomb 12

Photo 8. Znojmo, the Rotunda of St. Catherine: Overall view of the building from the southwest 13

Photo 9. Olomouc: Drawn reconstruction of the church area by the St. Wenceslas Cathedral in the 12th century 15

Photo 10. Nebovidy, the Church of St. Cross: View from the northwest 16

Photo 11. Nebovidy, the Church of St. Cross: View of the interior from the east 16

Photo 12. Topanov, c.d. Rybníky, the Chapel of St. Margaret: View from the southeast 18

Photo 13. Topanov, c.d. Rybníky, the Chapel of St. Margaret: The original Topanov church before 1859 18

Photo 14. Bohušov, the Church of St. Martin: General view from the west 20

Photo 15. Bohušov, the Church of St. Martin: Tombstones in situ and uncovered tomb 21

Photo 16. Kurdějov, the Church of St. John the Baptist: View from the south 21

Photo 17. Přepychy, the Church of St. Prokop: View from the south 24

Photo 18. Přepychy, the Church of St. Prokop: View of the interior with the place of the tomb 24

Photo 19. Tasov by Velké Meziříčí, the Church of St. George: General view of the present parsonage 26

Photo 20. Tasov by Velké Meziříčí, the Church of St. George: Relic of the rotunda masonry at the west side of the building detected by research 28

Photo 21. Tasov by Velké Meziříčí, the Church of St. George: Uncovered graves
in the area of the former Church of St. George 28

Photo 22. Tasov, the Church of St. Peter and Paul: Aerial photograph.
View from the north 28

Photo 23. Hustopeče, the Chuch of St. Wenceslas: New church building
in the place of the original one 30

Photo 24. Olomouc, the Church of St. Moritz: General view from the southeast 31

Photo 25. Český Krumlov, the Church of St. Vitus: View from the southwest 33

Photo 26. Český Krumlov, the Church of St. Vitus: Interior from the west 34

Photo 27. Český Krumlov, the Church of St. Vitus: Tomb of Eleonora Amalia
of Schwarzenberg, photograph from an exploratory borehole 36

Photo 28. Český Krumlov, the Church of St. Vitus: Coffin of Eleonora Amalia
of Schwarzenberg, photograph from an exploratory borehole 36

Photo 29. Uherský Brod, the Church of Master John Huss: Situation of
the reconstructed church building from 1920 from the southwest 38

Photo 30. Uherský Brod, the Church of Master John Huss:
Grave from the 13th century 38

Photo 31. Uherský Brod, the Church of Master John Huss:
Uncovering of the brick tomb from the 17th century 38

Photo 32. Uherský Brod, the Church of Master John Huss: Tomb of Jan Trchalík 39

Photo 33. Olomouc, the Cathedral of St. Wenceslas: View from the southwest 39

Photo 34. Olomouc, the Cathedral of St. Wenceslas: Church interior
with positions of entrances into tombs from the west 39

Photo 35. Třebíč, the Basilica of St. Prokop: View from the southwest 42

Photo 36. Třebíč, the Basilica of St. Prokop: Church interior from the west 42

Photo 37. Třebíč, the Basilica of St. Prokop: the Romanesque-Gothic crypt 42

Photo 38. Předklášteří, the convent of Porta Coeli with the Church
of the Assumption of the Virgin: The area from the west 46

Photo 39. Předklášteří, the convent of Porta Coeli, the Chapel of St. Catherine:
View of the archaeological research 49

Photo 40. Vyšší Brod, the convent with the Church of the Assumprion
of the Virgin Mary: The area of the convent from the north 49

Photo 41. Vyšší Brod, the conventual Church of the Assumption of the Virgin Mary:
Church interior from the west 49

Photo 42. Vyšší Brod, the conventual Church of the Assumtion of the Virgin Mary:
Relief tombstone of John, Count of Zrin 53

Photo 43. Znojmo-Louka, the Church of Virgin Mary and St. Wenceslas 53

Photo 44. Znojmo-Louka, the Church of Virgin Mary and St. Wenceslas:
Character of floor sagging in the crypt 55

Photo 45. Želiv, the monastic Church of Birth of the Virgin: View from the west 56

Photo 46. Želiv, the monastic Church of Birth of the Virgin: Church interior 56

Photo 47. Želiv, the monastic Church of Birth of the Virgin: 3D model
of the monastic church with plotting of the tombs 57

Photo 48. Želiv, the monastic Church of Birth of the Virgin: The tomb of abbots 57

Photo 49. Želiv, the monastic Church of Birth of the Virgin:
The tomb of the brethern from the east 59

Photo 50. Želiv, the monastic Church of Birth of the Virgin:
Decomposed painted coffin in the tomb of the brethren 59

Photo 51. Brno, monastic Church of St. Thomas: General view from the southwest 60

Photo 52. Brno, the monastic Church of St. Thomas:
Uncovered tomb of Margrave Jost 62

Photo 53. Šternberk, the monastic Church of the Annunciation:
View of the front from the west 62

Photo 54. Šternberk, the monastic Church of the Annunciation: Tin box
with remains of an andult man – perhaps Albert II of Šternberk 65

Photo 55. Doubravník, the Church of Finding of the Holy Cross:
View from the southwest 65

Photo 56. Šumice, the new Church of Birth of the Virgin:
View from the southwest 67

Photo 57. Uherské Hradiště, the Chapel of St. Roch: View from the west 69

Photo 58. Uherské Hradiště, the Chapel of St. Roch:
Aerial photograph of the archeology excavation 71

Photo 59. Uherské Hradiště, the Chapel of St. Roch:
3D model of the archaeology excavation 72

Photo 60. Blansko, the Church of St. Martin: View from the south 72

Photo 61. Blansko, the Church of St. Martin: Interior from the West 74

Photo 62. Blansko, the Church of St. Martin: Test pit in the northwest part
with uncovered wall 74

Photo 63. Brno, the Church of St. Joseph: Vew from the west 75

Photo 64. Uherské Hradiště, the Church of St. Francis Xavier:
View from the west 76

Photo 65. Uherské Hradiště, the Church of St. Francis Xavier: Barrel Vault
of the west wing of the tomb, vaults and chambers on the left 78

Photo 66. Uherské Hradiště, the Church of St. Francis Xavier: View of
the northwest corner of the tomb C. Positions of the skeletons
and remains of coffins after lowering of the flood waters 78

Photo 67. Jihlava: The studied area of the extinct synagogue
near the city fortifications 78

Photo 68. Jihlava: The building of the synagogue in 1920 78

Photo 69. Tábor: The studied area of the extinct synagogue
in the area of the lower car park 82

Photo 70. Tábor: The south side of the Tábor synagogue according
to the planned documentation of J.V. Staněk from 1883 82

Photo 71. Tábor: The west side of the Tábor synagogue according
to the planned documentation of J.V. Staněk from 1883 82

Photo 72. Tábor: Foundation walling of the extinct synagogue
in probes I-III and VIII-X. View from the northeast 86

Photo 73. Tábor: Detailed view of the extinct synagogue masonry relics 86

LIST OF FIGURES

Fig. 1. Religious buildings of the Czech Republic investigated
by geophysical prospection in various stages of these works
and realized archaeology excavation 5

Fig. 2. Prague, the Church of the Holiest Trinity: Map of Bouguer isanomals
with added gravitational effects of the masonry and the ground plan
of the uncovered crypt 8

Fig. 3. Křtiny, the Church of Virgin Mary: Situation of geophysical profiles and
interpretation profiles A- A´, B-B´ in the place of the main tomb and
of smaller objects 8

Fig. 4. Brno-Královo Pole, the Chapel of St. Vitus: Ground plan of the localized
extinct church building from the GPR method and an example of interpreted
radarogram 10

Fig. 5. Znojmo, the Rotunda of St. Catherine: Correlation scheme of results
of geophysical works from microgravimetry and the GPR (a, b), interpreted
radarogram (C) in places of identified inhomogeneities E, A (A3) and C 14

Fig. 6. Nebovidy, the Church of St. Cross: Correlation scheme of results
of geophysical works (a), one of possible variants of interpretation
of the prospection (b) and an example of interpreted radarograms
in the W-E (c) and N-S direction (d) 17

Fig. 7. Topanov, c.d. of Rybníky, the Chapel of St. Margaret: Correlation scheme of
geophysical works (a) and interpretation of results of measuring (b) 19

Fig. 8. Bohušov, the Church of St. Martin: Correlation scheme of results
of geophysical works (a), interpretation of the measured data (b),
manifestation of tombs by the southern outer walling of the church
from the GPR (c), tombs under the triumphal arch in the nave (d) 21

Fig. 9. Kurdějov, the Church of St. John the Baptist: Map of isolines σ_{app} according
to the DEMP and their comparison with the course of the underground corridor 23

Fig. 10. Přepychy, the Church of St. Prokop: Correlation scheme of results
of geophysical works with course of the interpreted and partly verified
underground corridors 25

Fig. 11. Tasov by Velké Meziříčí, the Church of St. George: Ground plan situational
scheme of the results of prospection and excavation 27

Fig. 12. Tasov by Velké Meziříčí, the Church of St. Peter and Paul:
Correlation scheme of the results of the GPR measuring (a), interpretation
of prospection results (b), manifestation of a tomb in the radarogram
in the proximity of the altar (c), inhomogeneities (tombs, graves,
accumulations of stones) under the triumphal arch (d) 29

Fig. 13. Hustopeče, the Church of St. Wenceslas: Comparison of results
of geophysical measuring with the situation of the church. A- VDV-R method;
B- DEMP method 30

Fig. 14. Olomouc, the Church of St. Moritz. Correlation scheme
of the GPR prospection results (a), interpretation of the measured data (b),
manifestation of crypts and tombs in the east part of the church (c, d) 32

Fig. 15. Český Krumlov, the Church of st. Vitus: Correlation scheme of results of
geophysical works (a), one of possible variants of interpretation of the measured
data (b), manifestation of tombs of Eleonora Amalia of Schwarzenberg (A)
in the interpreted radarogram (c), so far unknown tombs (C) under the triumphal
arch (d) and the tomb of the Ronenbergs (B) in the radarogram (e) 35

Fig. 16. Uherský Brod, the Church of Master John Huss: Correlation scheme
of the results of the GPR measuring (a), interpreted manifestation
of the near-surface inhomogeneities (b), presentation of tombs
and other structural elements in processed radarograms (c, d, e) 37

Fig. 17. Olomouc, the Cathedral of St. Wenceslas: Correlation scheme of results
of the GPR method from 2003-2007 (a), interpretation of the measured data
and section of the current objects in the east part of the cathedral (b),
manifestation of the filled-up Romanesque crypt of St. Adalbert (c),
presentation of modern tombs under the presbytery (d), modern tomb
in the main nave (e) 40

Fig. 18. Třebíč, the Basilica of St. Prokop: Correlation scheme of results of the GPR
measuring (a), one of possible variants of inhomogeneities interpretation in
the church area (b) and manifestation of crypt in the interpreted radarogram (c) 43

Fig. 19. Třebíč, the Basilica of St. Prokop- the crypt: Correlation scheme of results
of the GPR measuring (a), one of possible variants of interpretation of near-
surface inhomogeneities (b) and manifestation of indications
of various structures in the processed radarogram (c) 44

Fig. 20. Předklášteří, the Church of the Assumption of the Virgin Mary:
Correlation scheme of results of the geophysical works (a), interpreted
areal inhomogeneities in the building interior (b), manifestation
of tombs in the main nave axis (c) and the space of the tomb
in the northeast part of the main nave (d) 47

Fig. 21. Předklášteří, the Church of the Assumption of the Virgin Mary:
3D presentation of areal inhomogeneities – tombs, graves in the area
of the presbytery 48

Fig. 22. Předklášteří, the Chapel of St. Catherine: map of ρ_{app} isolines
and ground plan of the uncovered building 48

Fig. 23. Vyšší Brod, the Cistercian convent: Correlation scheme of the GPR
measuring results, interpreted radarogram from the presbytery area
of the Church of the Assumption of the Virgin Mary – indication
of the tomb A (a), from the transept – indication of the tomb E (b),
from the south side nave – tomb C (c), from the capitular hall – indication
of the grave G (d) and from the north-south cloister – graves D, L (e) 50

Fig. 24. Vyšší Brod, the Cistercian convent: One of possible variants
of interpretation of the prospection results 52

Fig. 25. Znojmo-Louka, the Church of the Virgin Mary and St. Wenceslas:
Correlation scheme of results of the geophysical works (a), interpretation
of inhomogeneities in the church interior (b) and in the crypt interior (c).
Presentation of a crypt in the radarograms (d) and smaller tombs
in the side northwest chapel (e) and in the crypt (f) 54

Fig. 26. Želiv, the Church of the Birth of the Virgin: Correlation scheme of the radar
measuring results (a), one of the variants of geophysical interpretation (b) and
manifestations of tombs and graves (B, C, E, G, H) in radarograms (c, d, e) 58

Fig. 27. Želiv, the Church of the Birth of the Virgin: Positions of the localized tombs 59

Fig. 28. Brno, the Church of St. Thomas: Correlation scheme of results of the geophysical works and interpreted tombs (a), tomb of Margrave Jost in the interpreted radarogram (b), manifestation of the Baroque tombs in the GPR (c), interpreted tomb in the church nave (d) 61

Fig. 29. Šternberk, the Church of the Annunciation: Results of the geophysical prospection and archaeological excavation (a), gauged profile in the north part of the nave and indication of inhomogeneities from the GPR method (b) 63

Fig. 30. Šternberk, the Church of the Annunciation: Map of σ_{app} isolines for $h = 1.5$ m in the area of the Chapel of Virgin Mary the Helper, where a smaller tomb was localized 64

Fig. 31. Doubravník, the Church of Finding of the Holy Cross: Map of ρ_{app}^{anom} isolines in the church area 66

Fig. 32. Doubravník, the Church of Finding of the Holy Cross: Correlation scheme of results of the geophysical works 67

Fig. 33. Šumice, the Church of Birth of the Virgin: Correlation scheme of results of the geophysical works and map of DEMp ρ_{app} isolines for $h = 3-5$ m 68

Fig. 34. Šumice, the Church of Birth of the Virgin: Performed archaeological research in the area of the building 69

Fig. 35. Uherské Hradiště, the Chapel of St. Roch: Correlation scheme of results of GPR measuring with marking of positions of verifying GPR measurings with marking of positions of verifying pedological probes (a), one of possible variants of the prospection interpretation (b) and interpreted radarogram with manifestation of brick masonry relics (c) 70

Fig. 36. Blansko, the Church of St. Martin: Correlation scheme of the results from the GPR method (a), presumed position of the older building (b), image of the newer tomb (c) 73

Fig. 37. Brno, the Church of St. Joseph: Map of DEMP ρ_{app} isolines for $h = 3-5$ m and correlation scheme of results of the geophysical works 75

Fig. 38. Uherské Hradiště, the Church of St. Francis Xavier: Correlation scheme of results of the geophysical works 77

Fig. 39. Uherské Hradiště, the Church of St. Francis Xavier: Interpretation of inhomogeneities from the GPR method, some of which were verified by archaeological excavation. 77

Fig. 40. Jihlava, the synagogue: Correlation scheme of geophysical works (a) and an example of interpreted radarograms with manifestation of identified inhomogeneities (b) 79

Fig. 41. Jihlava, the synagogue: Map of σ_{app} isolines from the DEMP method 80

Fig. 42. Jihlava, the synagogue: Probable situation of the synagogue 81

Fig. 43. Tábor, the synagogue: Correlation scheme of results of the geophysical works (a) and interpretation of radarograms on the profile 10 – 250 MHz antenna 83

Fig. 44. Tábor, the synagogue: generally archaeologically excavated area (probes I-V and VIII-XII) with marking of the most significant objects 84

Fig. 45. Tábor, the synagogue: Results of the geophysical research of the Tábor syenite massif under archaeological probes, in which hollows were discovered in several places (probes III and IV) in otherwise compact firm base 85

1. INTRODUCTION

Archaeology of church monuments is a part of archaeoreligionistics, which is considered a borderline interdisciplinary branch of science, its task being to examine religion on the basis of archaeological, ethnological, historical, scientific or possibly other sources with the use of general laws of religionistics. It illuminates the human religiosity and its changes in the connection with changes in the economic, cultural and social sphere.

The subject of the archaeology of church monuments is study of the church on the basis of material monuments obtained by the methods of archaeological investigation, while the church can be understood as either a religious organization or a community of believers. Therefore not only monuments connected with the clergy are in question, but also those associated with manifestations of Christianity in the lives of people – laymen. The objects of interest are thus not only buildings related with the worship, their equipment etc., but also manifestations of Christianity in the way of burying and dealing with the bodies of the deceased. When studying monuments reflecting religious notions of people, it is necessary to realize that these can be manifested in various ways in archaeological sources. Church buildings are documented quite distinctively, unlike the reflection in the burial rite, which varies in individual periods and sometimes can be difficult to interpret (Unger 2008).

The Christian religious architecture in the Czech Republic is represented by a relatively wide area of monuments within study of history of material civilization. It is primarily a large spectrum of various types of churches, chapels, monastery complexes and smaller cultic shapes from the period since the 9th century until the present. Archaeological and constructionally-historical research of these objects, which are situated in areas of town agglomerations and villages, deals with specifying their general ground plan situation together with determining locations of possible older defunct buildings, also with some problems related with determining static dislocation caused by both geological situation in the area and mechanical behavior of the foundation soils, by ground water surface level etc. (Hašek/Měřínský 1997, 425; Hašek/Peška/Unger 2009). At the present time, localization of tombs and simple graves in interiors of individual buildings has an important place in archaeological investigation on this field. The burial rite, subsequent archaeological research of the skeletal remains and time consequence are being watched (Hašek/Unger 2001, 87), also masonry relics of older pulled down buildings in places of later stages of construction (or reconstruction) of the churches etc.

In order for this task to be solved successfully, nondestructive geophysical methods and geology have been used apart from exposure works, or, in the last years, also camera research is being applied to give a clearer picture or clarify the view of the structure. These methods can, to a large extent, substitute other approaches, which are in most cases both capital and labour intensive and which are often randomly chosen – the aim is to gradually limit these and direct them primarily into the areas chosen by prospecting. Moreover, in interiors of church buildings it is not possible, in most cases, to carry out various excavation and other probing works, unless their general reconstruction is being done.

Brief characteristics of the religious architecture itself, burying in interiors of these objects and development of the applied methodology of geophysical works and also situations and experience which can be helpful for solving problems associated with archaeogeophysical researches and their interpretation are presented through a number of practical examples from various areas of the Czech Republic, time periods and locations from the point of view of the geological situation, or provenance of building materials.

This publication is a result of many years of cooperation of both authors on solving the presented problems. It could not have been written without the support of individual researchers in this field. Among archaeologists and art historians let us mention especially PhDr. J. Bláha, PhDr. L. Konečný, doc. PhDr. J. Kovárník, PhDr. K. Dvořáková, PhDr. J. Pavelčík, CSc., PhDr. J. Peška, PhD., among geophysicists Mgr. J. Tomešek, among geologists RNDr. L. Maštera, CSc. and a number of others. Our thanks belong to all these cooperators. We also thank to L. Švandová for preparing graphic documentation.

2. BASIC CHARACTERISTIC FEATURES OF RELIGIOUS BUILDINGS FROM THE 9TH UNTIL THE 18TH CENTURY IN BOHEMIA AND MORAVIA

Pre-Romanesque Church Buildings (9th – 10th century)

Irish-Scottish missionaries could have worked in Moravia already in the 8th century, however, there is no reliable evidence so far of their staying there. After the end of the Avar Kaganate at the end of the 8th century, missionaries from Salzburg, Passau and Aquileia become interested in the area of Moravia. From this environment a number of churches are known, whose appearance is made clear by archaeological researches and which could have served as models for the oldest Great Moravian churches. As soon as in the 1st half of the 9th century, Christianity was widespread especially in social elites, who built first churches in the areas of their residences. In the 860s, Byzantine mission led by Constantine and Methodius took part in organizing Moravian church and building houses of worship; Methodius even became metropolitan bishop in 880.

After the World War II, a number of churches datable back to the 9th century and connected with centres of power of the Great Moravian Empire were archaeologically uncovered and explored. In view of the fact that the above-grade masonry and mostly also the foundation masonry were taken away already before the research during exploitation of stone, it was necessary to develop a method of studying this type of monuments.

Remains of Great Moravian churches (both churches with longitudinal axis subdivided into presbytery and nave and rotundas on a circular ground plan) managed to be discovered so far in centers of power in the area of Uherské Hradiště, "Valy" in Mikulčice and Pohansko by Břeclav. So far disputable are churches at "Hradisko" by Znojmo, "Hradisko of St. Kliment" by Osvětimany, some buildings at "Valy" in Mikulčice and also in the vicinity of Uherské Hradiště. Only an uncertain note was made about the possibility of the Great Moravian masonry architecture at "Staré Zámky" by Brno – Líšeň. Traces of wooden architecture are so far only very uncertain, although it can be hardly imagined that this material was not used for building the oldest Christian sanctuaries in Moravia.

The oldest Christian churches in Bohemia were built under the influence of the Great Moravian architecture. Prince Bořivoj I. let built a church consecrated to St. Kliment on Levý Hradec and a church consecrated to Virgin Mary at the Prague Castle was built probably between the years 882 and 884. Another church, consecrated to St. Peter, was founded by Prince Spytihněv after 895 at Budeč.

The end of power structures of the Great Moravian Empire at the beginning of the 10th century meant a bad blow also for Christianity in Moravia, there was less burying at cemeteries by churches, which decayed gradually, but in Bohemia, under the government of the Przemyslids, the Christianity kept developing, especially after the Prague bishopric was established in 973.

New churches and monasteries originated at centres of power. Prince Vratislav let built the Church of St. George at the Prague Castle; the first Benedictine convent was later founded by this church, too. Prince St. Wenceslas built a rotunda consecrated to St. Vitus, in whose southern annex he was eventually buried. After the half of the 10th century, a church consecrated to Virgin Mary was built at the Budeč hillfort and several churches stood in Stará Boleslav. In the 10th century, churches stood at Vyšehrad in Prague, Žatec, Libice, Malín and probably also elsewhere. Before the end of the 10th century, Benedictine monasteries were founded in Břevnov and at Ostrov by Davle.

Adjunction of Moravia to the state of the Przemyslids created conditions for church organization connected with new centres of power. Around 1063, bishopric in Moravia with its site in Olomouc was established or reconstituted. Church administration was centered in several large parish churches, e.g. Olomouc, Brno, Znojmo. In the 11th century also sites of three monastic institutions were built which conformed to certain rules. Colonizing monasteries of Benedictines, Cistercians and Premonstratensians, founded by the monarch or the aristocracy, contributed to more even population distribution in their vicinity (Olomouc, Třebíč).

Together with the progress of Christianity, massive development of masonry church architecture is taking place in Bohemia and Moravia. A number of the buildings, however, later failed to serve their intended purpose due to unsuitable space arrangements and therefore some of them were included in new Gothic buildings or only parts of them were kept – peripheral walling of naves etc.

Romanesque Church Buildings (11th – 13th century)

Builders of churches were the ruler, feudal lords and church institutions. Typical simple central Romanesque churches are smaller sanctuaries – rotundas with cylindrical nave and usually one apse, sometimes provided with a lantern and an added cylindrical or prismatic tower. Oblong churches with cylindrical apse or quadratic presbytery can be single-nave or multi-nave.

Single-nave churches with apses or squared presbyteries were at first small and with flat ceilings, without towers. After 1100, this type of smaller castle and village churches becomes more spacious. An apse vaulted with concha and sometimes also a tower by the west front (Újezd u Černé Hory) is connected with a tall, mostly flat-ceiling nave. A tribune is usually built in the western part of the nave. Multi-nave buildings, especially three-nave basilical types with raised main central nave, are usually monastic churches or cathedrals – domes (Olomouc). They usually have a two-towered front and the transept (tranverse nave) of the same height and width as the main nave. The presbytery with the advanced choir in the transept is elevated because a crypt vaulted by crossings is situated underneath (Třebíč, Znojmo, Fig. 1).

Monasteries are independent economic units in this time. Their base is a large church, neighboured on the side by a cloister garth with a well, surrounded by an ambulatory (a cloister) and a building with the capitular hall, dormitory, library, kitchen. Economic buildings, workrooms and a hospital are present, too. Large late Romanesque monastic complexes represent a significant part of medieval religious buildings (Předklášteří, Vyšší Brod, Želiv).

Gothic Cathedrals (13th – 16th Century)

In the 13th century the church organization changed remarkably. Small parishes originated with churches as their centres where baptisms and burials took place. Concentration of a large amount of people in cities made it necessary for parish administrations to establish town monastic institutions. Monks who engaged in spiritual work in cities were chiefly Franciscans (friars minor) and Dominicans. A special form of monastic life were so-called knight orders combining the medieval ideal of monkhood and knighthood. These orders, whose main task was to fight against pagans and take care of pilgrims, had their sites called commendams, with several friars-knights, priests and servants in it. Church institutions gathered voluminous land property, which was an economic base of their activity (spiritual administration, charitable and cultural activity). Some orders, mainly the Cistercians, organized also extensive colonization of so far unoccupied territories. From the end of the 14th century, the property of church institutions aroused envy of especially the poorer aristocracy, who were experiencing great economic troubles. The disintegration of property of the church institutions (secularization) reached its peak in the 1st half of the 15th century in the times of the Hussite Revolution. Restitutions and recovery of the monastic life in some monasteries began as late as during the reign of George of Poděbrady.

The main feature of village parish churches of the 2nd half of the 13th century and the beginning of the 14th century are simple buildings consisting of a presbytery, sometimes still semi-circular or U-shaped, later usually polygonal. The vaulted presbytery was in most cases provided with supporting piers. A rectangular nave with a flat ceiling was continuation of the presbytery. In some cases, the choir was placed between the presbytery and the nave. The sacristy was attached to the presbytery and the tower to the west part of the nave (Brno, Nebovidy, Bohušov, Přepychy).

In the 14th century, efforts were made for a lightsome preaching space in city churches. Basilica is giving way to one-nave hall-like form, which is getting shorter and more compact by leaving out the arcades between the naves. Long cylindrical columns without capitals support the vault. Also presbyteries are shorter and wider and in the last third of the 14th century they form the type with the flat end. From the 14th century the triple-nave halls are roofed by a single pyramid roof culminating with a pinnacle and also position of usually only one tower is in the axis of the front or asymmetrically above the corner or at the side (Hustopeče, Kurdějov).

Monastic way of life developed strongly in the 13th century. Still more notable feudal lords took part in founding monasteries and a number of monastic houses were established in towns as well. The basic scheme of a monastic complex was essentially the same – a church and an adjoining cloister. This scheme was modified depending on the specialization of individual orders. Although a monastery meant usually a whole complex of buildings, some of which served for economical provision of the complex, attention is drawn specifically to the enclosure including the monastic church.

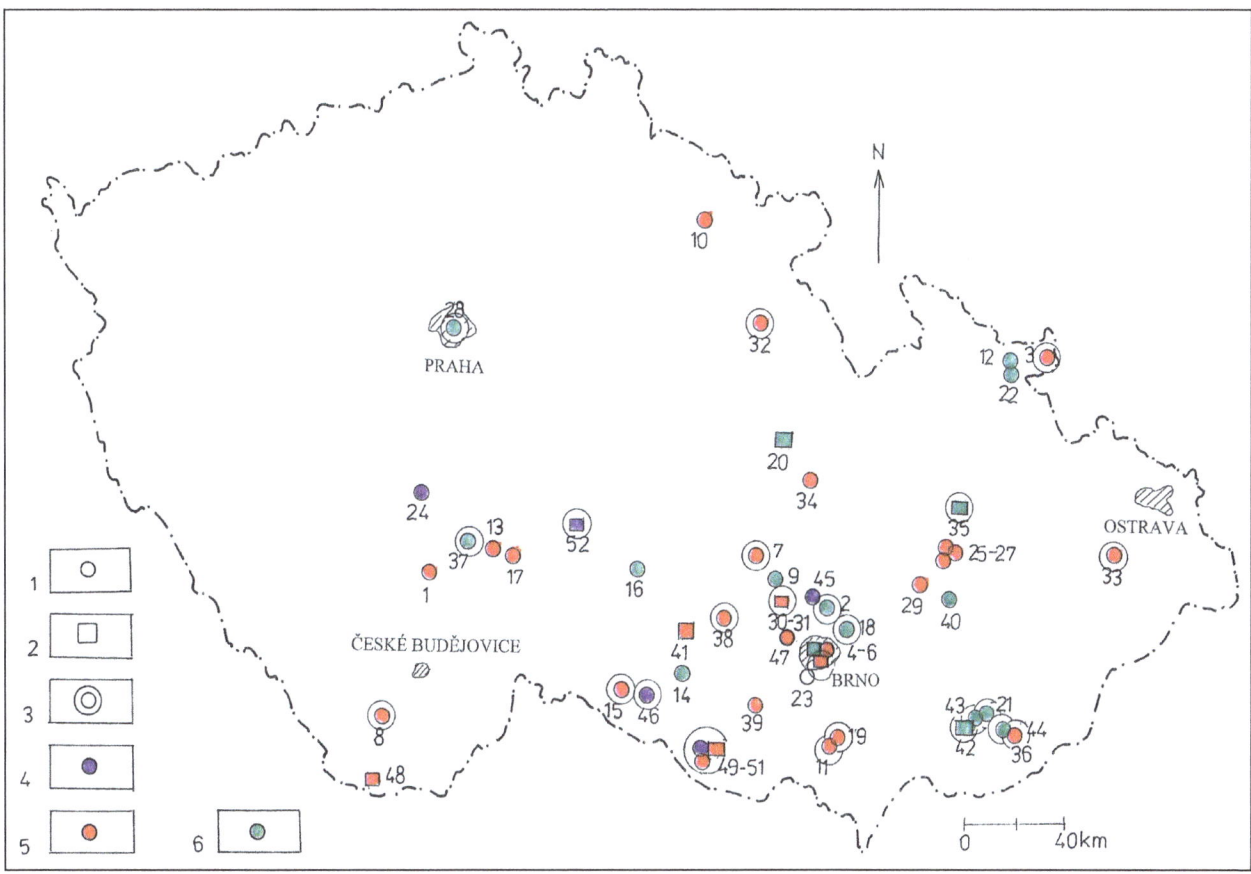

Fig. 1. Religious buildings of the Czech Republic investigated by geophysical prospection in various stages of these works and realized archaeology excavation. Explanatory notes 1 – church, 2 – monastery, 3 – archeology excavation, 4 – Romanesque building, 5 – Gothic building, 6 – modern building. 1-Bechyně, the Church of St. George; 2- Blansko, the Church of St. Martin; 3- Bohušov, the Church of St. Martin; 4, 5, 6- Brno, the Chapel of St. Vitus, Church of St. Thomas and of St. Joseph; 7- Bystřice nad Pernštejnem, the Church of St. Lawrence; 8- Český Krumlov, the Church of St. Vitus; 9- Doubravník, the Church of Finding of the Holy Cross; 10- Hostinné, the Church of the Holiest Trinity; 11– Hustopeče, the Church of St. Wenceslas; 12– Hynčice, the Church of St. Nicholas; 13- Chýnov, the Church of the Holiest Trinity; 14- Jaroměřice nad Rokytnou, the Chapel of St. Catherine; 15- Jemnice, the Church of St. Vitus; 16- Jihlava, the synagogue; 17- Křeč, the Church of St. James the Greater; 18- Křtiny, the Church of Virgin Mary; 19- Kurdějov, the Church of St. John the Baptist; 20- Litomyšl, the Piaristic College; 21- Mařatice, the Church of Assumption of the Virgin Mary; 22- the City of Albrechtice, the Church of the Visitation of the Virgin Mary; 23- Nebovidy, the Church of St. Cross; 24- Obděnice, the Church of the Assumption of the Virgin Mary; 25, 26, 27- Olomouc, the Cathedral of St. Wenceslas, the Church of st. Moritz and of St. Blažej; 28- Prague, the Church of the Holiest Trinity; 29- Prostějov, the Church of the Elevation of the Holy Cross; 30,31- Předklášteří, the Church of the Assumption of the Virgin Mary; the Chapel of St. Catherine; 32- Přepychy, the Church of St. Prokop; 33- Příbor, the Church of Birth of the Virgin; 34- Svitavy, the Church of Visitation of the Virgin Mary; 35- Šternberk, the Church of the Annunciation; 36- Šumice, the Church of Birth of the Virgin; 37- Tábor, the synagogue; 38- Tasov, the Church of St. Peter and Paul, of St. George; 39- Topanov, cadastral district of Rybníky, the Chapel of St. Margaret; 40- Tovačov, the Church of St. Wenceslas; 41- Třebíč, the Basilica of St. Prokop; 42, 43- Uherské Hradiště, the Church of St. Francis Xavier, the Chapel of St. Roch; 44- Uherský Brod, the Church of Master John Huss; 45- Újezd u Černé Hory, the Church of All Saints; 46- Újezd u Jemnice, the rotunda; 47- Veveří u Veverské Bítýšky, the Chapel of Assumption of the Virgin Mary; 48- Vyšší Brod, the Church of the Assumption of the Virgin Mary; 49, 50, 51- Znojmo, the Rotunda of St. Catherine, the Church of St. Nicholas and of St. Wenceslas; 52- Želiv, the Church of Birth of the Virgin

Layout of cathedrals (Olomouc) has a special position among types of churches. In these bishops' churches – domes an ambit with attached chapels is built around the tall choir. The width of the choir corresponds to the main nave and it is complemented by the so-called triforium between the arcades and the windows.

In the 16th and the 17th century, there are less churches being built because the construction activity focused primarily on the secular architecture. There are new cemetery chapels being founded outside the town walls and side tribunes – galleries are being built into the existing churches. Mausoleums of aristocrats are being constructed at cemeteries. New buildings adhere to the Gothic style in the polygonal presbytery, often also with supporting piers (Doubravník). Large unified hall-like rooms with polygonal ending without separated narrower presbytery occur sporadically. Renaissance elements (ellipsis, elongated polygon etc.) appear as late as at the end of the 16th century and were applied primarily in chapels. Larger non-traditional buildings of this time are even indicative of Baroque (Brno).

After the Battle of White Mountain in 1620, emphasis is put on church architecture in connection with recatholization. Churches from the earlier time are baroquized in the 17th and 18th century during necessary reconstructions (Blansko). From the 1340's, church orders, especially the Jesuits, develop building activities. In the 17th century, the type of a Jesuitical church prevails – a one-nave church with lower side chapels and sometimes with transept. The front is usually two-towered and in early times divided into several horizontal layers by distinctive sills (Uherské Hradiště).

The High Baroque creates both longitudinal and central layouts of churches of bent and mostly unified ground plan (Prague, Blansko). Pilgrim churches are either two-towered or with a central layout of the church itself surrounded by ambits with chapels (Křtiny). The chapels are one-naved (Mařatice).

There is still difference between village monasteries and those built in towns, as it was in the Middle Ages. Village monasteries are provided with large economic complexes (Šternberk). Among the town monasteries, Jesuitical colleges stand out for their extensiveness (Uherské Hradiště). (Dvorský 1989; Herout 1961; Chadraba 1984; Krsek 1996; Merhautová/Třeštík 1984).

2.1. BURIAL RITE IN RELIGIOUS ARCHITECTURE

In connection with burials in interiors of churches, it is suitable to address this specific issue in general and somewhat more closely. There are several possibilities how a grave can come to be inside a cathedral. In the first place, when the church had been built on an older burial ground, or when older graves got into the newly interpreted interior during its extension. This is, however, not a burial into the church interior. Another possibility is that the privileged individual was buried into a cathedral already existing or under construction. The endeavor of the church was to reserve the area of the house of God for praying and liturgy but the interest of the privileged classes to be buried inside the cathedral stood against this endeavor. The place for the founder was usually in the axis of the building in front of the altar and the place for other family members including close persons was in the nave. Graves of founders are really found in these places during archaeological excavations in interiors of churches. In some cases, burials in deserted churches were done. Problems with burials of dissenters arose in the 15th century, but primarily in the 16th century. They were refused burials at cemeteries administered by persons of a different religious belief. The dissenters wanted (or were forced) to bury at different places. Former parish churches in extinct villages were apparently suitable for this. It is evident from the above mentioned that there is a number of various possibilities of burials in church interiors and every case needs to be judged and interpreted individually.

At first, burials were done in tombs for one person. Large tombs for more people were not built until the 2nd half of the 14th century. From the 16th century, tombs for more people, "camouflet chambers", were built in cathedrals, the cause being interest of the nobility in family traditions. Entrances into these spaces were covered with slabs with circles enabling their lifting. Since the 17th century connection with newly established Loretan or other chapels appears and the chapels acquire the character of family burial grounds.

The rising economic potential of the bourgeoisie since the 16th century manifests itself in them being buried in churches, where various gravestones, epitaphs and sometimes even specially built chapels of bourgeoisie appear. This way of burying was formerly reserved to the monarch, higher nobility and the church hierarchy.

It was common for clergymen and monks to be buried inside a church. Bishops of the Western Church often used to be buried at pride of place – either in the residential church or in the church of the monastery they were connected with in some way. Monks used both monastic cemeteries and the area of the monastery for burying. Also lay benefactors were buried here, though. From the end of the 15th century larger tombs were built for burying monks in churches. Similarly, the effort of all chapter members since the 15th/16th century was to build a common tomb, as monks did. Superiors of monasteries used to be buried in capitular halls but if the abbot had a special relation to a certain building, his wish could be obeyed and he could be buried outside his own monastery. Also abbesses were entitled to a special burial. Orientation of graves of priests essentially concurred with that of churches and graves of other buried in keeping basically the west-east direction. As late as the 17th century burying of the clergymen in the opposite direction began – so that the faces of the deceased be turned towards the believers even after their death and this way their exceptional position be emphasized. The impulse for this change in the burial rite was Rituale Romanum passed by the Catholic Church in 1614, which however was slow to come into effect.

In the 18th century, the excess demand for burials in churches (which could not be satisfied because of insufficient space capacities) called in some cases (e.g. in Bratislava, the Cathedral of St. Martin) for building underground spaces in the form of wide corridors with niches at sides for placing the coffins, as it had been in the old Christian catacombs.

One phase of burial rite ends with the imperial decrees of the 1780's, ordering burials outside the municipal lands and thus also outside the interiors of the churches, even though exceptions are known up to the present (Unger 2006).

3. GEOPHYSICAL RESEARCH

3.1. HISTORICAL SURVEY OF APPLYING GEOPHYSICAL METHODS IN PROSPECTION OF RELIGIOUS BUILDINGS

The first experimental geophysical works for the purposes of archaeology excavation and static consolidation of a church building in Bohemia took place in Prague, in the Church of the Holiest Trinity in 1979 (Bednář/Novotný/Švancara 1980, 24) and 1983 (Domanský 1983). A distinctive closed gravity anomaly and changes in temperature gradients were detected by microgravimetric and temperature measuring in the western and central part of the building (Fig. 2). Consequent excavation uncovered an extensive crypt near the surface under the church floor. In Moravia, these investigations were made in the beginning of the 1970's in the wider area of the Chapel of the Assumption of the Virgin (Photo 1) near the Veveří Castle near Brno (Bernat/Hašek 1973, 8). The task of detecting expected graves, tombs and other inhomogeneities in the interior of the feature and its vicinity was solved by resistivity profiling, vertical electric sounding, shallow refraction seismics, microgravimetry and drilling works. A number of weakened zones of various origins and near-surface hollows – tombs, which are the probable cause of static dislocation of the studied Late Romanesque building from the beginning of the 13th century, were detected by the measuring.

One of the projects of this type, which can also be marked as experimental action aiming to localize tombs, is microgravimetric research realized in interiors of the Church of St. Wenceslas in Tovačov, district of Přerov, and the Church of Virgin Mary in Křtiny, district of Blansko in 1976 (Bednář/Novotný/Švancara 1980, 23 – 24). Results of the measuring proved the existence of a known tomb and an indication of another, so far unknown structure in the area of the presbytery in the first church, in the second case the measuring specified the location of a larger tomb and localized a hollow southwest of the tomb (Fig. 3). Consequent earth-removing works detected a charnel house with larger amount of skeletal remains. Later complementary DEMP measuring, performed in the

Photo 1. Veveří by Veverská Bítýška: The Late Romanesque Chapel of Assumption of the Virgin, view from the northeast (Photograph by V. Hašek)

main nave of the church, localized a near-surface inhomogeneity of increased specific resistance, which, after research, turned out to be the tomb of the abbot of Zábrdovice monastery Kryštof Matuška (Šebela et al. 1991).

Experimental geophysical measuring aiming to detect foundations of a supposed Romanesque rotunda in the area of the present cemetery was done in the vicinity of the parish church in Velký Újezd by Jemnice in 1980. Geoelectric method SOP with double depth range was used to solve the task; it could however be applied, in view of the presented situation, only on a limited space (Hašek/Měřínský 1991, 164).

It followed from the data obtained that there are distinctive changes in intensities of specific resistivity in the studied area, ranging from 90 to 250 ohms. It is caused probably by the abovementioned anthropogenic activity, maybe also by possible stone masonry relics. The most distinctive zones of high resistivities, which could localize remains of buildings, were proposed for archeolo-

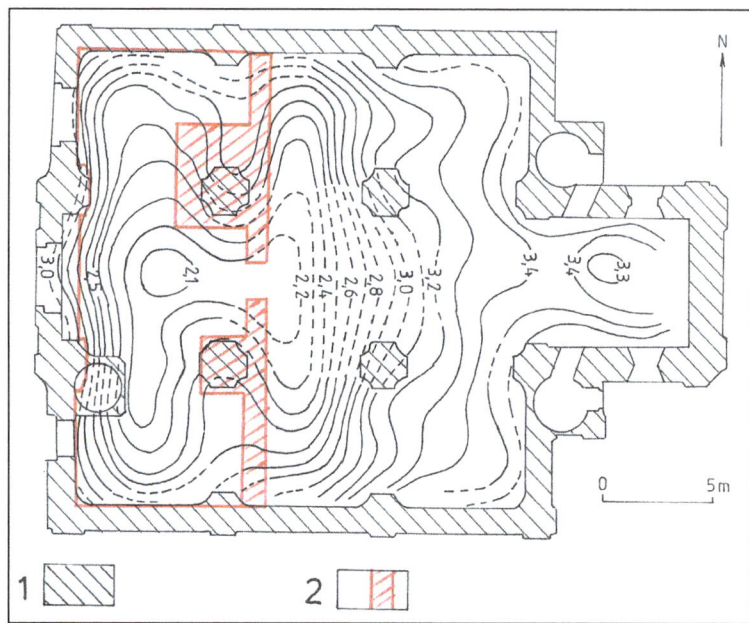

Fig. 2. Prague, the Church of the Holiest Trinity: Map of Bouguer isanomals with added gravitational effects of the masonry and the ground plan of the uncovered crypt (Bednář-Novotný-Švancara 1980)

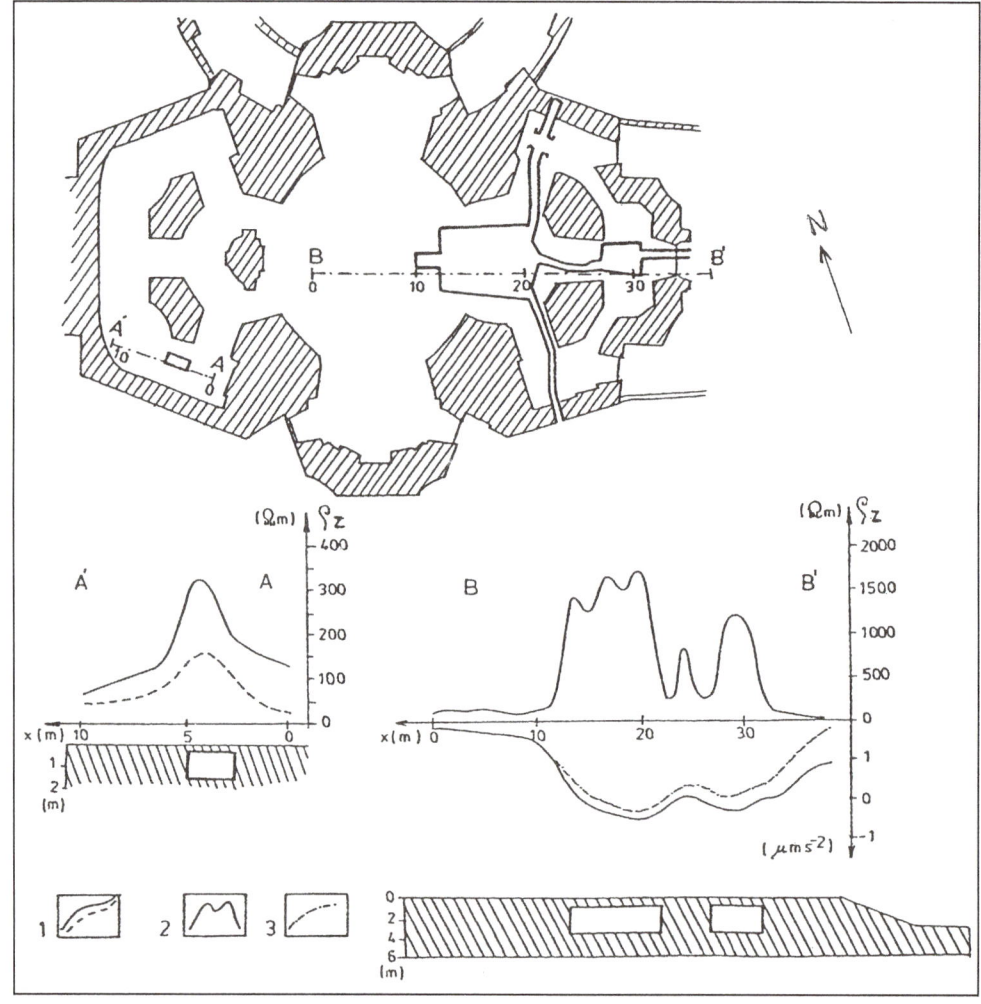

Fig. 3. Křtiny, the Church of Virgin Mary: Situation of geophysical profiles and interpretation profiles A- A´, B-B´ in the place of the main tomb and of smaller objects.
1-curves ρ_{app} from the DEMP method for h = 1.5 m, or h = 3-5 m; 2- Δg_{mes} curve; 3- Δg_{red} curve

gical verification. Masonry relics were detected in one of three sounds during probing performed on the basis of results of the geophysical measuring in 1980. This contributed (together with older written records) to specification of localizing the religious building and identifying its position. It was a rotunda with a cylindrical nave, probably with a U-shaped apse and a prismatic tower on the opposite western side, perhaps with a tribune. The whole formation can be dated generally back to the end of the 12th – the first third of the 13th century (Kudělka/Kalinová/Konečný/Samek 1982-83, 86-87).

In the years 1990 – 2008, more than 40 medieval (or modern) religious buildings were researched in the whole Czech Republic territory by systematic geophysical prospecting (see Fig. 1). The measurings were done by Geofyzika n.p. Brno (Geofyzika a.s. Brno) until 1993, later by the Archaeological Institute of the Czech Academy of Sciences in Brno (1994-2004) in cooperation with the company Geodrill s.r.o. Brno and consequently Geopek, spol.s r.o. Brno (since 2005). The aim of this future prospecting was to localize individual tombs and graves, determine their depth (and size), observe relics of masonries from older pulled-down features, specify the homogeneity of the environment and lithological properties of the near-surface layers of soils, but also to suggest both perspective and negative locations for situating surface exposures or test-pits. A complex of methods depending on the nature of the task, character of the environment and intensity of interference was used to solve these problems.

In 1990 – 1994, when method of dipole electromagnetic profiling (DEMP) was primarily applied, in contrast to experimental works, for solving the abovementioned tasks (it was only complemented by microgravimetry in some places) 9 such features were explored. As for localizing tombs and graves, some of these buildings can be considered as particularly significant: e.g. churches in Bystřice nad Pernštejnem, Doubravník (district of Žďár nad Sázavou), Jemnice (district of Třebíč) and Prostějov; the most significant ones as for observing foundation walls of the buildings are Kurdějov (district of Břeclav), Předklášteří u Tišnova (district of Brno) etc. (Hašek/ Unger 2001) (Fig. 1).

Localization of the extinct Chapel of St. Vitus, which stood in the northern segment of the Brno district Královo Pole in the wider are of the cast-iron cross at the Mojmír Square, was among the first proving works by the GPR method. The chapel was built around 1263, shut in 1783 and pulled down two years later (Bukovský 1994, 8–9). The aim of the performed geophysical measuring by the GPR method (Fig. 4) was to verify the general ground plan situation of this sacral building, because its position, size and inner structure are not known exactly (Hašek/Unger/Záhora 1997, 99). It was found out that the feature sized ca 20 x 9 m is further divided into three parts – the presbytery and the double area of the nave itself. Later construction work is possible, too. In the middle part of the presbytery a shallower grave sized ca 2 x 1 m can be expected. The outer wall was probably discontinued by the entrance into the then cemetery area in the middle part of the northern enclosing. The total size of the built-up area is ca 600 m^2. The conclusions of the geophysical measuring also correspond to the well-known image of the locality (Photo 2).

Photo 2. Brno – Královo Pole: The veduta of the Carthusian monastery area with a picture of the Chapel of St. Vitus

Since 1995, after obtaining the georadar (GPR), mostly combination of the both abovementioned methods (DEMP and GPR) has been used up to the present. Nearly 30 such features were thus explored by prospecting and in some places also by consequent probing. Good results in localizing crypts, tombs and graves, were achieved in the church areas in Brno, Český Krumlov, Chýnov (district of Tábor), Olomouc, Šumice (district of Uherské Hradiště), Šternberk (district of Olomouc), Třebíč, Uherské Hradiště, Uherský Brod (district of Uherské Hradiště) and Želiv (district of Pelhřimov), solid results in determining relics of masonries and hollows in general were also achieved in Blansko, Přepychy (district of Rychnov nad Kněžnou), Znojmo and in a number of others (Hašek/ Šindelář/Thomová/Tomešek 2008 etc.) (see Fig. 1). Archaeological verification was done so far in 28 of these buildings (53.8 % of the exploratory operations).

3.2. METHODOLOGY OF THE FIELD WORKS

During the test measurings in the beginning of the 1980's, primarily microgravimetry, but also resistivity profiling, shallow refraction seismics and thermometry were applied, i.e. geophysical methods which had corresponding apparatus equipment in the Czech Republic at that time. It ensued from these more detailed researches that microgravimetry showed itself to be suitable for solving tasks in interiors of buildings (Hašek/Měřínský

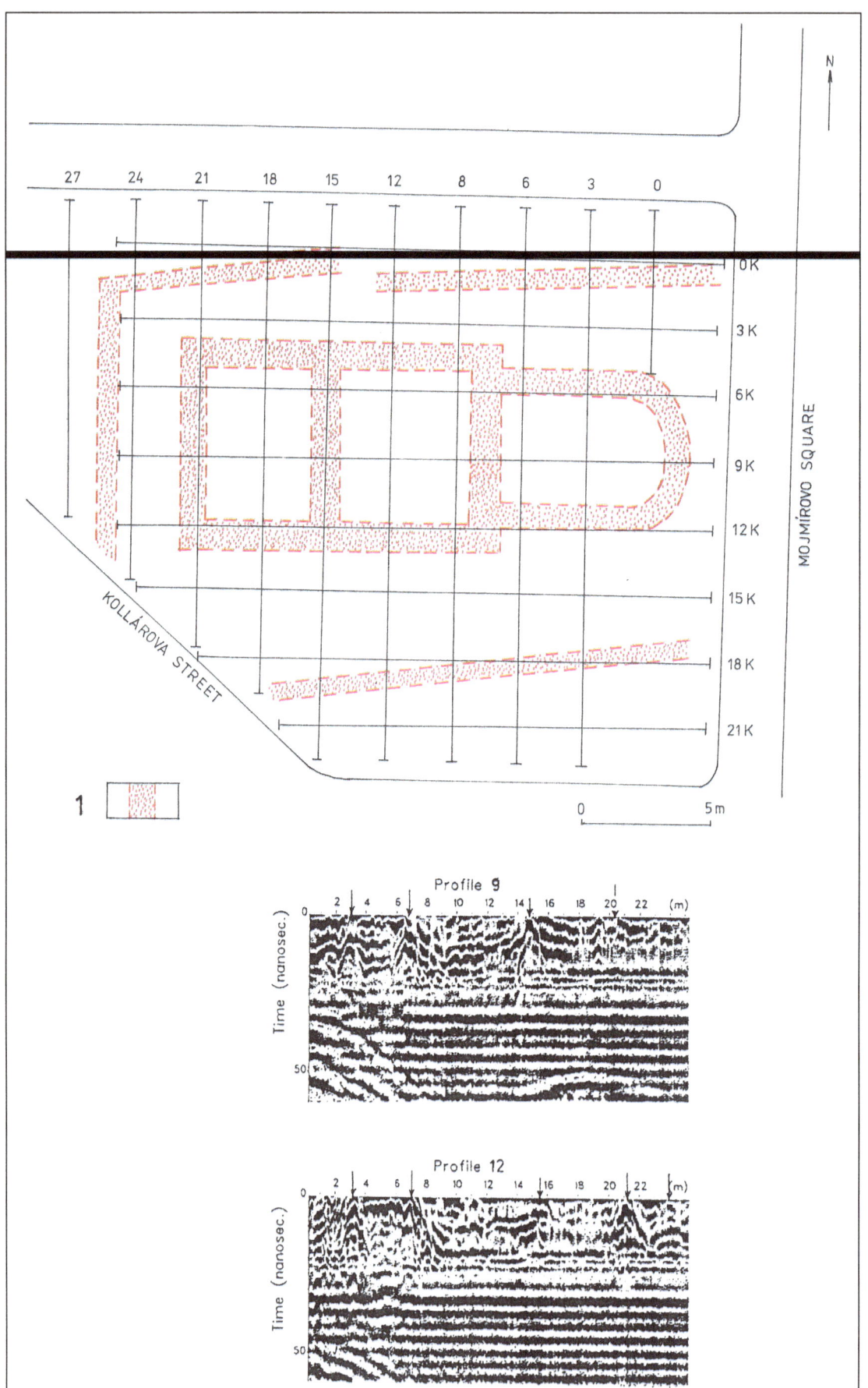

Fig. 4. Brno-Královo Pole, the Chapel of St. Vitus: Ground plan of the localized extinct church building from the GPR method and an example of interpreted radarogram. 1- relics of stone masonry; 2- an interpreted inhomogeneity

1991). However, these often both capital and labour intensive disciplines were gradually replaced by more mobile and exact methods already in the first stage of the systematic research of medieval and modern tombs and graves (1991 – 1994). These methods concededly include DEMP and after acquiring appropriate equipment in the second stage (1995 – 2008) especially the soil radar (GPR) (Hašek/Unger/Záhora 1997).

Microgravimetry based on differentiation of natural densities of rocks or anthropogenous features was used mainly for localizing various types of near-surface hollows. Changes of gravity acceleration (gravity) is measured on chosen points in respect to values on the basic gravimetric points. The gravity effect of anomalous near-surface density inhomogeneities was acquired from the measured gravity by subtracting theoretical effect of homogeneous earth and reduction of gravity to the chosen altitude (Odstrčil in Hašek/Měřínský 1991, 45-46). For the measuring itself, gravimeters with quartz measuring system, which enables to measure the gravity accurately to $\pm 0{,}15 \; \mu \; m.s^{-2}$, were used. Gravity anomalies caused by density inhomogeneities of the interest features – crypts, tombs etc., reach, according to modeling, up to values of $\pm 0{,}1$ až $\pm 2{,}0 \; \mu \; ms^{-2}$. To make it possible to detect such small anomalies, special methodology of measuring and processing the measured data was used. The gravity points were marked out in a net with a pitch of 0.5 to 3 m. Their altitudes, coordinates and gravities had to be measured more exactly.

The method of dipole electromagnetic profiling (DEMP) has been used since 1990 in observing foundation stone (or brick) masonries of extinct buildings, tombs, graves, or other elements connected with these features, whose conductivity properties differ from those of the surrounding environment, which is formed by loamy-sandy earths, various types of landfills etc. The field measurings were made at first by apparatuses of various depth ranges and operating frequencies (Hašek/Ungera/Záhora 1997,98). It is primarily the digital conductometer KD-1, operating at the frequency of 9.8 KHz with fixed distance between sending and receiving dipoles 3.66 m and depth range ca 3-5 m and KD-2, whose frequency is 13.2 KHz, the distance between dipoles 1 m, depth range with ZZ – polarization ca 1.5 m. In the last few years, namely multifrequency conductometer GEM-2 GEOPHEX (USA) (Photo 3) began to be applied in the research; it registers the electric and magnetic component of the electromagnetic field at a number of optional frequencies. The distance between dipoles is 2 m. The interval of the measuring on profiles depends on the nature of the solved task. It usually is within the nework of 1 x 1 m, or 2 x 1 m, however, it can as well be a network of 0.5 x 0.5 m. Evaluation of the measured values is made on the PC in the form of maps of isolines of apparent conductivities. Individual studied objects are displayed in them by both linearly oriented (masonry, underground services) and approximately isometric zones (tombs, graves) with mostly decreased conductivities.

Photo 3. Terrain measuring by the DEMP method. Multifrequency conductometer GEM-3 of the firm GEOPHEX (USA) (Photograph by V. Hašek)

Photo 4. Preparation of the apparatus RAMAC/GPR X3M GEOSCIENCE MALA´ for terrain measuring outside of the sacral building (Photograph by V. Hašek)

The **georadar** (GPR, soil radar), used in combination with DEMP for localizing tombs, graves and relics of masonries, ensues from the general principle that transmitter of electromagnetic waves of the frequency of 100 to 500 MHz and at the same time also receiver of the signal reflected from the conductivity boundary in the rock massif is a movable antenna placed at the zero level (Photo 4). The apparatus receives and processes the reflection in an appropriate recording device, so that it is possible, after drawing the reflected waves, to determine time of arrival of individual waves from the time of the transmitting of the electromagnetic pulse. During the field works, the antenna is relocated in certain distance intervals, e.g. $0.2 \div 0.5$ m, above the studied rock medium, or it is moved on the surface of the terrain (Photo 5). Distance between the profiles is 1-2 m. The result is the time profile of the gauged profile (equivalent of the seismic recording), acquired already during the measuring. It can be tentatively evaluated right in the site (Hašek/Unger/Záhora 1997,95). Practical usage of the

Photo 5. Radar measuring in the church interior by the apparatus RAMAC/GPR X 3M GEOSCIENCE MALA´ (Sweden)

georadar is based on detected differing relative permitivities and resistivities of the medium. Radius of the method depends also on the radiated impulse power, antenna and sensitivity of the receiver. In our conditions it is usually not greater than 4 – 5 m. For fieldworks, various apparatuses of foreign provenance were used. In 1990's, it was SIR – 7 of the company Geophysical Survey Inc and PULSE ECCO 100 of the company Sensors and Software, Inc. (Canada). Now it is RAMAC X3M/GPR made in Sweden (Geoscience Mala) and shielded 100 – 500 MHz antennas.

Positions of local inhomogeneities – cellars, tombs, graves near the surface manifest themselves on individual gauged profiles by reflections of electromagnetic waves shaped as curves situated under one another, similar to a single-leg hyperbolas of varying width and orientation (depending on the direction of the profile and angle of the searched structure), or also by interruption of the course of the reflective horizons. Also e.g. greater incline of the bedrock can reveal itself in similar way, or a near housing (outer walls of a building), where distinct diffraction of electromagnetic waves occurs.

3.3. OTHER NON-DESTRUCTIVE METHODS OF PROSPECTION

Since 2007, results of the geophysical works are checked by visual research when archaeological exposure itself cannot be realized in the object or in its vicinity (Photo 6). For this purpose a special exploring element, constructed for camera documentation of the old royal tomb in the St. Vitus Cathedral at the Prague Castle in 2005, is used. The exploring element consists of a sensitive minicamera, laser diastimeters, an incremental reader and sampling device. The whole system is worked by a robotic arm with radius of 10 m from the entrance hole (Photo 7). For the complete research of the underground it is therefore sufficient to make only a borehole with 3 cm in diameter. The result is quality color video recording of the underground feature (visual research) and detailed plans (in the form of ground plan, section and above standard also 3D model of the object). For mapping of the researched object we chose combination of polar method and intersection photometry. A sufficient number of natural impression points are targeted in the interior by laser diastimeters and incremental reader which are used for orienting the photograms made by calibrated camera. This way it is possible, in coordinates X, Y, Z, to target even the smallest details inside the inaccessible object.

Photo 6. Proving pedological holes – rig LSS-25

Photo 7. Camera research of the tomb
(Photograph by V. Hašek)

4. DISCUSSION OF PRACTICAL RESULTS AND OBSERVATIONS

The following paragraphs will present, on a number of examples, main data acquired by geophysical prospection in combination with exposing works and documentation when dealing with the issue of religious architecture from various time periods in the whole territory of the Czech Republic, which can be helpful for solving this issue connected with archaeological field excavations and their interpretation.

These features were further divided into three main groups – village, town and monastic church buildings. During the whole period from 1973 to 2009, 10 monastic and 42 parish city or village churches and chapels were researched by nondestructive methods (see Fig. 1).

4.1. CHURCH BUILDINGS FROM THE 11TH TO 12TH CENTURY

Christianity of the 11th and 12th century manifests itself most distinctively in church architecture, which was in some cases subject to geophysical research and archaeological excavation. This was done by boreholes and probes by standing buildings on one hand, by surface exposures of extinct features on the other hand. Apart from positive findings, only uncertain indications of the existence of various architectural and component structural elements are available in many cases. The Rotunda of St. Catherine in Znojmo is presented as an example from the first group, the second group is represented by a building in the area of the Olomouc cathedral.

ZNOJMO, the Rotunda of St. Catherine, District of Znojmo

A hillfort on the spur above the river of Dyje (providing the southern border) was let built by Prince Břetislav as soon as in the 11th century. The centre of the Znojmo appanage was here until the 12th century. The rotunda with unique painting decorations (Photo 8) stands in the

Photo 8. Znojmo, the Rotunda of St. Catherine: Overall view of the building from the southwest (Photograph by V. Hašek)

area of the outer ward. The significant monument brought about not only archaeological research in the interior and its vicinity, but also discussion concerning its dating and interpretation (Klíma 1995, Konečný 2005).

A Brief Overview of Geological Situation of the Locality

The area of interest belongs geomorphologically to the Jevišovice Highland (a subunit of the Znojmo Highland) and it is built by tectonically damaged magmatites of the Dyje Massif and in its superincumbent bed by Quaternary mantle rock. The pre-Quaternary subbasement is represented by granitoids (amphibolite-biotite granodiorite, biotite granite, veins of aplite and pegmatite) which are cataclazed (Proterozoic) towards the west. The rocks of the Dyje Massif (the most eastern part of the Moravic) were tectonically damaged during the geological development of the area. Apart from the system of the steep primary cracks, a system of aslope foliations developed here as a result of oriented pressure in the NE-SW and NW-SE directions because of mural jointing. Except for these finely tectonic elements influencing cohesiveness and breaking characteristic of rocks there

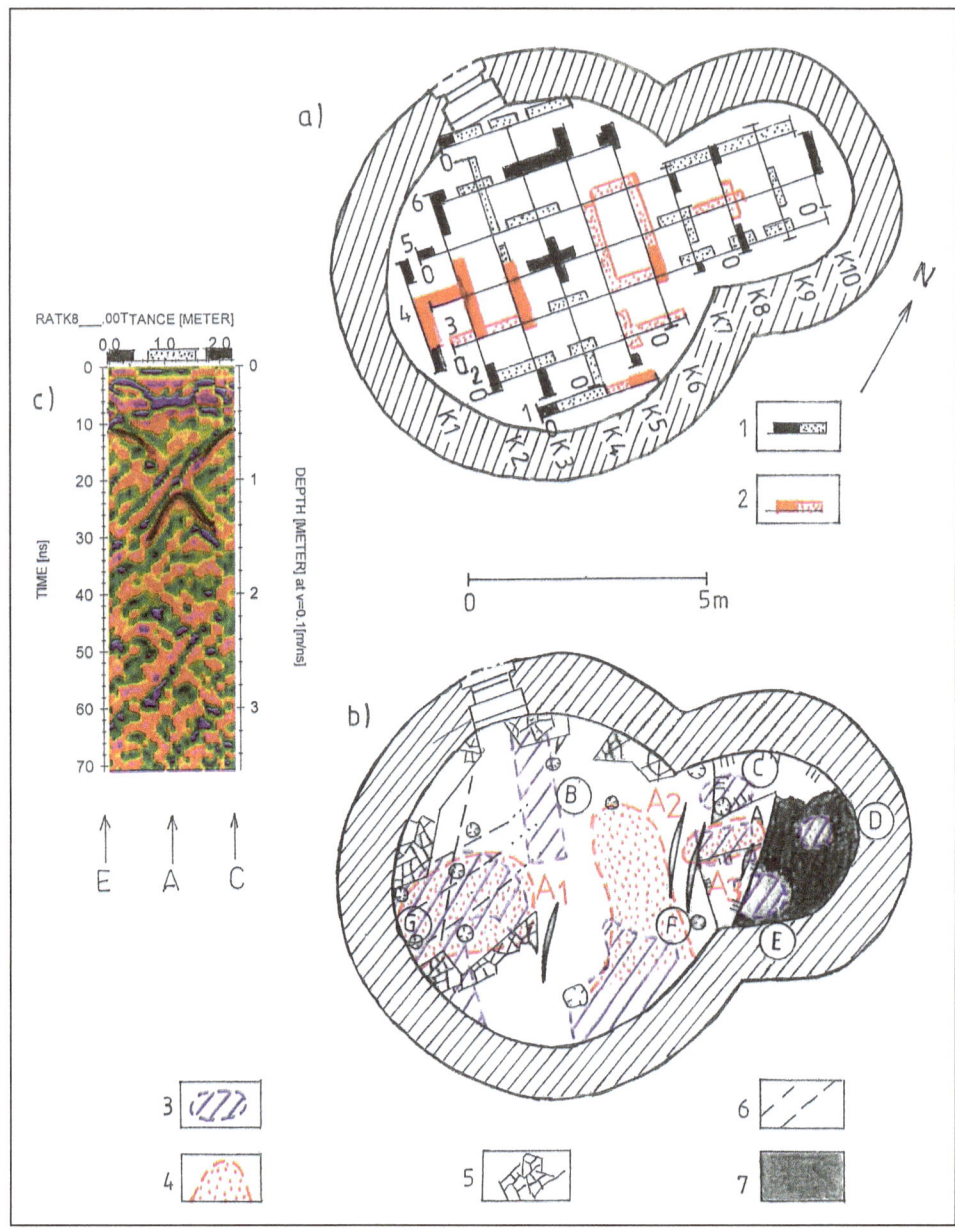

Fig. 5. Znojmo, the Rotunda of St. Catherine: Correlation scheme of results of geophysical works from microgravimetry and the GPR (a, b), interpreted radarogram (C) in places of identified inhomogeneities E, A (A3) and C.
1- near-surface inhomogeneities according to their distinctiveness (h=0.3-0.8m); 2-near-surface inhomogeneities according to their distinctiveness (h = > 1 m); 3- interpreted gravity anomalies (A-G); 4- identified inhomogeneities according to the GPR (A1, A2, A3); 5- masonry; 6- faulted (crack) zones; 7- aplite

are also small dislocations, i.e. planes of discontinuity, according to which either shift of rock masses or crushing of the rock occurred. The blankets consist mostly of mechanical wastes of varying grain-size composition developed on rocks of crystalline complex and influenced by Quaternary weathering, possilbly also of anthropogenous deposits.

Geophysical Prospection and Archaeological Interpretation of the Results

The main aim of the geophysical measuring performed in the area of the building by various organizations and methods in 1985-87, evaluated in the publication of Höschl/Puffr/Bílý/Kovárník (1996) and partly verified by drilling research (Woznica 1993), was to detect positions of possible graves. After processing all at the time available geological and archaeological data it was stated that such structures most probably do not occur in the interior of the building up to the depth of 3 to 4 m from the floor. Geophysical anomalies can therefore be caused mostly by system of fissure and otherwise damaged zones in the weathered bedrock. On the basis of complementary information, microgravimetric measuring was done in the interior of the building in question in 2007 (Mrlina 2007) and consequently also radar research the same year

(Hašek/Kovárník/Tomešek 2007), which were supposed to complement or further specify the knowledge obtained by the previous geophysical works.

From the results of microgravimetry, 7 main anomalies of places, marked A to G were identified. They indicate positions of various near-surface inhomogeneities, representing either possible manifestation of a hollow (A, B), or other anomalies (C to G). These were not archaeologically evaluated by the author for their small amplitude.

It was found out by evaluating the data of the gravimeter survey with GPR (Fig. 5a, b) that:

a) the gravimetric anomaly A in the apse proved to be, also by radar, the only possible even half-caved hollow of smaller size marked A3 (1.8 x 1.0 x 0.9) in the depth of 1.1 m;

b) the anomaly B interpreted from microgravimetry as a possible corridor (?) manifests itself in the GPR method only by a shallower linear indication in the depth of 0.3 – 0.4 m. Only a route of underground services – a cable – is assumed. However, its impact may overshadow the impact of a possible corridor, even though its course seems to be less probable from the GPR;

c) more local and less distinctive anomalies C, D, E in the apse are caused probably by morphology of the bedrock – its greater damage (depth of 0.6 to 0.7 m);

d) sources of anomalies F, G (size 2 x 1.5 m) can be thicker layers of landfill (A1), intensive lack of ventilation, possibly also weathering or even decomposition of granitoids. Also a shorter route of a high corridor (A2), crossing of the crack zones of the NE-SW and NW-SE directions etc. (Fig. 5c) is considered.

Archaeological Evaluation

From the correlation of the results of all geophysical works with the boreholes made it can be stated that possible inhomogeneities of more local character – hollows (half-caved or caved) would have to occur, according to the last research, probably only in the shallow parts of the granitoid massif in the proximity of the present surface of the terrain, because the boreholes are situated into the depths of ca 3.4 to 7.7 m, where the abovementioned structures were not localized by the works.

OLOMOUC – the Complex of the Cathedral, District of Olomouc

Existence of a princely residence is assumed on the Cathedral Rise in Olomouc from the 2nd half of the 11th century. A church stood here from the beginning of the 12th century, the bishop's seat was moved here in 1141. A whole number of events connected with archaeological excavations and construction-historical researches ended in reconstruction of the position of the Episcopal area, bringing about discussion on the topic of its dating and appearance (Photo 9) (Michna/Pojsl 1998).

Photo 9. Olomouc: Drawn reconstruction of the church area by the St. Wenceslas Cathedral in the 12th century (according to Michna-Pojsl 1988, 106)

A semicircular apse and a part of the church walling was managed to be discovered in the so-called "Small Yard". The church stood here until the destruction of the wooden-loamy fortification from the 10th century and was concealed by building of the presbytery of the cathedral built at the time of the bishop Henry Zdík in 1131. The method of soil radar was used in the area of the vicarious sacristy to give a clearer picture of the general situation and the size of the structure.

Geophysical Prospection and Archaeological Interpretation of the Results

The geophysical works identified two narrower and less distinctive linearly oriented anomalies in the studied area (Fig. 16), which probably represent further continuation of the outer foundation wall of the abovementioned religious building. Some data acquired by measuring in the northern side nave of the cathedral partly indicate possible southern limitation of this building by later development (Drobílková/Hašek/Hlobil/Zapletal/Zatloukal 2004, 73).

Archaeological Evaluation

It can be stated on the basis of archaeological excavations that a building constructed no sooner than in the final quarter of the 11th century and no later than in the first third of the 12th century was found in the small yard. According to some signs and results of the geophysics, the feature can be interpreted as a one-nave church ended by an apse ca 10-11 m wide and probably 14 m long (see Fig. 17). It is of course necessary to take into account the possibility that it was an unfinished construction project (Drobílková/Hašek/Hlobil/Zapletal/Zatloukal 2004, 75).

4.2. CHURCH BUILDINGS FROM THE 13 TO 15TH CENTURY

In the 13th century the church organization changed remarkably. Small parishes originated with churches as their centres where baptisms and burials took place. Concentration of a large amount of people in cities made it necessary for parish administrations to establish town monastic institutions (Unger 2008, 55). It is also in this period that the church monuments manifest themselves most distinctively in architecture. Many churches and monasteries are still standing but the archaeological research itself can in many aspects complete or even totally change the opinion on the development of the individual features.

Photo 10. Nebovidy, the Church of St. Cross: View from the northwest (Photograph by M. Hotárek)

4.2.1. Village Parish Churches

A whole number of archaeological excavations of this cathegory of monuments was initiated by construction or reconstruction activity. If conditions allowed, results obtained this way were sometimes very surprising. Results of works in the churches of villages of Nebovidy, Topanov (cadastral district of Rybníky), Bohušov, Kurdějov, Přepychy and Tasov may be instructive.

NEBOVIDY – Church of the Holy Cross, District of Brno

The building of the Church of the Holy Cross (Photo 10) is located on a small rise in the upper part of the village of Nebovidy in the district of Brno, on the crossing of the road with the main way leading in the direction from Brno. The late Romanesque base of the building – outer stone walling of the nave – is from the early 2nd half of 13th century. Dating of the reconstruction of the church depends on datation of painting decorations of its interior, today already completely restored. Style analysis put them to the 1370's – 1380's (Samek 1999, 645). The original presbytery was pulled down or extended before they were created and was replaced by relatively extensive Gothic formation of a rectangular ground plan ended by supporting piers. A sacristy was built by the south wall of the presbytery. The church was enlarged in 1936. According to the project made, east part of the presbytery was pulled down and the presbytery was extended to its double length (Photo 11).

A Brief Overview of Geological Situation of the Locality

The wider area of Nebovidy belongs, according to the Regional Structuring of the Czech Republic (Czudek

Photo 11. Nebovidy, the Church of St. Cross: View of the interior from the east (Photograph by M. Hotárek)

1973), into the Bobrava Upland, into the subunit of the Lipov Upland. The studied area is situated on the meeting point of two significant geological units – the Czech Massif and the West Carpathians. Also the regional unit of the Brno Massif belongs, among others, to the eastern margin of the Czech Massif. Units of outer West Carpathians – the Carpathian Foredeep and flysch belts of the Carpathians emerge southeast of Brno. The Pre-Quaternary base is represented by leucocratic to biotite granite of the Brno Massif – Proterozoic to lower Paleozoic, calcareous clays (tegels) – Lower Baden (morav), fluvial sandy gravels – Pliocene, Miocene. The Quaternary cover is represented by loesses, loess loams (Pleistocene – Würm), deluvial mostly loamy-sandy

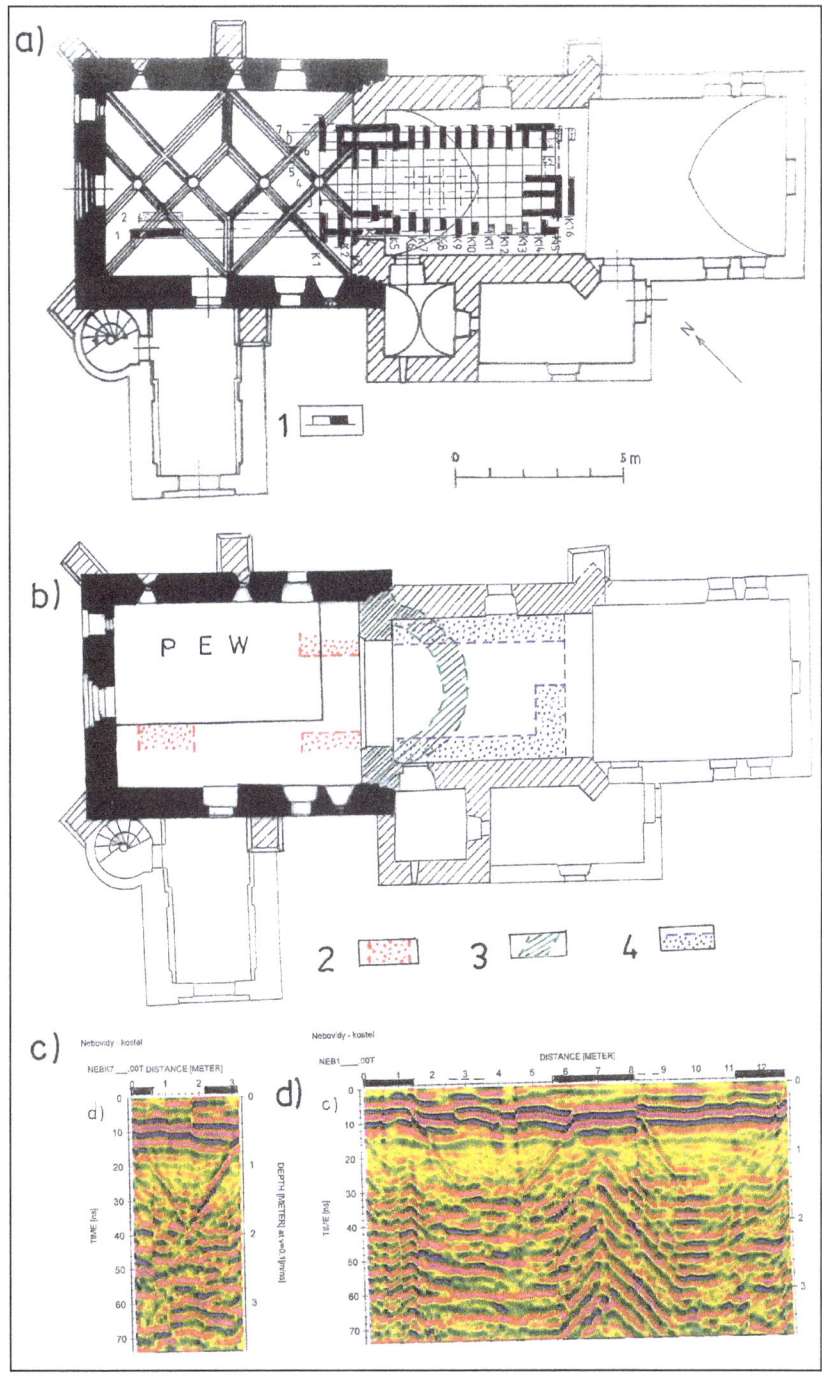

Fig. 6. Nebovidy, the Church of St. Cross: Correlation scheme of results of geophysical works (a), one of possible variants of interpretation of the prospection (b) and an example of interpreted radarograms in the W-E (c) and N-S direction (d) 1- indication of inhomogeneities according to their distinctiveness; 2- graves, accumulations of stones, etc.; 3- masonry relics- apse; 4- gravel sands with channels preventing penetration of humidity in the wall

sediments (Holocene, Pleistocene), black and brown soils (Holocene) and anthropogenous deposits of variable thicknesses.

Geophysical Prospection and Archaeological Interpretation of the Results

The task of geophysical research by the GPR method in 2009 was to provide information about existence of possible relics of the original presbytery walling, graves and other constructional elements under the church floor made up by glazed tiles.

Two boundaries can be identified from the data of the soil radar method. They occur at the times $t_1 = 8\text{--}10$ ns $t_2 = 36\text{--}40$ ns. If constant speeds $vr_1 = 0.10$ m/ns a $v_r = 0.12$ m/ns are assumed, in the first case it may be tile flooring with its inhomogeneous anthropogeneous base of fictive thicknesses h_1 = 0.4–0.5 m (0.48–0.60 m) in the superincumbent bed of the lithologically variable Quaternary layer of sandy-clayey sediments above the Brno Massif, whose relatively broken relief is located very roughly in the depths of h_2 = 1.8–2.0 m, or possibly h = (2.16–2.40 m).

After interpreting the radarograms, three more distinctive anomalies (marked in colour) are presented in the Fig. 6. They can be assigned to possible manifestations of grave backfills, various lithological changes in the landfill, masonry relics, or possibly other related architectural elements. Tops of all near-surface inhomogeneities are concentrated, as stated above, in depths of ca 0.5 to 0.7 m, or 0.6 to 0.8 m; their width oscillates from 0.7 to 2.3 m.

Archaeological Evaluation

More distinctive changes in the landfill (Qaternary) under the present floor show up especially in the part of the late Romanesque nave by the triumphal arch – on the right under the escutcheon of Ješek of Křižinkov and on the left under his wife's escutcheon and also in the southwest part of the nave. Images of inhomogeneities can thus only indicate (because of limited realization of the measuring procedure) possible positions of the graves, larger accumulations of stones etc. (Fig. 6a). Also the ledger of the parish priest Virgilius might be originally placed by the localized spot of anomaly in the southwestern part of the building (Mojžíš/Ptáčková/Bartl 2004, 35).

In the area of the Gothic presbytery several linearly oriented inhomogeneities (Fig. 6b) can be expected. Masonry of the semicircular apse from the original Romanesque church is assumed to be here. It is believed to be partly preserved in the negative print as well, according to less distinctive reflections. Effect of gravel-sand with channels preventing penetration of humidity into the wall is visible in the course of the inhomogeneities on the inner side of the outer wall of the presbytery (the north and south sides).

Areal inhomogeneity sized ca 2.5 x 1.0 m with a NE-SW axe by the stairs to the new presbytery (20th century) may be caused by existence of walling from the east end of the Gothic presbytery, by a mensa or an altar (see Fig. 6a, b).

TOPANOV, Chapel of St. Margaret, District of Znojmo

The late Romanesque cemetery Chapel of St. Margaret from the first half of the 13th century (Photo 12) is a torso of the original parish church of the extinct Medieval village of Topanov. It is located ca 1.3 km east of the village of Rybníky by Moravský Krumlov. According to the 1859 drawing (Photo 13), only a separate choir of an oblong ground plan and a U-shaped apse remained out of the oriented oblong one-nave building. The presbytery was originally a part of a tower-type formation (see Photo

Photo 12. Topanov, c.d. Rybníky, the Chapel of St. Margaret: View from the southeast (Photograph by V. Hašek)

Photo 13. Topanov, c.d. Rybníky, the Chapel of St. Margaret: The original Topanov church before 1859 (according to Moritz Wilhelm Trapp 1859)

13). The stone nave was pulled down in 1877 and the chapel got the present appearance in 1895; it was repaired in 1910 and after 1945 (Samek 1999, 601).

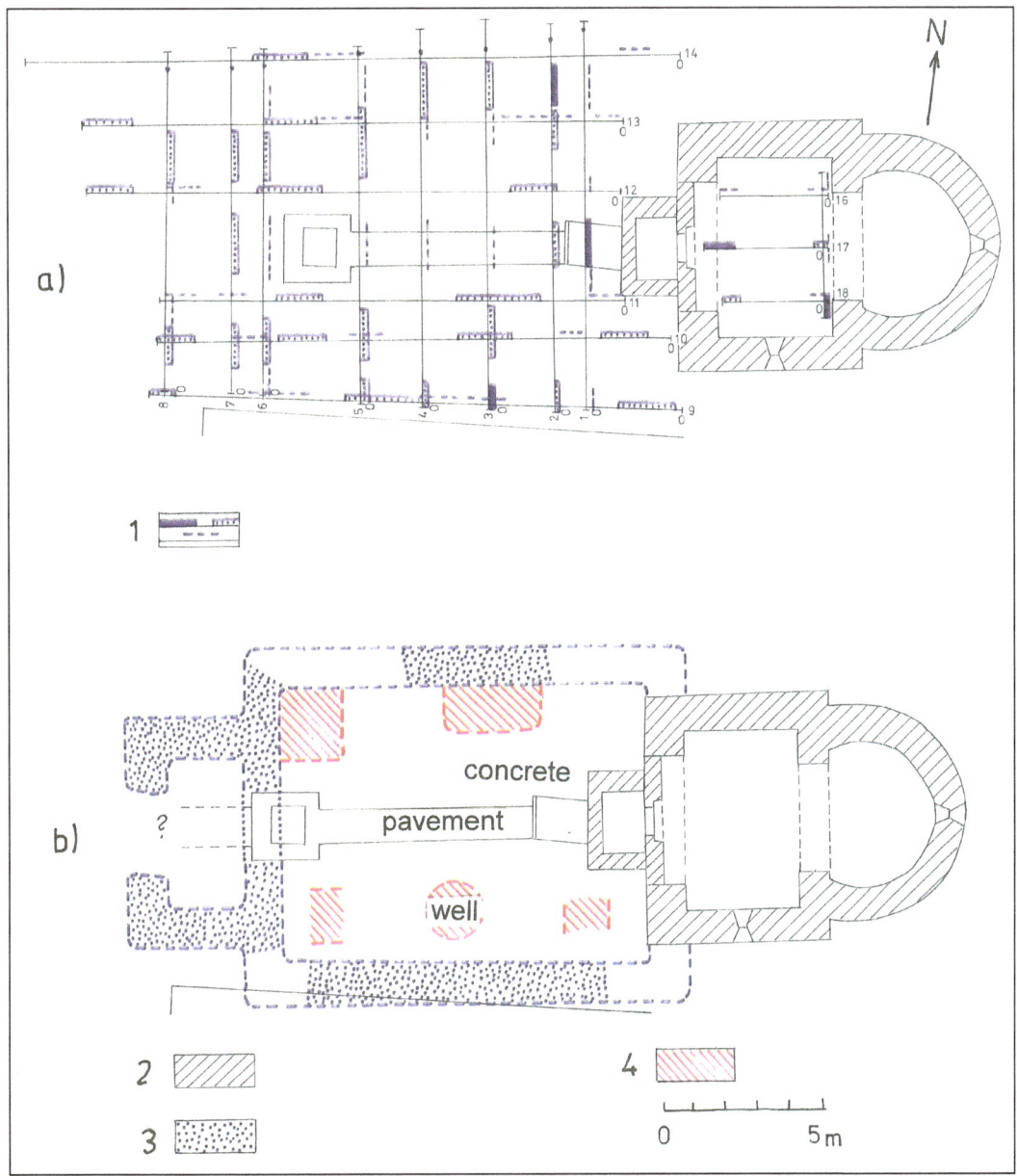

Fig. 7. Topanov, c.d. of Rybníky, the Chapel of St. Margaret: Correlation scheme of geophysical works (a) and interpretation of results of measuring (b) 1- interpreted inhomogeneities according to their distinctiveness; 2- the current walling; 3- interpreted relics of the walling; 4- accumulations of stones, graves, well

A Brief Overview of Geological Situation of the Locality

The wider area of the Chapel of St. Margaret lies on the boundary of the Boskovice Furrow and Jevišovice Highland, in the subunit of Znojmo Highland, built by rocks of Moravian Moldanubic and by Quaternary cover in their superincumbent bed. The studied area itself is located in the area of the left terrace of the river Rokytná. The pre-Quaternary base (Cryptozoic) is represented by biotite and sillimanite-biotite paragneisses, leucocratic migmatites and granulites with garnet and biotite. The quaternary cover is represented by loesses, deluvial (mostly stony-loamy) sediments, fluvial sandy gravels – Riss, Günz (Pleistocene – Holocene), deluviofluvial sandy-stony complexes, the black and brown soils (Holocene) and anthropogenous deposits of variable thicknesses.

Geophysical Prospection and Archaeological Interpretation of the Results

The main task of the detailed GPR measuring in 2009 was to map out the course of the relics of the outer walling of the original church nave (Hašek/Tomešek 2009).

Several more distinctive anomalies (marked in colour) are presented in the Fig. 7a. According to their mutual correlation, they can be considered possible manifestations of masonry relics, grave backfills, various lithological changes in landfill etc. Tops of all these near-surface inhomogeneities are concentrated in the depths of ca 0.50 – 1.30 m, or 0.60 – 1.56 m; their width varies from 1 to 2.50 m. Fictive depth of the base of the landfills (Quaternary?) and of the surface of the weathered to partly weathered base rocks of the Moravian Moldanubic period (?) or gravel-sand is, given t =30–44 ns a vr = 0.10 m/ns, h = 1.50–2.20 m; vr = 0.12 m/ns, h = 1.80 – 2.64 m.

From the point of view of possible detaching the stone masonry relics from the extinct nave of the parish church, situated WSW of the presbytery, we can interpret the course of these inhomogeneities of linear character (marked in blue) as ca 11.50 m long and 8.50 m wide (inner size of the building), which also corresponds approximately to the original size of the assumed feature (Samek 1999, 600). Thickness of the walling is 1.20 m, depth is 0.70 – 1.00 m. They are two less distinctive parallel indications with ENE-WSW axis and one perpendicular (western) wall with NNW-SSE axis, which will be probably adjoined by a smaller "entrance hall" sized ca 4 x 2 m (Fig. 7b). It is possible that it is partly also a negative imprint of the masonry in places as a consequence of total removal of the material for newer buildings.

Inside and outside this part of the original church, several more local, areal inhomogeneities were identified (marked in red), corresponding to positions of present graves and larger accumulation of stones on the one hand and near-surface inhomogeneities – paving, plinths, a well (marked in black) on the other hand.

The aim of the prospection on several profiles in the interior of the presbytery was to verify whether the semicircular apse could have been a remnant of an older rotunda. This hypothesis, however, was not proved by geophysical measuring.

Archaeological Evaluation

As results of the geophysical works indicate, the original length of the parish church of the extinct village of Topanov, reminded in the years 1273-1503, was ca 25 m including the entrance hall, maximum width was ca 11 m. Also positions of several graves in the interior of the nave are possible.

During the duration of the village, whose origin is tied with an order of German knights, Topanov could have also a lightly fortified residence. In the early 2nd half of the 13th century, German knights moved the site to the newly founded city of Krumlov. The village thus loses the character of a local center (Gruna/Grunová 2008).

BOHUŠOV, the Church of St. Martin, District of Bruntál

Bohušov is located in Osoblaha Promontory, approximately 2 km from the state border with Poland. The Gothic Church of St. Martin is in the urban area of the village; it is a one-nave building with an oblong presbytery, probably from the 1st half of the 14th century (Photo 14). The presbytery was vaulted and supporting piers added on the outer side in the 15th century. Other adjustments took place in the 17th and 19th century (Samek 1994, 85).

Photo 14. Bohušov, the Church of St. Martin: General view from the west

A Brief Overview of Geological Situation of the Locality

Geomofphologically the region belongs to Jindřichovice Highland, a part of Zlaté Hory Upland. The village spreads along the left margin of the wide Osoblaha river flood plain. Because of the flat surrounding terrain and gradual descent of the watercourse the thickness of the Holocene loamy fluvial filling of the flood plain is several meters. The surrounding peneplain is covered by Upper Pleistocene loess and loess loam drifts. Bassets of Middle Pleistocene gravel sands covered with loamy-sandy tills protrude from the drifts, especially along the valleys of the watercourses. These deposits represent residues of Middle Pleistocene Saal glaciation. South of Bohušov, in the Osoblaha basin, residues of Cenomanian sediments emerge still more out of the loess covers. They consist, apart from sandstones with hornstones, of sands and cardazytic sandy clays resting on Lower Carboniferous (Upper Visean) sediments with rhythmic bedding of fine-grained graywackes, siltites and slates. In the stratigraphic division, rocks of the Moravice Formation are a part of the co-called Moravian-Silesian Culm. The foundations of the church are for the most part on fluvial sediments, or in the deposits coming from the Saal glaciation.

Geophysical Prospection and Archaeological Interpretation of the Results

From the data of the GPR method, using an unshielded antenna 250 MHz, positions of known, mostly brick tombs (marked H1 to H4, Fig. 8c, Photo 15), and another tomb on the epistle side (A), south from the mensa of the main altar, can be localized in the area of the presbytery,

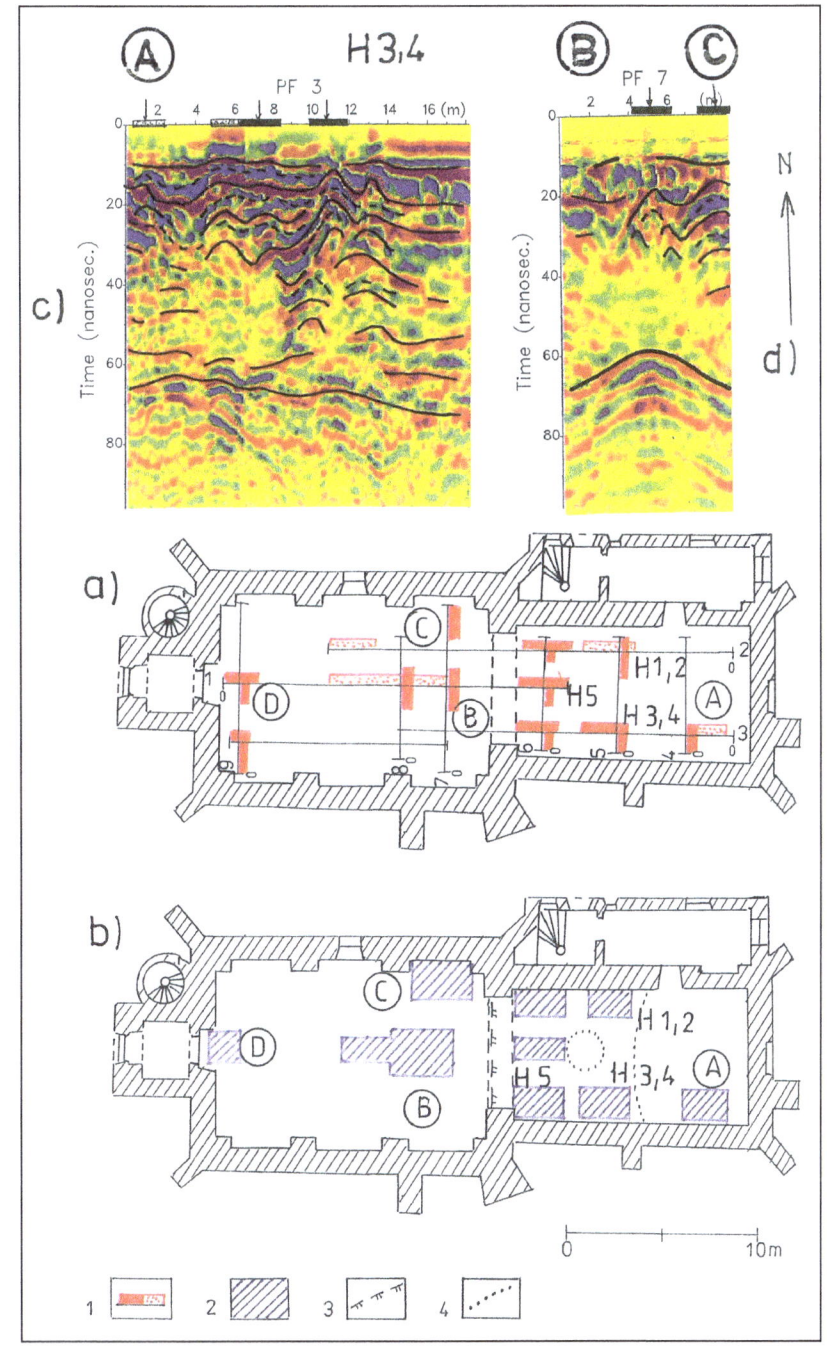

Fig. 8. Bohušov, the Church of St. Martin: Correlation scheme of results of geophysical works (a), interpretation of the measured data (b), manifestation of tombs by the southern outer walling of the church from the GPR (c), tombs under the triumphal arch in the nave (d). 1- manifestation of inhomogeneities according to their distinctiveness; 2- interpreted tombs; 3- scarp; 4- boundary in the removed paving

along both sides of the tomb uncovered by the excavation in 1999 – 2000 during the rehabilitation of the floor and static securing of the building walling (Zezula 2001, 197). The tombs lie under three Renaissance sepulchral slabs (16th to the beginning of the 17th century) located on the surface of the original brick paving by the peripheral masonry of the object (Fig. 8a, b). A smaller step-shaped entrance (H5), covered with a stone slab to the height of the abovementioned larger known tomb (Hašek/Unger 2001, 94) was detected close to the triumphal arch. A larger inhomogeneity (B) sized ca 4 x 2.5 m can be identified in the center line of the nave near the triumphal arch. It corresponds to either more extensive accumulation of stones in the anthropogenic layer up to 0.8 m thick in the superincumbent bed of the clayey-sandy weathered rocks, or to a shallower tomb, or a grave (Fig. 8d). Similar situation occurs by its north margin (C), where an existence of a smaller tomb, or a grave, is also possible. The interpreted anomalies in the western section of the building near the entrance (D) are probably

Photo 15. Bohušov, the Church of St. Martin: Tombstones in situ and uncovered tomb (Photograph by V. Hašek)

Photo 16. Kurdějov, the Church of St. John the Baptist: View from the south (Photograph by V. Prokop)

connected only with smaller local architectural elements, or possibly with lithology of the backfill of local depressions (Hašek/Peška/Unger 2008, 18).

Archaeological Research

In the excavated part of the presbytery, altogether 18 funerals from the 13th to 17th century were uncovered by archaeological research of the State Institute of Monument Care in Ostrava. Some of them probably belonged to members of the noble family of Fulstein, which had a castle built above the village since the 13th century. Some members or relatives of the family could have been be buried into brick vaulted chambers during the 16th and in the beginning of the 17th century. Four grave chambers were uncovered in the east part of the presbytery, other similar ones together with a larger tomb occurred in its west part (Zezula 2001, 197).

KURDĚJOV, the Church of St. John the Baptist, District of Břeclav

A fortified church was a part of the village in the 13th century, according to written sources. It was found out by archaeological excavation and written sources that the Church of St. John the Baptist (Photo 16) that stands on a terrace above the middle of the village, was built around the turn of the 13th and 14th century as a relatively large building with a presbytery, whose appearance is not known, with a vaulted transept and a flat-ceiling nave. In the second building stage (2nd half of the 15th century), the original presbytery was replaced by a new and larger one, which already a had a defensive floor with loopholes. The archaeological excavation does not discard the possibility that also a tower added to the southwest side of the transept belongs to this building stage. At the turn of the 15th and 16th century, the church was fortified with a rampart, whose part was also a chapel with a defensive floor, a massive tower and a parsonage provided with loopholes. This fortified church is one of the best preserved churches on our territory. A bricked underground corridor dug in loess leads out of the presbytery of the church (Unger 2008, 63).

A Brief Overview of Geological Situation of the Locality

The wider area of interest belongs geomorphologically into the Ždánice Forest, consisting of Tertiary flysch rocks of the Ždánice unit and of Quaternary cover in their superincumbent bed. The pre-Quaternary base of the building is built by psammitic-lutaceous to psammitic facies with positions of conglomerates of the Ždánice-Hustopeče formation (Egger-Eggenburg). The Quaternary cover is represented by Pleistocene loesses, loess loams and fluvial Hologene sediments in the area of the Kurdějov stream.

Geophysical Prospection and Archaeological Interpretation of the Results

The geophysical works in the wider area of the fortified church in Kurdějov in 1992 aimed to prove possibilities of the DEMP method for localizing emergency corridors from the turn of the 16th and 17th century, 1.5 – 1.95 m tall and 0.7 – 1.6 m wide, dug in loess and bricked. The bottom of the corridors reaches up to the depth of 10.9 m, as compared with the presbytery floor level. The outer corridor leads under the ossarium and ends after about 30m by caving-in under the rampart in the place of the original gate (Unger 1987, 101, Hašek/Unger 1994, 32).

Results of geophysical measurings correspond very closely to the data of the archaeological excavation (Fig. 9). Routes of the underground corridors are strongly evident in the geophysical data in the form of narrow tones of increased specific resistivities, especially in the area of the church itself. In the SW segment of the area of interest, they also outlined continuation of the corridor in

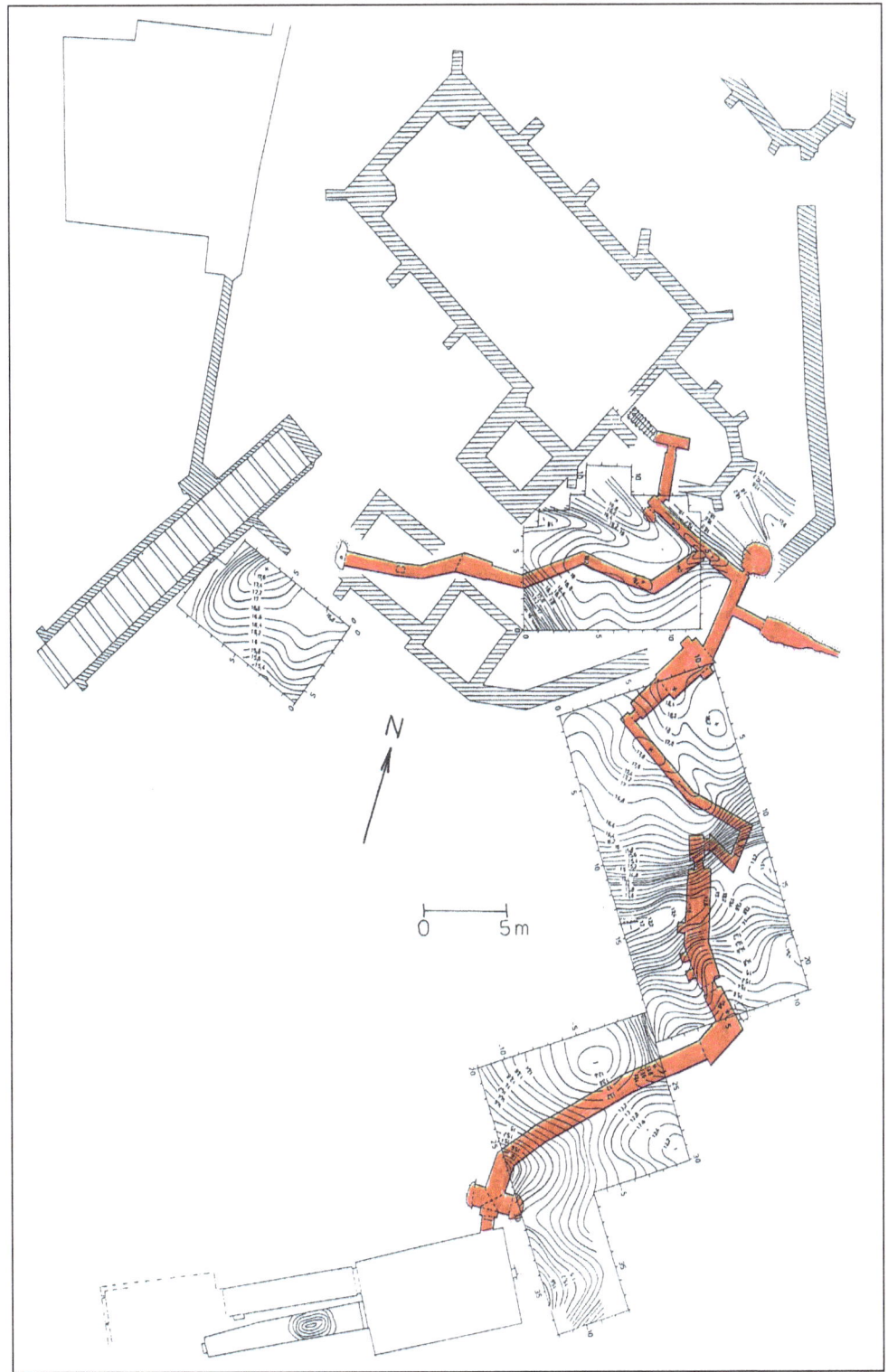

Fig. 9. Kurdějov, the Church of St. John the Baptist: Map of isolines σ_{app} according to the DEMP and their comparison with the course of the underground corridor

the slope behind the caving-in, with diversion from the original direction (E-W) to the NE-SW orientation.

Localization of the corridor is very distinctive also outside the fortification of the object, even though certain distortion of its course occurs in its middle part, which is caused probably by saturated weakened zone (NE – SW direction), or possibly by a lithological change in loesses. In the vicinity of the profile 10 of the spacing of 28m and 35 m, results of measuring are already influenced by the effect of the not caved in basement, into which the corridor leads.

PŘEPYCHY, the Church of St. Prokop, District of Rychnov nad Kněžnou

The parish Church of St. Prokop stands in the upper part of the village square in the middle of the old cemetery (Photo 17). A pentagonal presbytery with annexes at the north and south sides joins the one-nave building in the east, a tower does by the northwest corner. The nave is vaulted by a barrel vault (Photo 18).

Photo 17. Přepychy, the Church of St. Prokop: View from the south (Photograph by V. Hašek)

Photo 18. Přepychy, the Church of St. Prokop: View of the interior with the place of the tomb (Photograph by V. Hašek)

A local parson is mentioned as soon as in 1355. In 1506, a non-vaulted building with a polygonal presbytery was built in the place of the older, perhaps wooden church. Later a watchtower was added to the north wall of the nave. The church was rebuilt in the renaissance style and vaulted in 1574. After 1840, the original tower was pulled down and a new one was built (Poche 1980, 172). Gravestones of local gentry members, originally bedded in the floor, were a part of the interior. Currently five of them are built into walls of the nave under the choir and one is in the space under the tower (Hašek/Petera 2002, 317).

According to the oral tradition, written records and collapsed pieces of land, several corridors are assumed to be under the village, which were supposed to start in the church under the tower, or in some tomb, and end either by the deer park in Opočno or lead from the church south towards the parsonage.

A Brief Overview of Geological Situation of the Locality

The area of interest of the studied locality belongs to the Orlice Plateau, formed by Upper-Cretaceous rocks of the Czech Massif – Lower Turonian and by a Quaternary cover in their superincumbent bed. The pre-Quaternary base consists of white-grey to yellowy marlites, sandy and spiculitic marlites (opoka), sandy clays, marlitic sandstones etc. Quaternary blankets are represented by Pleistocene loesses, calcareous loesses and also rock mantle formed by mechanical wastes of varying grain-size composition, originated in mild to glacial climate on Mesozoic rocks.

Geophysical Prospection and Archaeological Interpretation of the Results

In the church interior and its nearest vicinity 18 profiles of total length of 495 m were identified and consequently geophysically gauged in two stages in 1999 and 2001 (Hašek/Tomešek 1999a, 2001a).

Several local inhomogeneities of maximum sizes of 2 x 1.5m to 3 x 2 m can be observed on the profiles in the interior of the building. They correspond to positions of tombs or graves marked with gravestones in the walls of the building on the gospel and epistle side of the presbytery by the triumphal arch and by the south outer margin of the tower (Fig. 10) and also, in case of omission of the reflection boundary in the nave under the choir (marked 3, Fig. 10), to some either larger insunk and buried feature from previous building conversions or to a redeveloped tomb.

Measuring in the area of the old churchyard and its wider vicinity indicated several ihomogeneities varying in extension, which, according to the density of the situated profiles, may indicate, due to the complicated landscape, especially positions of recent graves. In several cases, though, after mutual correlation of the "anomalies", their linear character also cannot be excluded (A, B, D?, see Fig. 10). Especially the linearly oriented zone A, 1.0 – 1.5 m wide, with its beginning approximately south of the church tower, can be considered as interesting from the

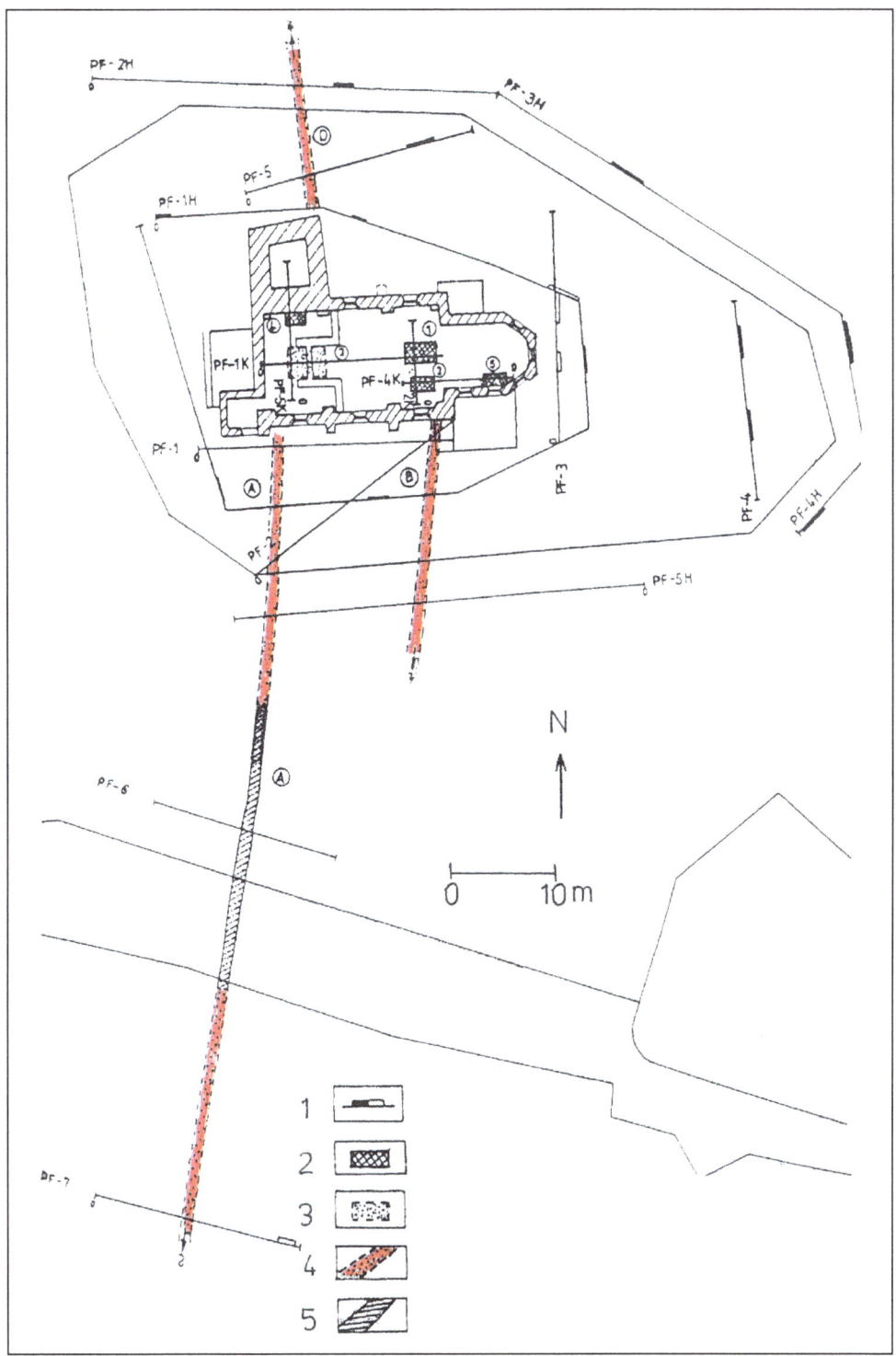

Fig. 10. Přepychy, the Church of St. Prokop: Correlation scheme of results of geophysical works with course of the interpreted and partly verified underground corridors. 1- manifestation of inhomogeneities according to their distinctiveness; 2- known tombs; 3- interpreted underground spaces; 4- course of corridors verified by research; 5- corridors assumed from the GPR results

point of view of possible localization of an underground corridor. Also those beginning at the area marked 3 and continuing along the parsonage towards the south cannot be excluded, possibly also a shorter zone beginning by the west corner of the south sacristy (B, see Fig. 10) and parallel with A. A certain indication of a similar structure can be identified north of the tower in the east direction (D), even though our (only probable) interpretation conclusions may play the role here due to having only a limited network of profiles for geophysical works to choose from. For all the above mentioned reasons, speculation of older inhabitants about existence of routes of possible corridors leading from the tomb or grave (1, 2) and continuing southwards towards the parsonage and northwards to the parcel No. 55 (Hašek/Petera 2001, 321) appears to be less credible.

Archaeological Excavation

The interpreted linear zone (A) was verified by archaeological sounding performed by the Municipality of Přepychy in 2001. A corridor was detected, so far 27 m long, leading towards the churchyard wall. It is however interrupted by a deposit from the side with the stream and by a caving from the other side with the parsonage. The bottom of the so-far cleared corridor, digged from the surface and masoned by sandy marlites, is approximately in the depth of 4 m. Its height is almost 230 cm near the parsonage, 160 cm in the area of the present entrance, the width is ca 100 cm. The ceiling consists of two flat opoka stones of minimum thickness of 15 cm. Dating of the building of the corridor is problematic but it may be connected with existence of the watchtower located in the area of the present church. The found route corresponds to the direction from the fortified church (tower) to the parsonage. Thus both the written sources and oral tradition claiming the existence of the corridor were verified.

TASOV, the Church of St. George and the Church of St. Peter and Paul, District of Žďár nad Sázavou

The village of Tasov lies ca 2.5 km SSW from the D1 highway, on which it is connected with Velké Meziříčí, 9 km distant. The housing of the village follows (in the length of approximately 1.5 km) a shallow valley, through which a smaller watercourse runs from the northwest to the southeast.

Tasov was founded in connection with colonization of the Czech-Moravian Upland no later than in the first half of the 13th century by a noble family, from which we know Záviš from 1233 and until 1240 also Mladota, Bohuslav and Budislav. In the Middle Ages, Tasov had three churches in certain period: the Churches of St. Peter and Paul, St. Wenceslas and St. George. The Romanesque church of St. Wenceslas was closed down and pulled down in 1784; St. George, whose masonry is a part of the present parsonage (Photo 19), is mentioned as a deserted church in 1550 and 1561. It was adapted into a parsonage in 1730. Around the end of the 14th century the Church of St. George did not serve the purpose anymore and a new High Gothic church was built with the help of Sazema of Tasov, which, slightly modified, serves the spiritual needs of the inhabitants up to the present day.

A Brief Overview of Geological Situation of the Locality

Tasov is located in Křižanovice Upland, which is a component orographic unit of the Czech-Moravia Upland. The bedrock is formed by eruptive rocks of the Třebíč

Photo 19. Tasov by Velké Meziříčí, the Church of St. George: General view of the present parsonage (Photograph by J. Unger)

Massif, which is of Variscan – Paleozoic (probably Lower Carboniferous) age. As for various facieses forming this durbachite complex, porphyric small-grained melanocratic amphibole-biotitic granites to quartz syenites occur in the wider area of the village. At the northwestern end of the village, the small-grained facies of porphyric type borders with the basic coarse-grained porphyric facies of magmatites of the same composition along the line of disturbance in the northeast – southwest direction. Again moldanubic, but this time leucocratic biotite magmatites with sillimanite reach into the vicinity of the village from the north. Narrow stream beds are filled with Holocene sandy-clayey sediments and thicker, perhaps Pleistocene, deluvial loamy-sandy and loamy-stony accumulations formed on their confluences in some places along their banks.

Geophysical Prospection and Archaeological Interpretation of the Results

The purpose of geophysical radar measuring was to find out the extension of the rotunda, whose masonry reaches under the building of the present parsonage. The apse, reaching under the building of the current parsonage, could have been as deep as is the size of the nave radius. South of the presbytery masonry appeared by complementary radar measuring. The real extension of the building to which the masonry belonged to is not clear yet (Fig. 11). On the basis of reinterpreting data of the GPR in the garden at the south side, and indication of a pulled-down building (A) sized 9 – 10 m x 5 – 5 m can be assumed, also a wall (B) of the WNW – ESE direction and a position of several graves. In the area of the north

DISCUSSION OF PRACTICAL RESULTS AND OBSERVATIONS

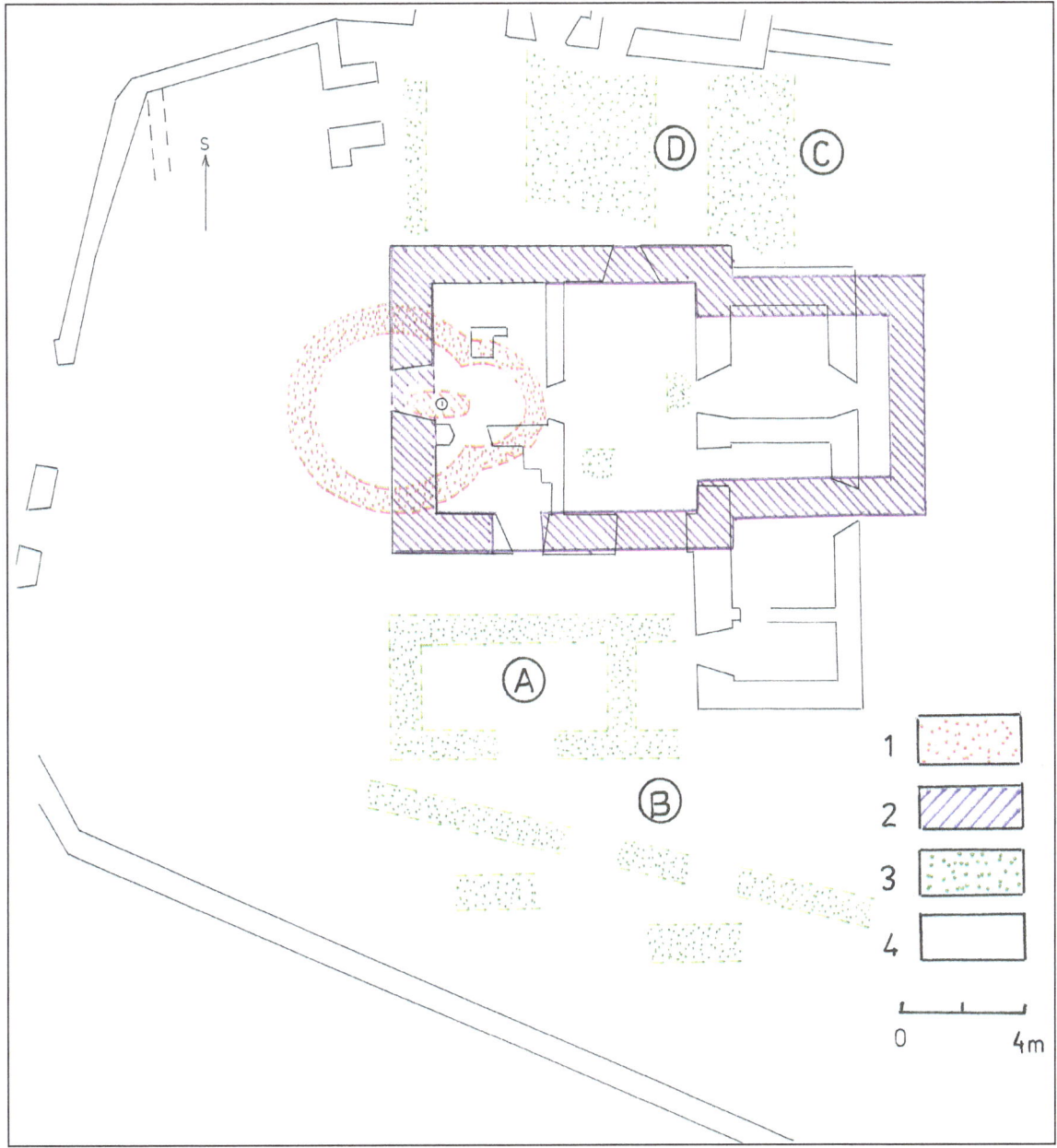

Fig. 11. Tasov by Velké Meziříčí, the Church of St. George: Ground plan situational scheme of the results of prospection and excavation. 1- the rotunda building; 2- the original walling of the small filial church of St. George; 3- interpreted inhomogeneities from the GPR; 4- the current house-building

yard there are two areal anomalies that we connect with recent activity (septic tank), indications of possible masonry (C) or cellar (D) etc.

Archaeological Excavation

The determinative research in the years 2007 – 2009 was initiated by discovery of walled portal on the south side of the present parsonage which confirmed that the current parsonage hides a substantial part of the original church of St. George known from written records. It was also discovered that intensive burying activity took place around the church and that it is necessary to archaeologically monitor and document all the excavation work. Archaeological research discovered the original presbytery of right-angled ground plan on the east side of the church nave. An absolutely unexpected finding was however done by a probe placed along the west front of the parsonage (Photo 20), which detected walling of an older rotunda, ca 0.8 m wide, whose part, together with an apse, lies under the parsonage building. A proof of the rotunda having been a church around which burials were made is the discovery of four skeletal graves damaged by newer masonry. Sometimes in the 2nd third of the 13th century it turned out that the original building did not meet the requirements put on a parish church, therefore it was pulled down and the building stone, except for the foundations, was used for building of a new church

Photo 20. Tasov by Velké Meziříčí, the Church of St. George: Relic of the rotunda masonry at the west side of the building detected by research (Photograph by J. Unger)

Photo 21. Tasov by Velké Meziříčí, the Church of St. George: Uncovered graves in the area of the former Church of St. George (Photograph by J. Unger)

consisting of the right-angled presbytery and an oblong nave. Also here, around the new church of an unchanged patrocinium, the burials were frequent, as is apparent from the multitude of grave sites, disturbed by one another (Photo 21).

The parish Church of St. Peter and Paul (Photo 22) is essentially a High Gothic building from the end of the 14th century, which was baroquised in the 18th century. There was a cemetery by the church from time immemorial.

Photo 22. Tasov, the Church of St. Peter and Paul: Aerial photograph. View from the north (Photograph by J. Kovárník)

Geophysical Prospection and Archaeological Interpretation of the Results

In the interior of the studied building on the area of 170 m^2, 21 perpendicular profiles of total length of 205.4 m were gauged by the soil radar method (Hašek/Maštera/Tomešek/Unger 2007). It is possible to identify, according to individual GPR findings, indications of various smaller structures (HR1-HR4; H1-H4 and K1-K5) in the abovementioned area. They can be attributed to tombs (HR1-HR4) and graves, larger accumulations of stones, variable lithology of the infill of depressions (H1-H4), relics of masonry (K1-K6) etc., situated mostly into the presbytery under the triumphal arch and in the axis of the church (Fig. 12a, b). One of the more significant ones, from our point of view, is the object HR1 located in the pride of place near the altar by its western margin (Fig. 12 c), also the tombs HR2 and HR3 west of the lintel – step (Fig. 12d), and maybe a possible tomb HR5 in the nave, too. Also the possibility of occurence of half-filled tombs (graves), which manifest themselves indistinctly in the results of geophysical works, cannot be excluded (Hašek/Peška/Unger 2008, 32).

Archaeological Excavation

Existence of probably Baroque tombs indicated by geophysical measuring was verified by determinative research in the church interior. Presence of original Gothic paving tiles and bricks was detected.

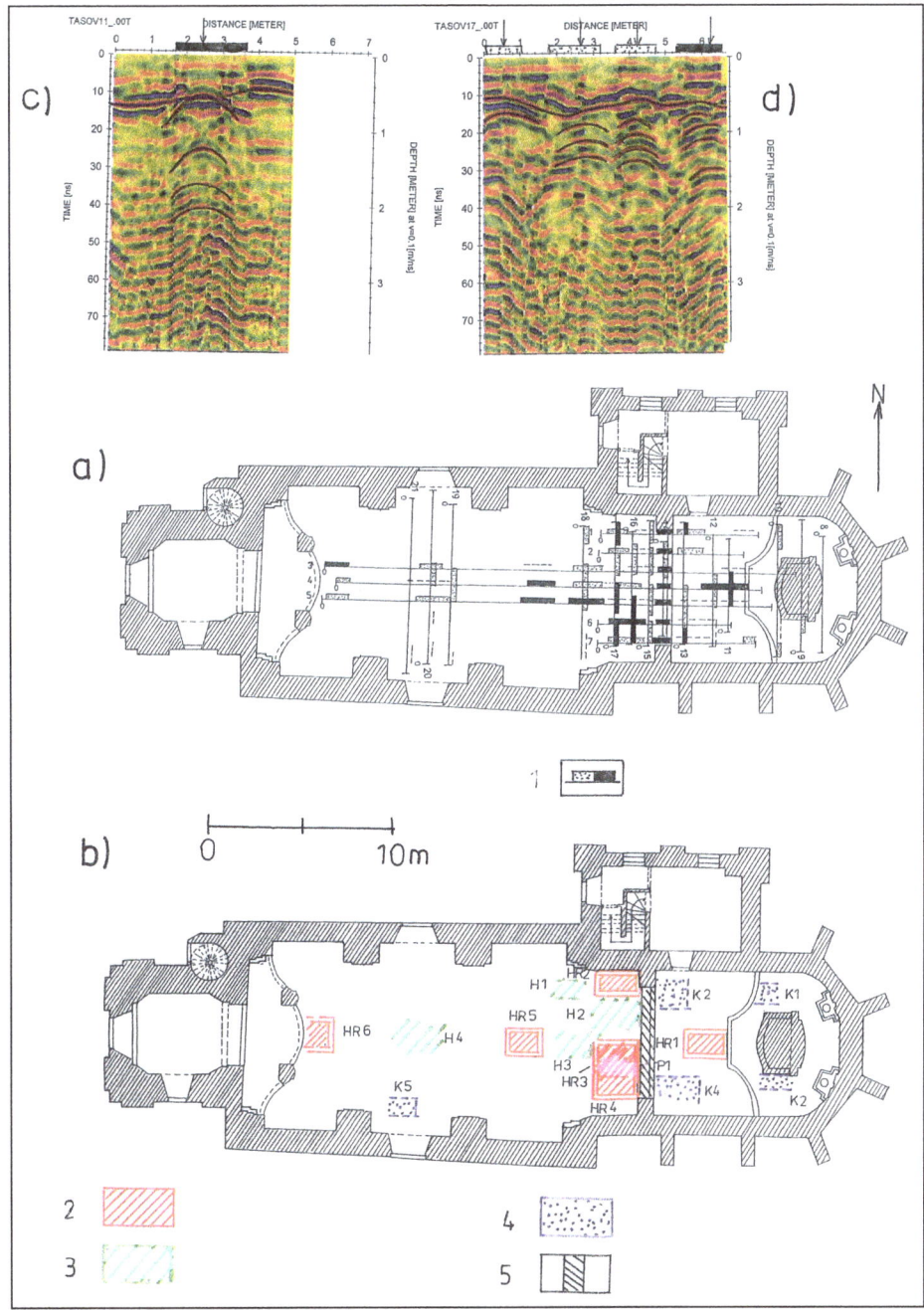

Fig. 12. Tasov by Velké Meziříčí, the Church of St. Peter and Paul: Correlation scheme of the results of the GPR measuring (a), interpretation of prospection results (b), manifestation of a tomb in the radarogram in the proximity of the altar (c), inhomogeneities (tombs, graves, accumulations of stones) under the triumphal arch (d).
1- interpreted inhomogeneities according to their distinctiveness; 2- tombs; 3- graves, accumulations of stones etc.;
4- shallower inhomogeneities (backfill, masonry relics, graves?); 5- lintel, stairs

4.2.2. City Parish Churches

Cities usually had one parish church and only large cities had more. For example, in medieval Brno there were two parish churches – Church of St. Peter and Paul and Church of St. James. In contrast to village churches, city churches are more palatial and more splendidly equipped. Within various construction activities, some interventions into the ground were used for specification of the constructional development of the church architecture (Unger 2008, 65). Churches in Hustopeče, Olomouc, Český Krumlov and Uherský Brod are examples.

HUSTOPEČE, the Church of St. Wenceslas, District of Břeclav

The Church of St. Wenceslas was built in the 13th century on the square of newly founded city of Hustopeče. It underwent a number of changes during next centuries, the

Photo 23. Hustopeče, the Chuch of St. Wenceslas: New church building in the place of the original one (Photograph by L. Pekárková)

most marked ones, that have left the greatest impression in the present appearance of the church, are those from the 15th and 16th centuries. In 1961 the tower collapsed and the two naves of the church were demolished. Only the presbytery stayed unharmed. The building was pulled down in 1962 and the whole area gradually turned into a park. At the end of the 20th century a new, modern church was built in the area of the original one (Photo 23) (Hašek/Unger 2001, 91).

A Brief Overview of Geological Situation of the Locality

The city of Hustopeče lies in the Dambořice Upland, which is a part of the Ždánice Forest. Its oldest part stands on ca 400 m wide flood plain of the stream of Stikovka consisting of fluvial Holocene deposits. Slightly elevated banks are formed by distinctly variable (as for facies) Eger Ždánice-Hustopeče formation of the nappe flysch Ždánice unit. It consists of psamitic, psamitic-pelitic and pelitic lithofacies, which often substitute each other laterally. Especially in the right-bank part of the city the formation is covered by Upper Pleistocene loesses and loess loams. It is possible to say that actually the whole wider vicinity of the town is covered by these Eolian sediments of variable thickness. Varying lithofacial developments of the above-characterized flysch base emerge alternately out of them.

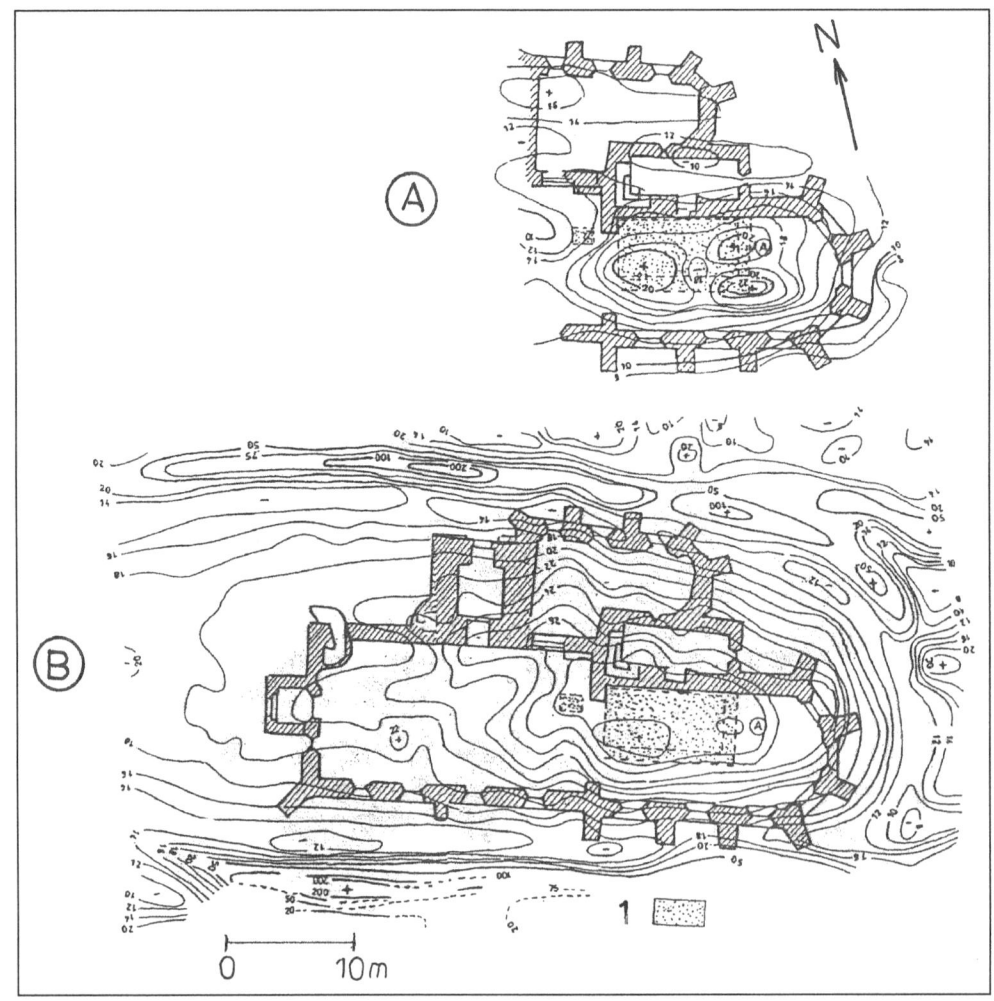

Fig. 13. Hustopeče, the Church of St. Wenceslas: Comparison of results of geophysical measuring with the situation of the church. A- VDV-R method; B- DEMP method; 1- localized tomb

Geophysical Prospection and Archaeological Interpretation of the Results

The aim of the DEMP works (h = 3÷5 m) – and experimentally also of resistance version of the very long waves method (VDV-R) – was to detect, in connection with projected new building construction, the exact situation of the original church and to localize a quite extensive tomb in the area of the presbytery. The position of the church is apparent in the results of the geophysical works through generally increased values of apparent specific resistance (Fig. 13). A minor diversion of linearly oriented anomaly ρ_{app} against the axis of the extinct religious building is caused by the effect of the iron frame of a panel by the northeast margin of the gauged area. A slight local arching of isolines of apparent resistances represents the course of the relics of the stone and brick walling of the component building elements. On the other hand, the more local, approximately isometrical zone of increased ρ_{app}, which are marked A in the ρDEMP map (29ohmm) and in the ρVDV map (22ohmm) is produced by manifestation of the tomb itself uncovered during consequent archaeological excavation. The course of two narrow weakened zones situated approximately to the centre of the explored area in the northeast – southwest direction could be the cause of static disturbance and subsequent collapse of the tower of the original church.

Archaeological Excavation

It was discovered by archaeological probing in the area of the extinct feature in 1990 that basement space sized 11 x 8 m, situated under the presbytery, has survived of the oldest building. This space was originally divided by a wall and its purpose is not quite clear. The chronogram 1747 at the door head dates probably its reconstruction into a Baroque tomb. Walling of the nave itself has not survived. An Early Gothic sacristy was added to the northern side of the presbytery relatively early. The building development in the 14th century continued by adding a new church nave, probably together with a tower. The last large reconstruction of the church was done at the turn of the 15th and 16th century. The Chapel of St. John was built at the north side, finished in 1496. In 1512 – 1517 a large Late Gothic presbytery vaulted by a net vault was built (Unger 1991, 67; 2008, 69).

OLOMOUC, the Church of St. Moritz, District of Olomouc

The city of Olomouc is located in the Upper Moravian Valley on the boundary line of the Middle Moravian flood plain and the Prostějov Highland. The course of the river Morava runs towards it from the northwest from Litovel through a water cut. In the often-winding riverbed, it flows through the eastern part of the city and heads towards Kroměříž.

The Gothic provost and parish church of St. Moritz (Photo 24) was built in the 2nd half of the 13th century. The building was damaged by several fires and therefore a new church began to be built in the 14th century. The southern prismatic tower survived from its older phase. Building of the smaller northern tower began in the beginning of the 15th century. The hall triple nave was built in 1435 – 53, its remaining part and the presbytery were finished in 1483. Also the west porch was built in this period. In 1572, a Renaissance behind-the-grave chapel of the Edelmann family was added to the church on its north side and in the 18th century also a total New Gothic rebuilding of the church was done and both spires of the west front were heightened (Hlobil/Toner/Hyhlík 1992).

Photo 24. Olomouc, the Church of St. Moritz: General view from the southeast (Photograph by V. Hašek)

A Brief Overview of Geological Situation of the Locality

The city lies in the several kilometres wide flood plain of Morava, which is widened in the east by flood plain of the river Bystřička. The city centre rests on elevation of the bedrock. The rock island is formed by Lower Carboniferous, Upper Viséan sediments of the Moravice formation. They are represented by partly uncovered bassets of outcrops with numerous thick areas of small-grained conglomerates. Housing in the Upper and Lower Square rests on sandy gravels with occurences of clays from Neogéne, which form the so-called motley Pliocene series. They line the western margin of the island. In their superincumbent bed, residues of many hundred years' building development of the city in the form of rubble and waste follow in the west direction. The centre of the city is lined with Holocene river sediments, which are namely sandy flood loams with variable admixture of gravels. The church building was probably founded in Neogéne sediments but it can be expected that the foundation walls already rest on the bedrock formed by massive Lower Carboniferous rocks, or near them.

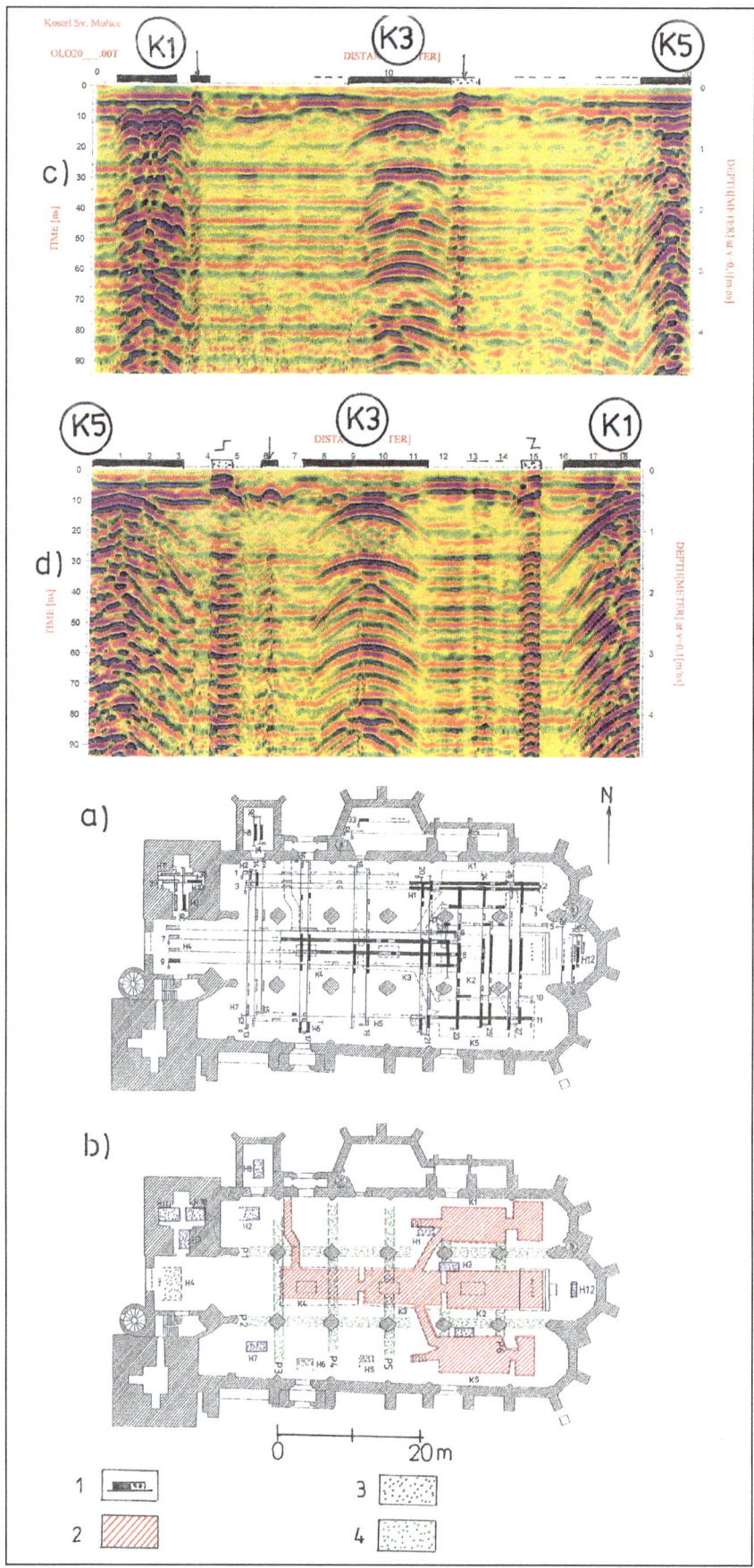

Fig. 14. Olomouc, the Church of St. Moritz. Correlation scheme of the GPR prospection results (a), interpretation of the measured data (b), manifestation of crypts and tombs in the east part of the church (c, d). 1- manifestation of inhomogeneities from the GPR according to their distinctiveness; 2- crypt; 3- graves; 4- continuous column foundations

Geophysical Prospection and Archaeological Interpretation of the Results

In the interior of the parish church of St. Moritz, several subsegments sized ca 1000 m² (the main and both side naves, presbytery, sacristy, the Marian chapel and Holy Trinity chapel) were geophysically gauged in 2007 (Hašek/Maštera/Tomešek 2007). A number of rather extensive anomalous zones can be identified here on the basis of the GPR method results. According to their extension and configuration, they correspond probably to positions of already known baroque crypts on the one hand, on the other hand to indications of graves, larger accumulations of stone material, continuous column foundations etc. (Fig. 14 a,b). Articulate and relatively well accessible baroque crypts (K1 to K5) occur in the area of all three naves. They are interconnected by three narrow, ca 1 m wide corridors and four entrances (Fig. 14 c, d).

Apart from the abovementioned area features, also indications of smaller structures (H1 to H12) can be identified in the gauged interior according to individual GPR indications. They can be assigned to graves (or walled tombs), larger accumulations of stones, relics of masonry etc., situated mostly near side altars, and areas of individual chapels (see Fig. 14). From our point of view, one of the most significant objects is the feature H4, located in the proximity of the main entrance by the western margin of the church, furthermore the grave or tomb H8 in the Marian chapel and the pit H12 behind the main altar, confirmed by the camera system. In the case of H4, there is a possibility that it can be a certain building component from the older extinct Romanesque church architecture placed probably outside the present object of the church, which was not intercepted by the geophysical measuring at the researched area. These could have been included in the baroque buildings of crypts. The orientation of possible graves is assumed to be E-W and sporadically also N-S. Continuous column foundations (P1 to P6) were partly localized in both the main and the side naves (Hašek/Peška/Unger 2008, 38).

Archaeological Evaluation

The geophysical prospection specified the system of the Baroque underground spaces – crypts, which extend under almost the whole church nave, positions of newer tombs in side chapels and detected indications of possible masonry relics also from the extinct older buildings in the researched area.

ČESKÝ KRUMLOV, the Church of St. Vitus, District of Český Krumlov

The Gothic Cathedral of St.Vitus (Photo 25) is situated in the outcrop above the river of Vltava in the historical part of the town. It was founded in 1329 and built in the first half of the 14th century during the political activity of

Photo 25. Český Krumlov, the Church of St. Vitus: View from the southwest (Photograph by J. Vandělík)

Peter of Rosenberg (Rožmberk) (Poche *et al*. 1977, 223). Its builder was Linhart of Aldenberk and afterwards also the master builder Staněk of Krumlov. The religious building was newly built in 1407-1439, expanded in 1638 and in 1725-26 and also in the 2nd half of the 18th century, adapted in 1893-94, renovated in 1899-1900 and 1936.

The building itself is a hall triple nave with a prolate pentagonally closed presbytery (Photo 26), storeyed sacristies, chapels of Resurrection and of St. John of Nepomuk. A spire with Romanesque windows in the ground floor is located in the west front, the last storey is Pseudo-Gothic. The Chapel of Resurrection, located by the north peripheral masonry, is an evidence of the Gothic building phase of the church. Krumlov archdeacons were buried here and its beginnings are connected with the period of consecration of the church (1439). During the Baroque adaptation ribs were removed and the chapel was opened into the side nave by a semicircular arch. The Chapel of St. John of Nepomuk itself was built in the first half of the 18th century. It is located on the north side of the left side wall of the church, east of the Chapel of Resurrection. Two gravestones of red marble, belonging to Wilhelm of Rosenberg (+1592) and his third wife Anna Maria of Baden (+1582), are placed by its entrance. These gravestones were moved here at the command of Joseph Adam of Schwarzenberg after taking apart and opening the tomb of the Rosenbergs in the church presbytery. Also Eleonora Amalia of Schwarzenberg is supposed to be buried in the chapel.

Photo 26. Český Krumlov, the Church of St. Vitus: Interior from the west (Photograph by J. Vandělík)

The foundations of the tomb of the Rosenbergs, which is placed west of the main altar in the middle of the presbytery, together with the entrance, are documented in 1583. In 1783, when this tomb was opened, it contained four coffins: of Wilhelm of Rosenberg, Anna Maria of Baden, Maria Johanna of the Dutch side of the Schwarzenbergs (+1670) and Francis Joseph, the son of Joseph Adam of Schwarzenberg (+1750), who founded the local chapel of St. John of Nepomuk together with his wife Eleonora Amalia.

A Brief Overview of Geological Situation of the Locality

The area of interest of the geophysical prospection is a part of the Český Krumlov Upland, formed of rocks of motley series of the Krumlov branch of the Moldanubicum and in its superincumbent bed by Quaternary rock mantle. The pre-Quaternary base is represented by its south margin by biotite paragneisses with interbeds of amphibolites and amphibolite gneisses. In higher locations, stripes and fairly wide positions of crystalline limestones with fine-grained paragneisses containing often higher abundance of quartz alternate. Amphibolites form abundant but thin bedded veins in all rocks. Graphite zones are either bound with formations of limestones or they jut right in the limestones. The abovementioned rocks constitute also building material of the religious building. The blankets are represented mostly by mechanical wastes of varying grain-size composition formed on the crystalline complex and influenced by Quaternary weathering.

Geophysical Prospection and Archaeological Interpretation of the Results

41 mutually perpendicular profiles of total length of 286.5 m were measured in the researched interior of the sacral building in 2007 (Hašek/Šindelář/Thomová/Tomešek 2008, 58). Variably homogeneous environment into depths of ca 1.2 to 2.9 m (vr = 0.10 m/ns) can be assumed on the gauged GPR profiles on the basis of distinctive linear reflections at shorter times (t' = 24–40 ns) by interpreting the geophysical data. It can be certain fictious borderline between a layer of recent deposits and a surface of weathered rocks of the Moldanubicum due to probable more gradual lithological transition between anthopogenous cover and Quaternary rock mantle (eluvium). From evaluation of the radarograms a number of local indications of variable depth level of their upper parts can be expected. They can be attributed, apart from the abovementioned geological causes, to manifestation of several tombs, possible graves, related building elements, depression character of underbed structures with varying sandy-clayey filling, larger accumulations of stones etc. All these near-surface inhomogeneities are concentrated in depths of ca 0.5 to 0.8 m; their width ranges from 1.3 to ca 4.0 m.

Three main kinds of near-surface inhomogeneities can be presumed to be in the interior of the excavated building according to the results of the GPR method: tombs, graves and continuous column foundations etc. In the area of the Baroque chapel of St. John of Nepomuk, a smaller structure (A) sized ca 2.3 x 1.4 x 1.5 m proved to be under the gravestone by interpreting the radarograms. It can correspond, according to the inscription, to the tomb of Eleonora Amalia of Schwarzenberg. A known larger tomb (B), sized ca 3.5 x 2.5 x 2.5 m, belonging to the Rosenbergs, was localized west of the main altar in the presbytery. The entrance is expected to be at its east margin near the altar (Fig. 15e). Another larger tomb (C) on a ground plan of ca 4.0-4.5 x 2.5 m is located under the triumphal arch and partly also under the presbytery (Fig. 15d). It has not been mentioned in written records so far. Its entrance (2 x 1 m) is expected to be in the main nave on the west side. Its continuation may be a grave marked + in a tile sized 2 x 1.2 m.

An indication of an areal structure, possibly correspondding to some unknown tomb (D), was detected under the wooden floor in the north sacristy (Fig. 15).

In the original Gothic Chapel of the Resurrection, possible position of a smaller, probably half-caved tomb (E) was interpreted by geophysical prospection. According to the results of the measuring, also positions of two graves with the E-W (or N-S) orientation come into consideration.

Except for the mentioned areal features, manifestation of several graves can be expected in the areas of the main and both side naves, located mostly to the long axis of the church (E-W orientation). They can be partly caved. On the basis of the prospection results, altogether 4 such places were identified here, sized 2.0-2.2 x 1.0-1.2 m.

On both sides of the entrance into the Chapel of St. John of Nepomuk, gravestones of Wilhelm of Rosenberg and Anna Maria of Baden are put into the inner side wall of the church, as mentioned above. Their location indicates,

DISCUSSION OF PRACTICAL RESULTS AND OBSERVATIONS

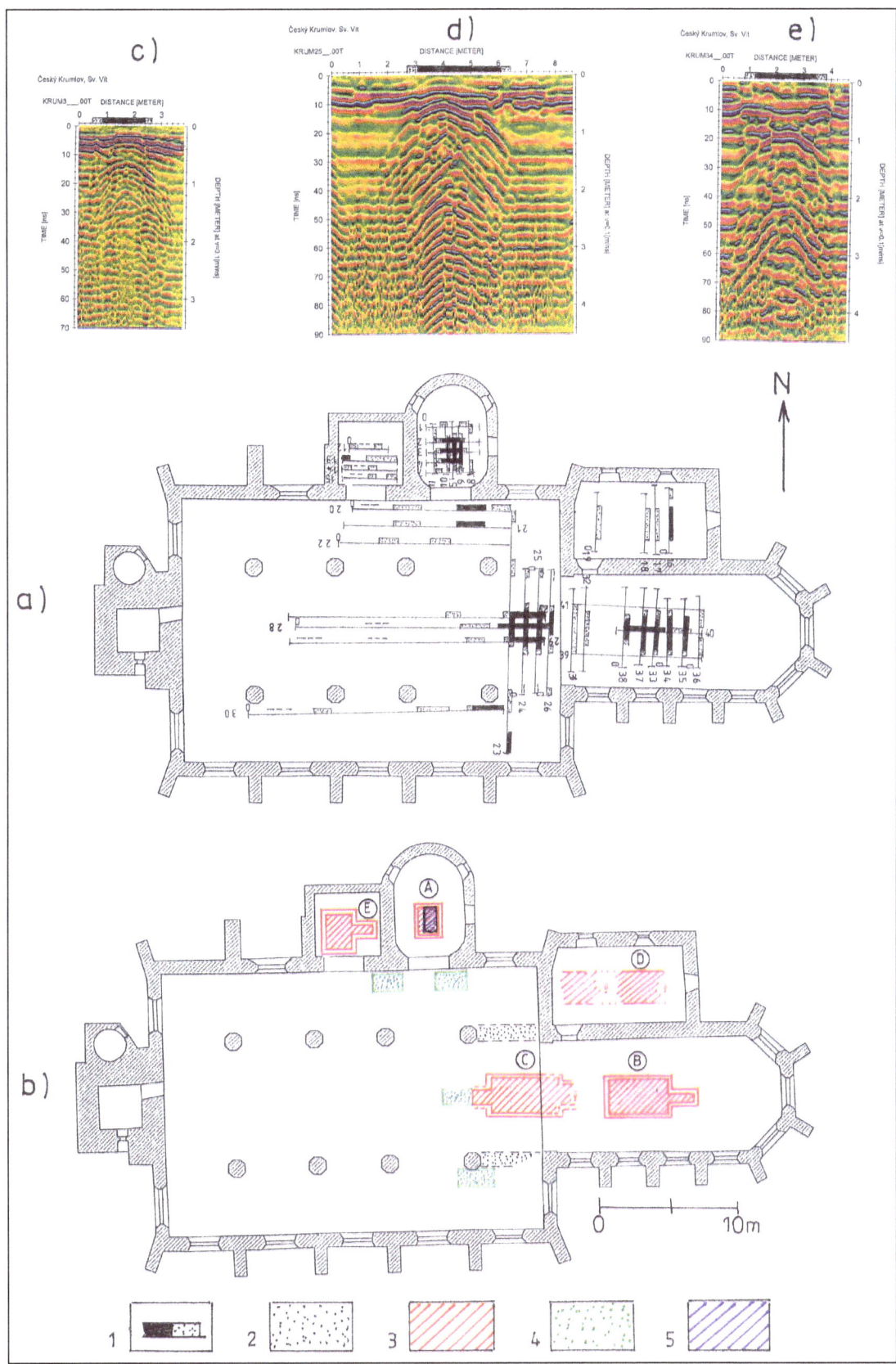

Fig. 15. Český Krumlov, the Church of st. Vitus: Correlation scheme of results of geophysical works (a), one of possible variants of interpretation of the measured data (b), manifestation of tombs of Eleonora Amalia of Schwarzenberg (A) in the interpreted radarogram (c), so far unknown tombs (C) under the triumphal arch (d) and the tomb of the Ronenbergs (B) in the radarogram (e). 1- near-surface inhomogeneities according to their distinctiveness; 2- relics of masonry, continuous column foundations; 3- interpreted tombs; 4- assumed graves, accumulations of stones; 5- tombstone of Eleonora Amalia of Schwarzenberg

according to GPR, possible existence of two close graves sized ca 2 x 1.2 m, or other possible secondary interferences into the church floor. Manifestations of continuous column foundations (see Fig. 15) were partly localized on both sides of the triumphal arch with the axis in the E-W direction.

Camera Research and Documentation of the Tomb of St. John of Nepomuk

A granodiorite tombstone sized 179 x 89 cm covering a walled vaulted tomb is located in the side chapel in front of the altar (Photo 27). A majuscule inscription of 7 lines (HER LIGET DIE ARME SÜNDERIN ELEONORA. BITTET FUR SIE. OBIJT DIE 5. MAJI A 1741) is on the tombstone, height of the letters is 5 to 10 cm. A princely crown is pleced above the first line, a skull and crossbones is above the penultimate line.

Photo 28. Český Krumlov, the Church of St. Vitus: Coffin of Eleonora Amalia of Schwarzenberg, photograph from an exploratory borehole (Photograph of J. Vandělík)

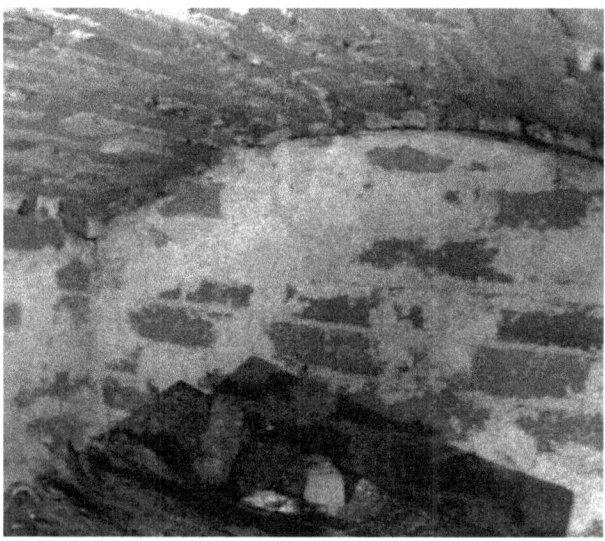

Photo 27. Český Krumlov, the Church of St. Vitus: Tomb of Eleonora Amalia of Schwarzenberg, photograph from an exploratory borehole (Photograph by J. Vandělík)

The tomb is a simple area of an oblong ground plan (with a longer N-S axis) and it is built of bricks and vaulted by simple brick vault. It is a shaft tomb of smaller sizes (1.40 x 2.30 m). The burial was laid into a simple wooden coffin of larger sizes, which takes most of the space of the tomb itself. The coffin is decorated by painted motifs of skull and bones and with a picture, which is already illegible today and from which only black beams have survived on the upper lid of the coffin (Photo 28). Thanks to disintegrated side boards, it was possible to penetrate into the coffin itself by an exploratory borehole at least partly research its contents. Apart from fragmented boards, also parts of the surviving skeleton (upper and lower limbs), remains of textile cover and perhaps also of the clothing of the deceased woman were managed to be photographed. The record is presently subject to further interpretation. The coffin is filled with many wood shavings to absorb the humidity. The funeral was not unique in any way and did not differ from the way of burying in the first half of the 18th century (Hašek/Šindelář/Thomová/Tomešek 2008, 59).

So according to the inscription on the tombstone on the west side of the chapel, Eleonora Amalia of Schwarzenberg, born of Lobkovice, was buried in the tomb. In 1710 she married prince Adam Francis of Schwarzenberg (1680 – 1732) who inherited the property of Eggenbergs when this family died out in 1719. Prince Adam Francis himself was shot dead by unfortunate coincidence by the Emperor Charles VI on a hunt in summer of 1732 and Eleonora Amalia took care of the family property for her juvenile son Joseph Adam. Eleonora Amalia died in 1741. Her tragically deceased husband is buried in several places. The deceased without his heart and insides is buried in the Church of St. Vitus in Český Krumlov, the insides in the cemetery Church of St. Giles in Třeboň.

UHERSKÝ BROD, the Church of Master John Huss, District of Uherské Hradiště

The wider area of the building in question occurs in the original historic and probably also the oldest centre of the city of Uherský Brod, founded in 1250's. The present Church of Master John Huss (or, more exactly, its oldest part) comes probably from the first half of the 13th century (Photo 29). It was originally consecrated to St. John the Baptist. The Romanesque building was being adapted and extended several times. Towards the end of the 15th century, the nave was adapted and the presbytery extended, the sacristy was added and in 1589 also the Renaissance spire. The last adaptation of the church, corresponding to the present appearance, comes from the years 1666 – 1667. It was deactivated and secularized in

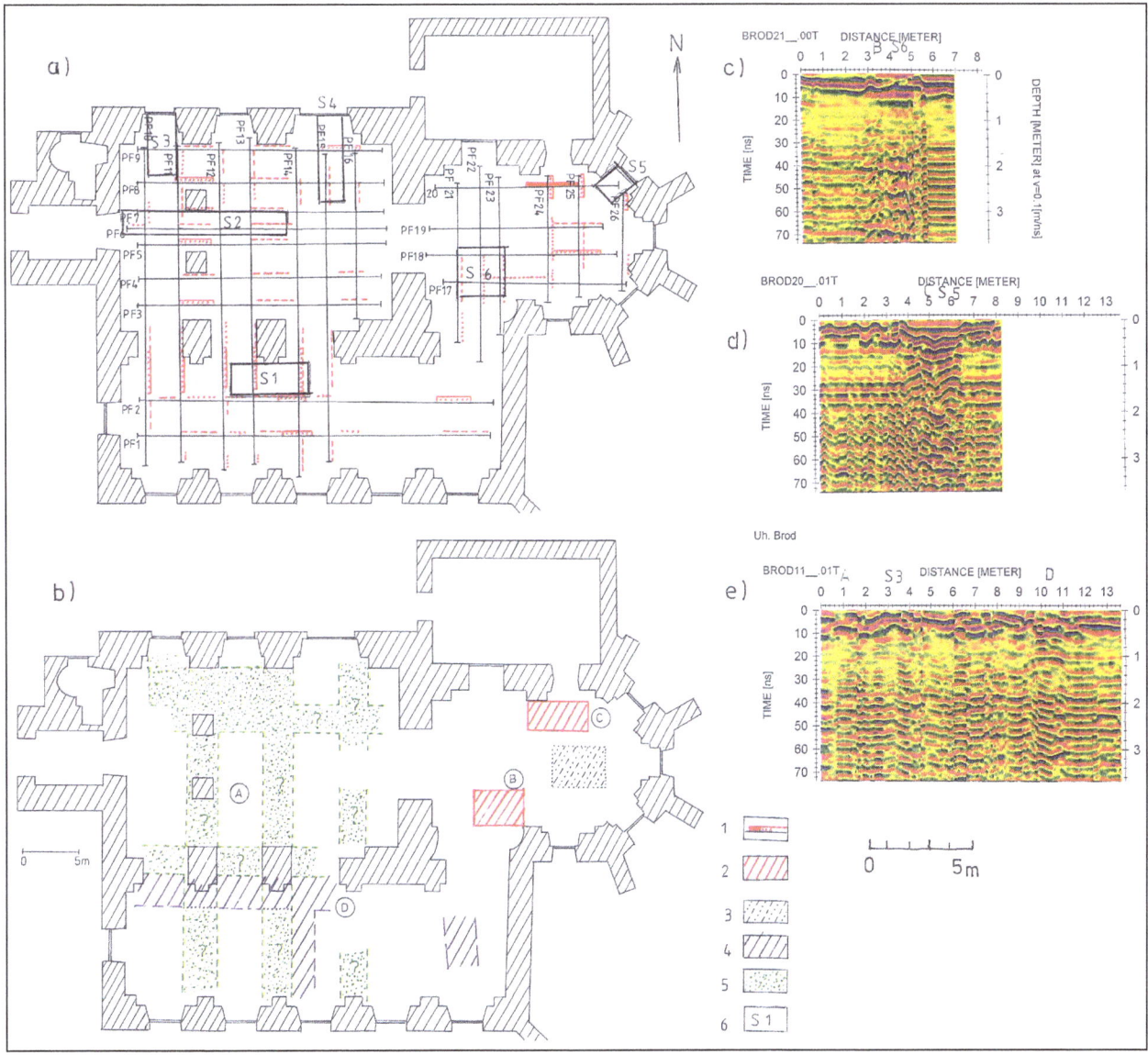

Fig. 16. Uherský Brod, the Church of Master John Huss: Correlation scheme of the results of the GPR measuring (a), interpreted manifestation of the near-surface inhomogeneities (b), presentation of tombs and other structural elements in processed radarograms (c, d, e). 1 – localized inhomogeneities according to their distinctiveness; 2- interpreted tombs; 3- probable manifestation of the stone plinth of the altar; 4- masonry relics; 5- simple graves, continuous column foundations; 6- archaeological probes

1784 but it has been serving to the Czechoslovak Hussite Church since 1920 (Hašek/Šindelář/Unger/Vaškových – in print).

A Brief Overview of Geological Situation of the Locality

It is a part of the Vizovice Upland, subunit of Hluk Highland, formed by rocks of the Magura Flysch Belt and by Quaternary cover in their superincumbent bed. The pre- Quaternary base is represented by Vsetín layers of the Zlín Formation (subunit of Račany), which is formed by medium to coarse-grained rhythmic flysch with calcareous claystones and glauconitic sandstones (lower Eocene – lower Oligocene). The Quaternary cover (Holocene) is represented by deluvial clayey-stony sediments and anthropogeneous deposits of variable thicknesses.

Geophysical Prospection and Archaeological Interpretation of the Results

The aim of the radar measurement performed here in 2008 was to check the remains of older walls, graves, hollow spaces etc. Several fairly distinctive anomalies (A, B, C, D) were localized by interpreting the radarograms. They can be manifestations of various lithological changes in the made-ground under the wooden church floor, such as backfills of simple graves (A), half-caved tombs (B, C), masonry relics (D), or other related building elements (Fig. 16a). All these near-surface inhomoge-

Photo 29. Uherský Brod, the Church of Master John Huss: Situation of the reconstructed church building from 1920 from the southwest (Photograph by J. Pavelčík)

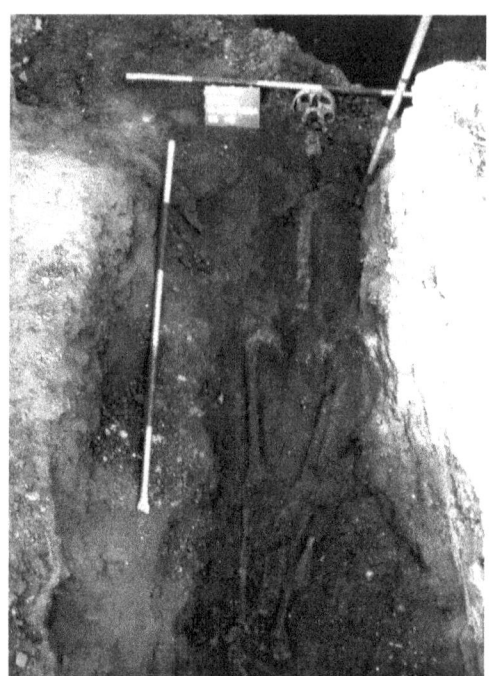

Photo 30. Uherský Brod, the Church of Master John Huss: Grave from the 13th century (Photograph by M. Vaškových)

neities are concentrated into depths of 0.4 – 1.0 m (tops); their widths range in the interval of 1.0 – 2.0 m.

Two interpreted indications of areal character of the total size of 2 x 2 m (B) and 2 x 1 m (C) are located on both sides of the presbytery. They indicate positions of walled-up and also probably partly caved tombs. The cause of other, geophysically less distinctive, inhomogeneities in the interior of the object, can be, apart from lithology of the anthropogeneous layer, also backfill of simple graves (such as the example A) or possibly combined with manifestation of continuous column foundations.

Archaeological Excavation

On the basis of the evaluation of the GPR, several test pits of various sizes and depths were placed in the space of the church by the South Moravian Museum in Uherské Hradiště (Fig. 16), which uncovered larger amount of simple inhumation graves from both the Late Medieval Period (14th century) and especially the Early Modern period (16th – 17th century), including two walled-up tombs (S-5, S-6) (see Fig. 16b). In the test pits S – 2, 3, 4, altogether 13 graves were excavated, some of which were laid separately (example in Photo 30), in one case there are as much as three individuals laid directly on one another. That could be connected with their burying during time of war events (17th century). At least 50 individuals were buried here. Limbs of many of them are missing and musket bullets can be found in their thoraxes.

Apart from graves in the church nave, a Baroque bricked tomb (17th century) (S-6) was discovered in the area of

Photo 31. Uherský Brod, the Church of Master John Huss: Uncovering of the brick tomb from the 17th century (Photograph by M. Vaškových)

the presbytery. It reached to the depth of ca 210 cm under the floor level (Photo 31, Fig. 16c). Except for several remains of human bones it contained interesting finds such as a part of a leather shoe, of a vestment, parts of rosaries, lockets and glass vessels. Also uncovering of the already known walled-up tomb of the last parish priest in the church, the dean Jan Trchlík, who was buried in it in 1739 (S-5), was interesting. Under the massive tombstone there are remains of oak coffin with a skeleton of a tall man, embroidered green vestment together with remains of a rosary and a pendant cross that he probably had in his clasped hands (Photo 32, Fig. 16d).

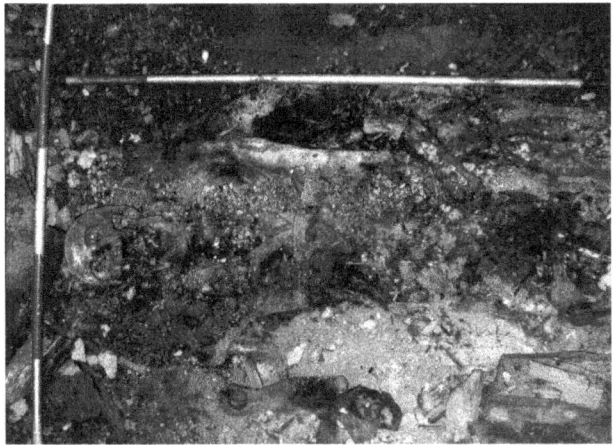

Photo 32. Uherský Brod, the Church of Master John Huss: Tomb of Jan Trchalík
(Photograph by M. Vaškových)

Apart from research of burials, the walling of the church foundations from the 13th century in the SW part of the building was successfully uncovered (Fig. 16e). The solidity of the building is obvious from the massive and carefully scabbled sandstone ashlars of the Magura Flysch laid on quality mortar (Hašek/Šindelář/Unger/Vaškových – in print).

OLOMOUC, the Cathedral of St. Wenceslas, District of Olomouc

The original Romanesque Cathedral of St. Wenceslas was a three-nave basilica. The main nave ended at the east side by a semicircular apse, and so probably did the side naves. The presbytery with choir in transept was elevated above the church level by nine degrees. A crypt was located under them, accessible by a narrow staircase from the north. The part of the crypt under the presbytery was uncovered as soon as in the 19th century. Its west outer wall was probably not detected. A newer tomb was established in this place, which probably destroyed the west part of the building. According to surviving written documentation, the total length of the building was ca 50 m and width more than 29 m (which also agrees with the Gothic disposition). The Romanesque part of the masonry disappeared gradually, first by Late Romanesque and Early Gothic rebuildings in the 13th century. The Early Gothic reconstruction of the cathedral kept the sizes of the original Romanesque triple nave, which was however razed. Only a crypt under the presbytery has survived. Bishop Bruno built an Early Gothic triple nave with a new inner vault axis and outer buttresses on the Romanesque foundations of the outer walls of the basilica triple nave. The High Gothic reconstruction of the Olomouc dome (Photo 33) was ended in the first decades of the 15th century, before the Hussite Wars. A new presbytery was supposed to be annexed to the triple nave, which was however probably not finished. The new presbytery of the cathedral was built as late as in 1616 – 1618. In 1636, two crypts had not been finished yet. They were built subsequently in 1661 (Photo 34). The Dietrichstein presbytery is now preserved only in the pseudo-Gothic masonry of the present presbytery. (Richter 1959, Michna/Pojsl 1988, Hašek/Tomešek/Zatloukal 2003).

Photo 33. Olomouc, the Cathedral of St. Wenceslas: View from the southwest (Photograph by L. Pekárková)

Photo 34. Olomouc, the Cathedral of St. Wenceslas: Church interior with positions of entrances into tombs from the west (Photograph by L. Pekárková)

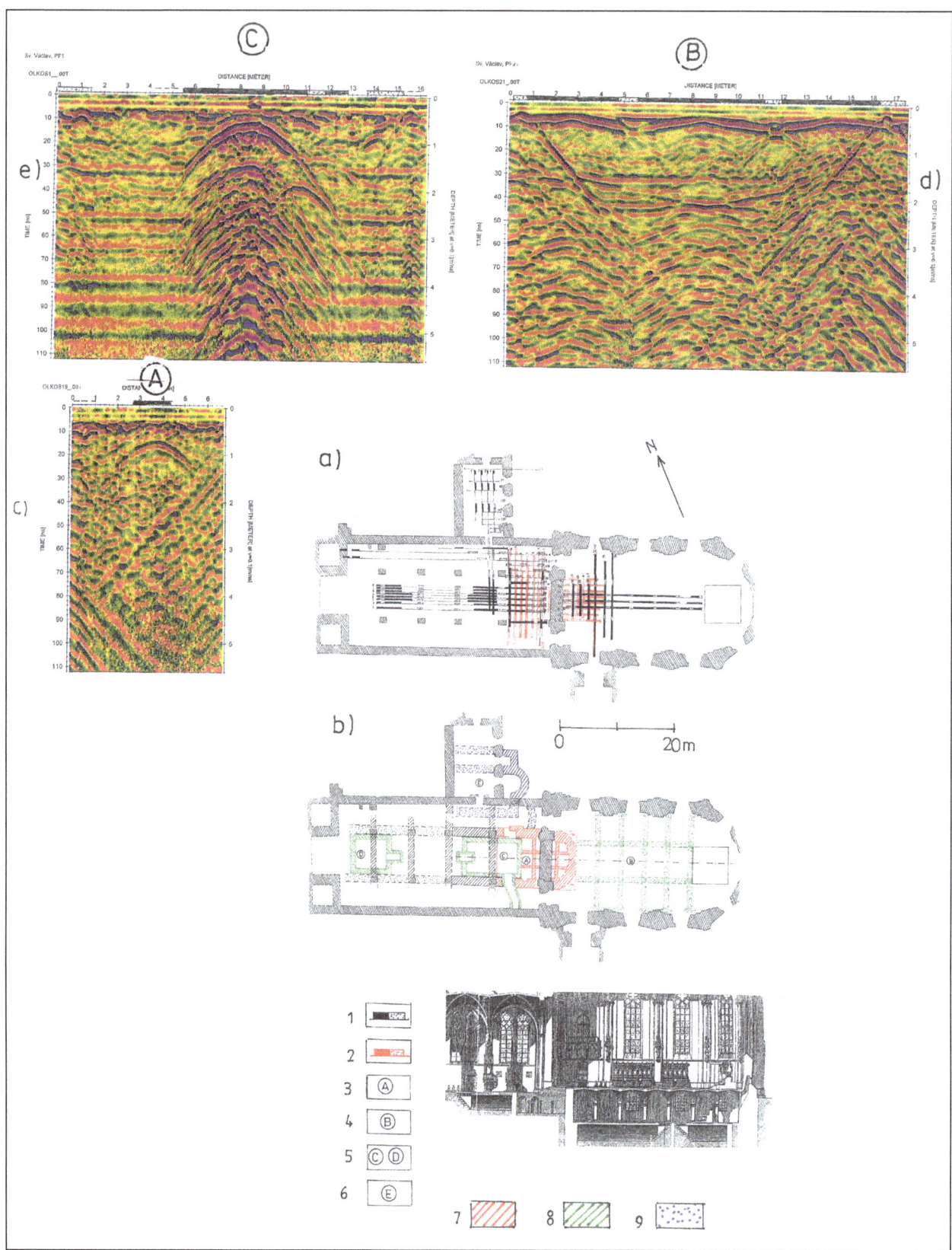

Fig. 17. Olomouc, the Cathedral of St. Wenceslas: Correlation scheme of results of the GPR method from 2003-2007 (a), interpretation of the measured data and section of the current objects in the east part of the cathedral (b), manifestation of the filled-up Romanesque crypt of St. Adalbert (c), presentation of modern tombs under the presbytery (d), modern tomb in the main nave (e). 1- near-surface inhomogeneities according to their distinctiveness from the GPR measuring in 2003; 2- near-surface inhomogeneities according to their distinctiveness from the GPR measuring in 2007; 3- Romanesque crypt; 4- modern tombs under the presbytery; 5- modern tombs in the main nave; 6- relics of the uncovered older Romanesque church; 7- the Romanesque crypt masonry; 8- modern tombs masonry; 9- the Romanesque church masonry relics

A Brief Overview of Geological Situation of the Locality

The wider area of the rise of the cathedral belongs, according to the Regional Structuring of the Czech Republic, into Middle Moravian floodplain of the Upper Moravian Valley (Czudek 1973). The site of interest is in the northeastern part of Olomouc. It is located on a rise, which is a part of the Hněvotín – Olomouc horst and at the same time also of the Čelechovice – Olomouc elevation zone of the NE-SW direction. The area of interest itself is terminated by steep slopes and it is by-passeed by one of the branches of the Morava River. The before-Quaternary base is formed by Lower Carboniferous sediments in the Culm facies. In the stratigraphically lowest position there are layers of compact wackes, in some places also conglomerate wackes and small conglomerates of pea gravel type, which pass into siltites and clayey shales (Barth *et al.* 1971). The Quaternary cover is formed, according to the archaeological test pit, laid out in the western corridor of the Gothic ambit, by relics of pleistocene loesses in the superincumbent bed of the bedrock. Stratigraphically higher, above the position of the yellow sand, primeval cultural layers lie, further is a 10th century horizon in the form of dense soil with ample residues of pottery, and finally also a thick layer of brown landfill, which used to overlain the rise north of the cathedral up to the Chapel of St. John the Baptist (Michna/Pojsl 1988). Anthropogenic layers might be spread all over the area of the Wenceslas Square due to intense building activity in the past.

Geophysical Prospection and Archaeological Interpretation of the Results

The aim of geophysical prospecting in 2006-2007 was to specify development of this monument and foreshadow possibilities of further research. From the total correlation of the GPR indications (Fig. 17a,b), altogether 5 fairly extensive zones can be identified here (A – the Romanesque crypt, B – the crypts in the presbytery from 1661, C and D – the Baroque tombs in the axis of the nave, E – masonry from the Romanesque sacral building) and 19 narrower structures of linear character (various vault chords of both crypts, continuous column foundations in the nave, walling of the vicarious sacristy, funeral objects).

In the anomalous zone A, detected by the prospecting under the triumphal arch, in the wider area of the stairway and at the west margin of the pseudo-Gothic presbytery, there is a manifestation of the Romanesque and currently buried crypt of St. Adalbert (the largest inner size 9 x 7 m, thickness of the walling ca 1.0 m, Fig. 17c). It was probably destroyed (walled in) at its west side during the process of building, or during the eastern limitation of the Baroque tomb (C). We expect indications of only relics of its outer walls and vault chords in the lengthwise and transverse direction. The depth of the tomb ceiling is ca 0.8 to 1.4 m, the floor of the object ca 2.8 – 3.4 m. The original east end was constituted of an apse, which was probably finished afterwards (during building of the crypt in 1661) to form a rectangle, as is apparent on the present ground plan (Fig. 17).

The position of large modern crypt (Fig. 17d) with the same sizes as the pseudo-Gothic presbytery (ca 28 x 16 m – marked B) is very interesting, in spite of relatively small extent of radar measuring in this area of the cathedral (intensely built-up area, pews). Indications of five vaults of the span of ca 4 m between the vault chords were detected here in the transverse direction and three vaults ca 5-6 m wide in the lengthwise direction. On both sides of the feature also manifestation of outer walls cannot be excluded. Another narrower and more extensive tomb can be expected under the building (see Fig. 17).

In the area of the axis of the main nave, two areal zones (C, D) can be interpreted from the intense reflections of electromagnetic waves, followed by narrow near-surface linear anomalies in both the lengthwise and transverse direction – continuous column foundations. The anomalous areas C and D indicate known larger walled-up modern (17th – 18th century) tombs (inner sizes 9 x 5.5 m; 5.5 x 5.5 m – walling thickness 0.6 – 0.7 m) placed in the middle (C) and west part (D) of the cathedral with ledgers apparent in the tile flooring. We expect two entrances in the relatively larger tomb (C) – on its west and south side. Fictive depths of ceilings of both objects are 0.7 m for C and 0.8 m for D (Fig. 17e).

An indication of a possible apse (?), terminating the north side nave can be assumed under the triumphal arch by the stone stairway into the crypt located under the present presbytery.

In the vicarious sacristy two narrower and less distinctive linear anomalies marked E were localized. They probably proved the existence of another continuation of the course of the north foundation walling from the older (Romanesque) sacral building with an apse (see Fig. 17), which was uncovered by excavation on a yard east of the studied area (Hašek/Tomešek/Zatloukal 2003). Results of works in the north side nave of the church partly indicated also possible southern and western limiting of this building (Hašek/Peška/Unger 2008, 39).

4.2.3. Monasteries

In the 13th century monastic way of life achieved an extraordinary development. Feudal lords participated still more in founding of monasteries and a whole number of monastic houses were built in cities. The basic scheme of a monastic complex was essentially the same – a church and an adjoining quadrature. Although a monastery was usually a whole complex of buildings, some of which served to ascertain the economic security, attention is focused especially on the enclosure including the monastic church (Unger 2008, 73).

4.2.3.1. The Benedictines

Beginnings of the Benedictine Order go back to the 6th century when St. Benedict of Nursia (480 – 547) founded a monastery in Monte Cassino. Appearance of the original monastery is not known but monks created principles of a building type in the course of centuries which has stayed in order architecture during the whole Middle Ages. The ideal ground plan of a monastic complex including economic buildings is known already from the 9th century. The central point of a monastery was a church with adjoining ambulatory and a cloister garth, around which necessary spaces of the cloister centre were concentrated, and other, mostly economic buildings nearby. The monastery in Třebíč in Moravia may be an example.

TŘEBÍČ, the Basilica of the Assumption of the Virgin Mary, District of Třebíč

In the 12th century, also churches of princely monasteries had basilican disposition, if they were built in this period. It could be also the case of the original Benedictine monastery, located on a rise above the river of Jihlava in the northwest part of the historic center of the city of Třebíč, founded sometime between 1101 and 1104. Later in the 13th century the smaller church was replaced by the large monastic church, finished in 1240 – 60 (Photo 35), which stylistically belongs to the final period of the Romanesque architecture in Moravia. It is an elongated three-nave basilica without a transept with a deep, strongly isolated presbytery (Photo 36) above a three-nave crypt (Photo 37), with a pair of towers in the west front (Chadraba *et al.* 1984, Foltýn *et al.* 2005, 686).

Photo 36. Třebíč, the Basilica of St. Prokop: Church interior from the west (Photograph by M. Heyduk)

Photo 37. Třebíč, the Basilica of St. Prokop: the Romanesque-Gothic crypt (Photograph by V. Hašek)

Photo 35. Třebíč, the Basilica of St. Prokop: View from the southwest (Photograph by V. Hašek)

A Brief Overview of Geological Situation of the Locality

According to the Regional Structuring of the Czech Republic (Czudek 1973), the area of interest of the geophysical prospection is a part of the Czech-Moravian Upland, subunit of the Jaroměřice basin formed by rocks of the Třebíč Massif and by Quaternary rock mantle in its superincumbent bed. The pre-Quaternary base consists of amphibolitic-biotitic melanocratic granite to medium-grained syenodiorite (the younger Paleozoic). Blankets are represented especially by mechanical wastes of varying grain-size composition that have originated on crystalline complex rocks and are influenced by Quaternary weathering.

Geophysical Prospection and Archaeological Interpretation of the Results

The main goal of the GPR method research in 2006 – 2007 was to localize positions of tombs and graves or possibly also the foundation wall of the Chapel of St. Benedict (consecrated in 1109), in spite of limited usage of geophysical methods due to rather complicated

DISCUSSION OF PRACTICAL RESULTS AND OBSERVATIONS

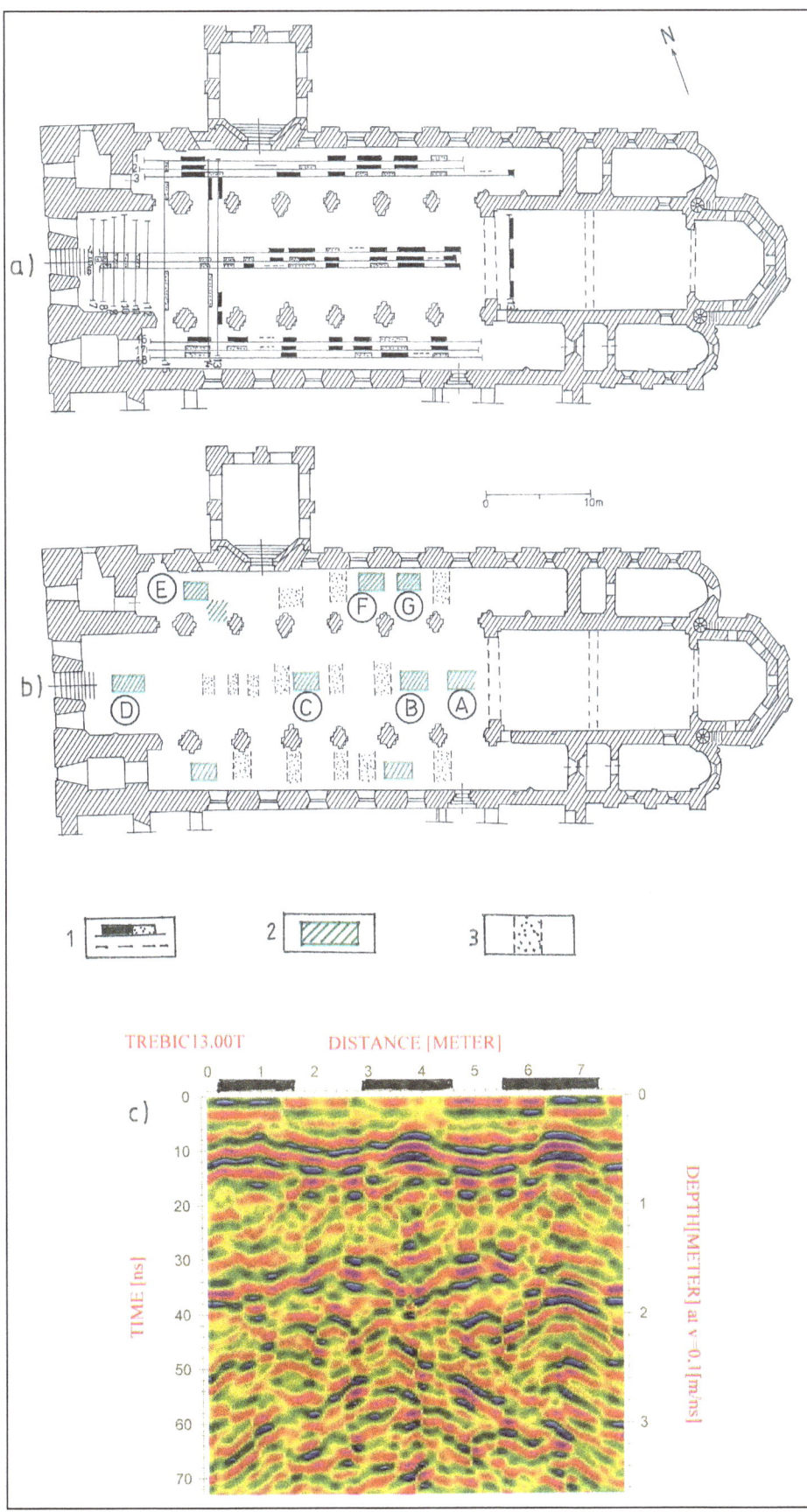

Fig. 18. Třebíč, the Basilica of St. Prokop: Correlation scheme of results of the GPR measuring (a), one of possible variants of inhomogeneities interpretation in the church area (b) and manifestation of crypt in the interpreted radarogram (c). 1- interpreted indications of inhomogeneities according to their distinctiveness; 2- graves, tombs, accumulations of stones; 3- probable masonry relics

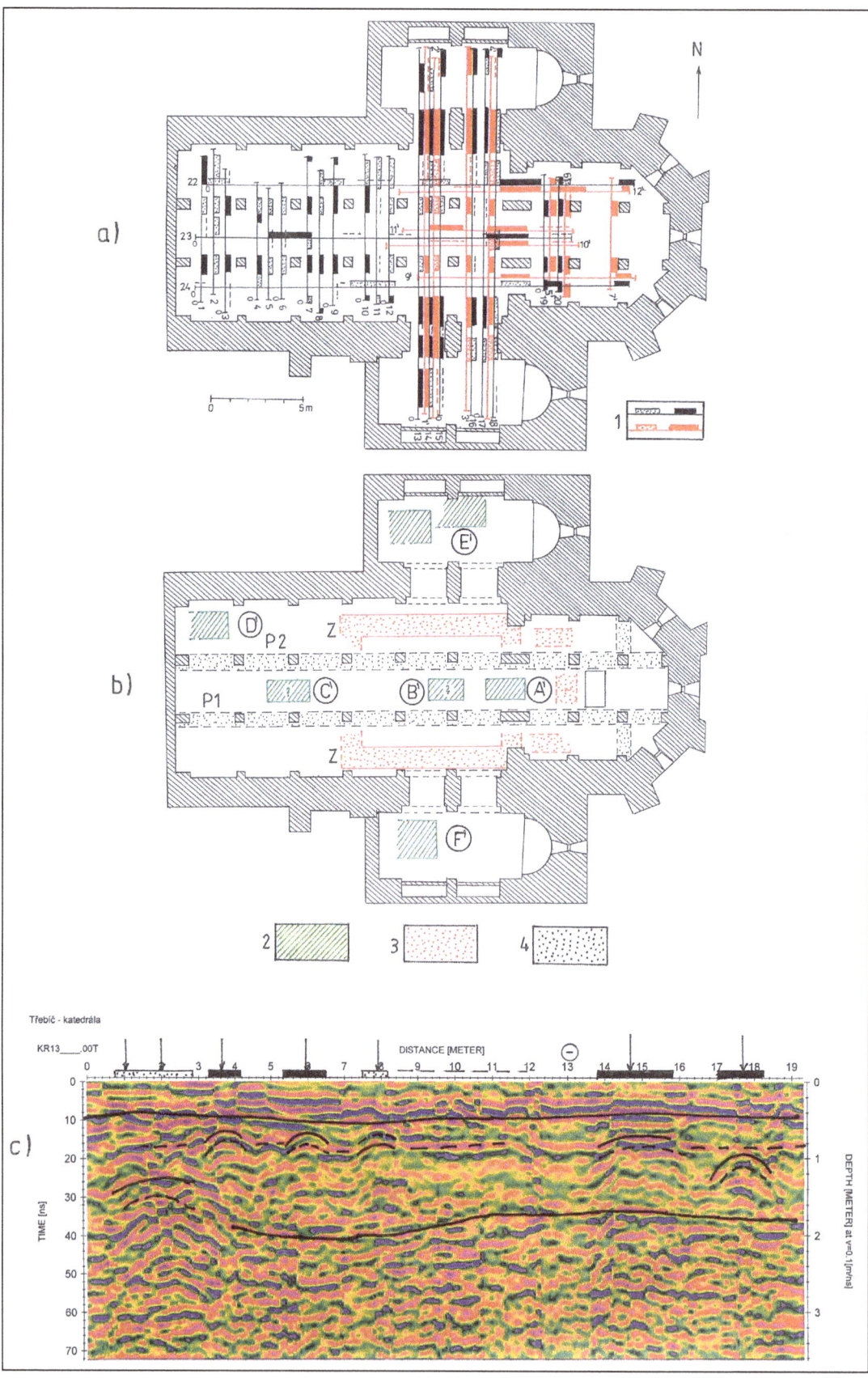

Fig. 19. Třebíč, the Basilica of St. Prokop- the crypt: Correlation scheme of results of the GPR measuring (a), one of possible variants of interpretation of near-surface inhomogeneities (b) and manifestation of indications of various structures in the processed radarogram (c). 1- interpreted indications of inhomogeneities according to their distinctiveness from the measuring in 2006 (black) and 2009 (red), 2- graves, tombs, accumulations of stones, 3- masonry relics of the assumed older building (?), 4- continuous column foundations

conditions for measuring (large built-up area, unremovable recent objects etc.). The prospection also aimed to localize other related inhomogeneities, characterized probably only by less different physical parameters (backfill of the structures) from the surrounding environment, which is formed mainly by sandy-loamy to stony-sandy earth (destructive layer, landfill, eluvium of the massif etc.).

After complex interpretation of all measured data from both stages of the prospection (Dostál/Hašek/Tomešek 2006, Hašek/Maštera/Tomešek 2007) with consideration of the feature layout surveying according to Kuthan (1994, 223), several inhomogeneities were identified in the studied area of the Basilica of St. Prokop, i.e. in the main and side naves and in the crypt. Some of them are recommended to be verified by drilling research.

From the GPR data, two or three (in some places) quite distinctive boundaries of reflected electromagnetic waves were identified in the both studied areas (the church, the crypt). The boundaries occur on times $t_1 = 8–4$ ns, $t_2 = 20-36$ ns, $t_3 = 46–64$ ns (the church) and $t_1 = 10–6$ ns; $t_2 = 30–36$ ns (the crypt). When introducing constant speed (2nd variant of the solution) $vr_1 = 0.10$ m /ns and $vr_2 = 0.12$ m/ns, the first case can be course of a near-surface inhomogeneous layer – the floor (tiles of one or more layers and their sandy base), with fictive thickness $h1 = 0.4–0.7$ m, or $0.48–0.84$ m ($h_1 = 0.50–0.80$ m and $0.60–0.96$ m) in the superincumbent bed of lithologically variable anthropological complex of stony-sandy or sandy-loamy earths lying above eluvium of syenite massif $h_2 = 1.0–1.8$ m, or $h_2 = 1.20–2.16$ m, whose fairly articulate relief occurs very approximately in depths $h_3 = 2.3–3.2$ m, or $2.76-3.87$ m (the basilica) and $h_2 = 1.50–1.80$ m, or $h_2 = 1.80-2.16$ m (the crypt). Greater increase of landfill thickness, of various destructive and other material as a whole is expected in both sectors of the development plan in the W – E direction.

A number of quite extensive anomalous zones (Fig. 18a) can be observed on the researched sub-areas of all three church naves. According to their size and configuration, they are probably indications of positions of mostly graves and larger accumulations of stone material features. Those marked A to G can be considered the most distinctive, the most dominant are structures A,B (Fig. 18) where places of rather large half-caved-in tombs are not excluded. Other, narrower, linearly oriented inhomogeneities, can indicate course of masonry (lengthwise and transverse continuous column foundations etc.).

In the area of the Romanesque crypt, distinctive indications with linear configuration (Fig. 19a) were interpreted by processing of the GPR data. They indicate positions of two lengthwise continuous column foundations (P1, P2); in the middle part of the feature they indicate probably thicker relics of masonry documenting perhaps an area of an extinct oblong building (Z) on the east side, possibly with an apse of an orthogonal or oval ground plan, but it cannot be unambiguously proven from the research made (a plinth of the altar). Outer length of the possible building is 13 cm, the width is 8 cm. According to the location of these anomalies we however do not exclude smaller simple graves, objects or other lithological structures randomly occurring in the abovementioned ground plan of the hypothetical building.

Other observed inhomogeneities of more local character (Fig. 19b) are indicative of positions of graves, destruction of stone material, morphology of the rock massif etc. (marked A' to F'- see Fig. 19b, c).

4.2.3.2. The Cistercians

Determirnation to keep strictly the Benedictine order's rules led to reform tendencies that eventuated in founding a monastery in Burgundian city of Citeaux (Cistercium). The ambition to reform the monastic life reflected also in architecture emphasizing austerity and simplicity. The most important part of a monastery was a church usually consecrated to Virgin Mary. The church is adjoined by an enclosure around a garth with a cloister. Individual rooms basically keep the older scheme and served as a sacristy, capitular hall, kitchen etc. Předklášteří u Tišnova in Moravia and Vyšší Brod in Bohemia are presented as examples.

PŘEDKLÁŠTEŘÍ u Tišnova, the convent of Porta Coeli, the Church of the Assumption of the Virgin Mary, District of Brno

Combination of the late Romanesque and the so-called transitory Burgundian-Cistercian style is characteristic for the whole convent area founded by Queen Constance and built in 1233 – 1239. Its centre – the church, the cloister and the capitular hall have survived in the original, partly restored condition. The Church of the Assumption of the Virgin Mary (Photo 38) is a three-nave basilican disposition with a transept from the time of founding the church. The conventual building has a cross-shaped ground plan with an elongated presbytery with a six-part vault field and a pentagonal end. One also pentagonal chapel is on each side of of the presbytery. A significant element of the austere outer facades is the main west portal in the advanced part of the main nave front from around 1250's. There are no records of the convent from the time of the Hussite Wars (1419–37) but it can be assumed that the Cistercian nuns left the convent and returned after settling of the situation. The convent was abolished in 1782 but restored in 1921. It was abolished again in 1950 and restored in 1990. Also the Chapel of St. Catherine stood in the convent area. It is probably older then the convent and during building of the convent it could have served as a temporary church, in which burials took place until the beginning of the 15th century. The chapel was liquidated in the 18th century. In the pride of

Geophysical Prospection and Archaeological Interpretation of the Results

The main task of the geophysical works in 2002 was to localize tombs of founders of the convent and other funeral structures located in the interior of the conventual church (Hašek/Tomešek/Unger 2002).

Three distinctive boundaries of reflected electromagnetic waves were detected on all gauged profiles from the GPR data. They occur on times $t_1 = 8–16$ ns, $t_2 = 34–46$ ns and $t_3 = 82-90$ ns. In the first case it is summary effect of the pavement, rubble with residues of mortar and bricks in the superincumbent bed of the loamy mound with fictive thickness of 0.4 to 0.8 m ($v_r = 0.1$ m/ns), in the second case it is probably subsurface water level, of depth of 1.7 to 2.3 m, in the third case it is either relief of the bedrock or of gravel-sand in depths of 4.1 to 4.5 m. Several anomalies were localized by interpreting the radarograms, which can be manifestation of primarily tombs and graves, whose ceilings (tops) are concentrated in depths of ca 0.7 m-1.40 m.

From the overall correlation of the GPR indications 8 areally and linearly oriented extensive structures (marked A to G, Z) can be observed in the interior of the religious building. They correspond to positions of various near-surface inhomogeneities.

In the space of the main nave and near the adjoining side chapels, zones marked A, B, C may be considered intensive reflections of electromagnetic waves. D and Z are less distinctive (Fig. 20a,b). The anomalous zone A (Fig. 20c), detected partly by the prospection, characterizes a fairly large Baroque tomb of provosts, placed in the church axis in the west sector of the main nave with an entrance sized ca 2.2 x 1.5 m visible in the tiled floor. Indication B (Fig. 20c) in the east part of the nave represents a Baroque tomb of the Cistercian nuns with the entrance sized ca 2.5 x 1.5 m located at its east margin.The ceiling is in the depth of 0.7 – 1.3 m. A distinctive tomb (probably Baroque as well) was situated somewhat more northways. Its sizes are ca 3 x 2 m, h = 1.1 m (C), it is however not visible on the surface of the church. The inhomogeneity D lying south of C indicates perhaps a grave sized ca 2.2 x 1.3 m and 1.3 m deep. Linear zones localized among columns (Z) may be brought about, among others, by existence of masonry relics ca 1.0 – 1.3 m wide, which puts them in connection with their continuous column foundations, too.

In the area of the presbytery, several less distinctive inhomogeneities were identified marked E, F, G (Fig. 20), corresponding most probably to positions of half-caved-in walled-up tombs or simple graves. The anomalous zone E, F near the triumphal arch can be indicative of tombs sized 2.2 x 1.6 m, h = 0.60 m and 2.4 x 1.7 m, h = 0.85 m, even though partial influence of a scarp is possible. The structure G located in the axis of the building in front of the main altar can indicate a walled-up half-caved-in tomb

Photo 38. Předklášteří, the convent of Porta Coeli with the Church of the Assumption of the Virgin: The area from the west (Photograph by V. Hašek)

place in the axis of the presbytery of the conventual church in front of the main altar, the founder of the convent Queen Constance (+1240), wife of Przemysl Otakar I is buried with her son Przemysl (+1239), Moravian margrave. In the east segment of the main nave there is the Baroque tomb of the Cistercian nuns, the tomb of provosts is in the west part (Belcredi 1993, Foltýn et al. 2005, 615).

A Brief Overview of Geological Situation of the Locality

The area of the convent of Porta Coeli in Předklášteří u Tišnova is, from the orthographic point of view, a part of the Křižanov Upland, of the subunit of the Bíteš Upland. Filling of the wide valley of the river of Svratka consists of Holocene fluvial loamy-sandy sediments. They are partly covered from the west by larger alluvial fan of deluviofluvial sediments which is formed by nameless streams. Bedrock of these sandy-loamy sediments are red Lower Devonian basal clastics consisting of petromict conglomerates and arcoses on the right bank. They rest on a near bared Proterozoic biotite paragneisses. Tectonically limited blocks of massive Middle Devonian (Frasnian) limestones appear in Devonian conglomerates on the opposite bank of Svratka. The course of the Svratka valley is predisposed by tectonic disturbance of the northwest direction. The conventual complex rests by its foundations on fluvial and deluviofluvial sediments of Svratka and Loučka.

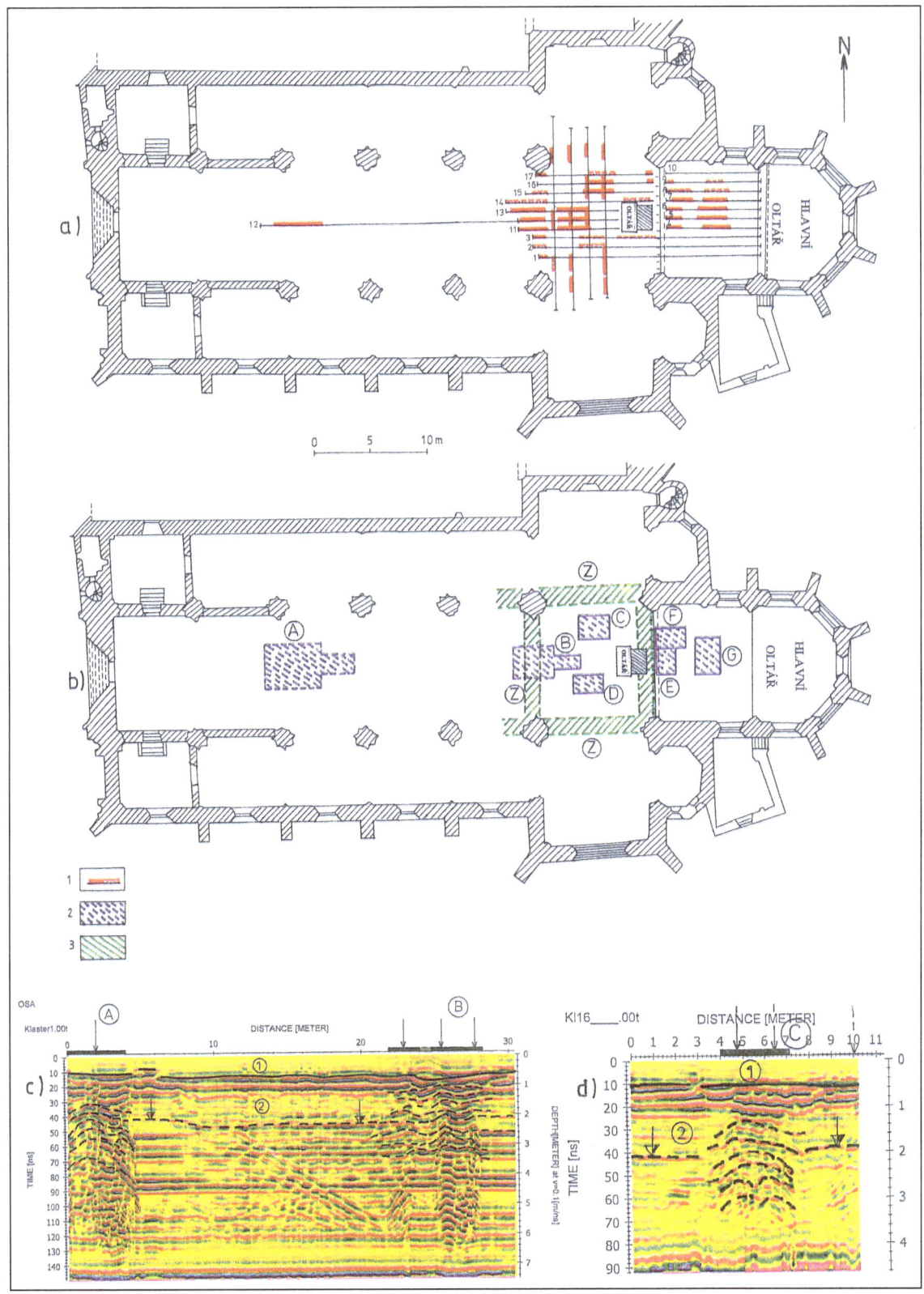

Fig. 20. Předklášteří, the Church of the Assumption of the Virgin Mary: Correlation scheme of results of the geophysical works (a), interpreted areal inhomogeneities in the building interior (b), manifestation of tombs in the main nave axis (c) and the space of the tomb in the northeast part of the main nave (d). 1- near-surface inhomogeneities according to their distinctiveness, 2- tombs, simple graves, 3- masonry relics, continuous column foundations

on a ground plan of 2.6 x 1.8 m and 1.2 m deep (Fig. 21). Its advanced position towards the presbytery is indicative of a tomb of an influential individual, maybe Queen Constance. The question of original location of the

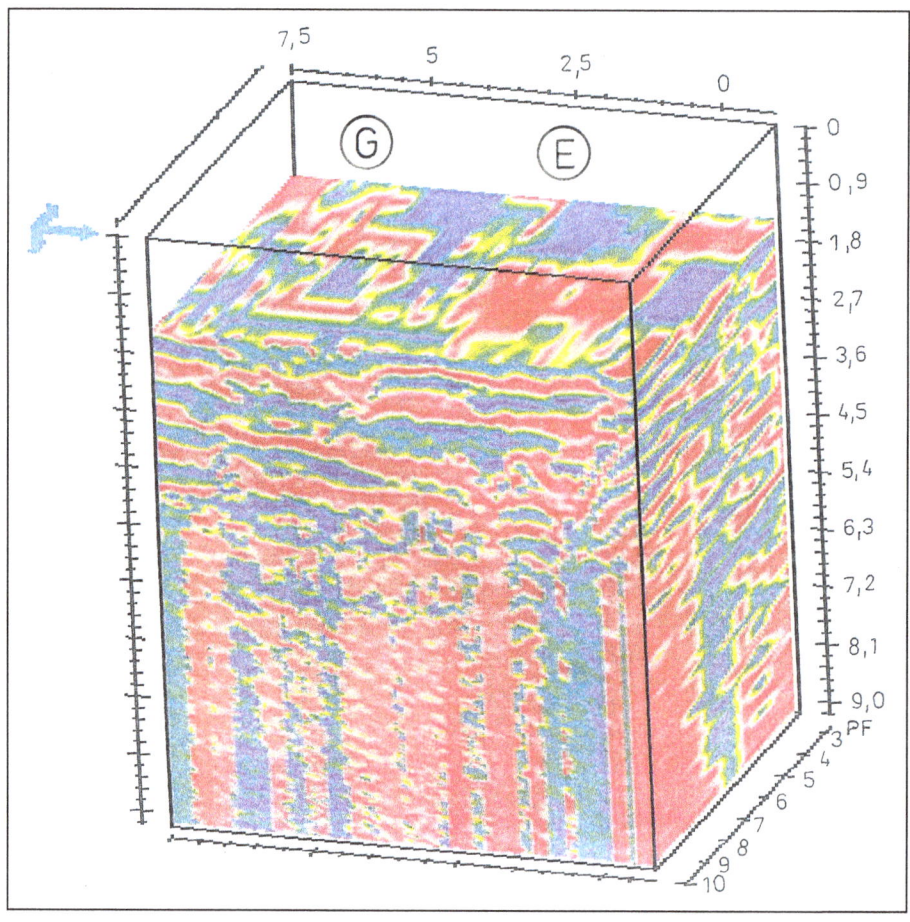

Fig. 21. Předklášteří, the Church of the Assumption of the Virgin Mary: 3D presentation of areal inhomogeneities – tombs, graves in the area of the presbytery

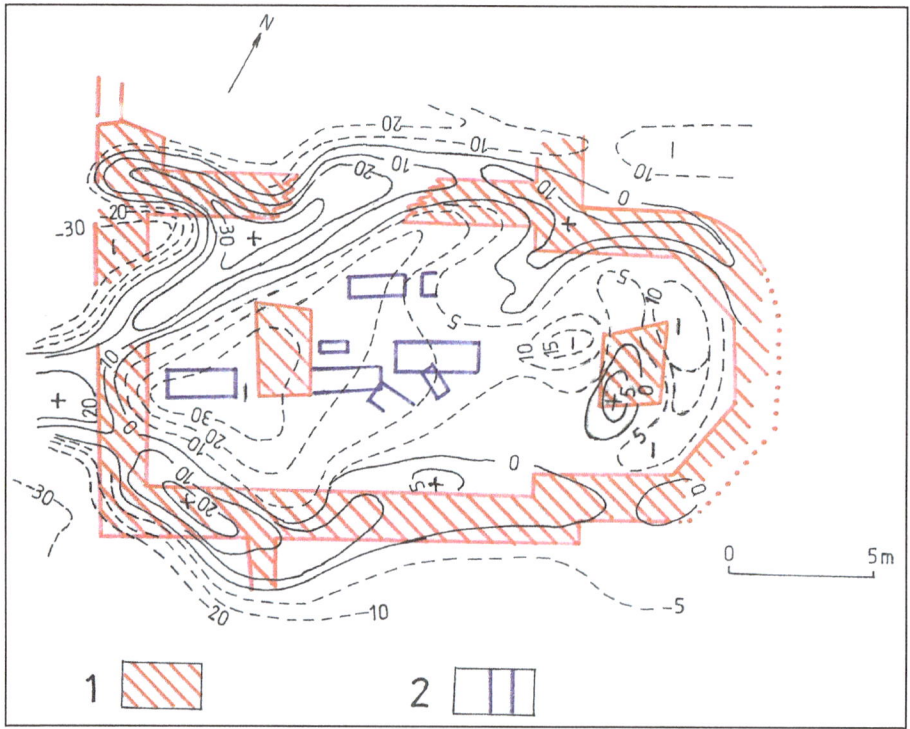

Fig. 22. Předklášteří, the Chapel of St. Catherine: map of ρ_{app} isolines and ground plan of the uncovered building. 1- stone masonry relics, 2- graves

abovementioned tomb stays open but the geophysical prospection marked out places which deserve maximum attention.

About 50 m NW from the portal into the conventual church detailed geoelectric measuring was performed which aimed to determine the supposed position and ground plan of the Chapel of St. Catherine, whose beginnings go back to the 1st half of the 13th century (Hašek/Kovárník 1996, 77).

The data of the DEMP method processed into a map of isolines $\rho_{appDEMP}$ (Fig. 22) indicated two narrower linearly oriented zones of increased resistivities with approximately NE – SW axis. The one that is more northern is disturbed by another zone of increased resistivities, oriented in the NNE – SSW direction. The anomalous elements get narrower towards the north and gradual connection can be expected (the end of the presbytery).

Archaeological Excavation

Areal exposure was situated in the anomalous spots detected by the research in the Chapel of St. Catherine. It found out relics of combined brick and stone foundation walls of the building with polygonal presbytery, oblong nave and a tribune in the west part of total size of 16 x 9 m (Photo 39). Mosaic two-coloured paving is indicative of connection with a Cistercian building ironworks. As in other Cistercian convents and monasteries this was a building serving to lay staff of the convent (Belcredi 1993).

Photo 40. Vyšší Brod, the convent with the Church of the Assumprion of the Virgin Mary: The area of the convent from the north (Photograph by J. Vandělík)

church on the east side and adjoining abbey in the NE. The conventual church with adjoining buildings was built gradually from the 1260's, it was finished in 1380's. In the 1260's – 1280's, east part of the church with a presbytery (Photo 41) and a transept was built with side north chapels of St. Benedict and St. Cross and south chapels of St. Bernard and Virgin Mary. A specific style manifestation is the capitular hall vault (around 1285). The cloister was built during the 14th century. The church was burnt down by the Hussites in 1422. Larger repairs and reconstructions in the New Gothic style were carried out in 1830-1860, when the spire was added as well. The convent was abolished in 1950 and restored in 1990. Ten generations of Rosenbergs were buried in the choir of the church (Poche *et al.* 1982; Vlček/Sommer/ Foltýn 1997, 688).

Photo 39. Předklášteří, the convent of Porta Coeli, the Chapel of St. Catherine: View of the archaeological research (Photo by L. Belcredi)

VYŠŠÍ BROD, the Convent with the Church of the Assumption of the Virgin Mary, District of Český Krumlov

The center of the convent founded by Vok of Rožmberk before 1259 consists of a church with an ambulatory on the south side (Photo 40), a smaller garth with an old

Photo 41. Vyšší Brod, the conventual Church of the Assumption of the Virgin Mary: Church interior from the west (Photograph by J. Vandělík)

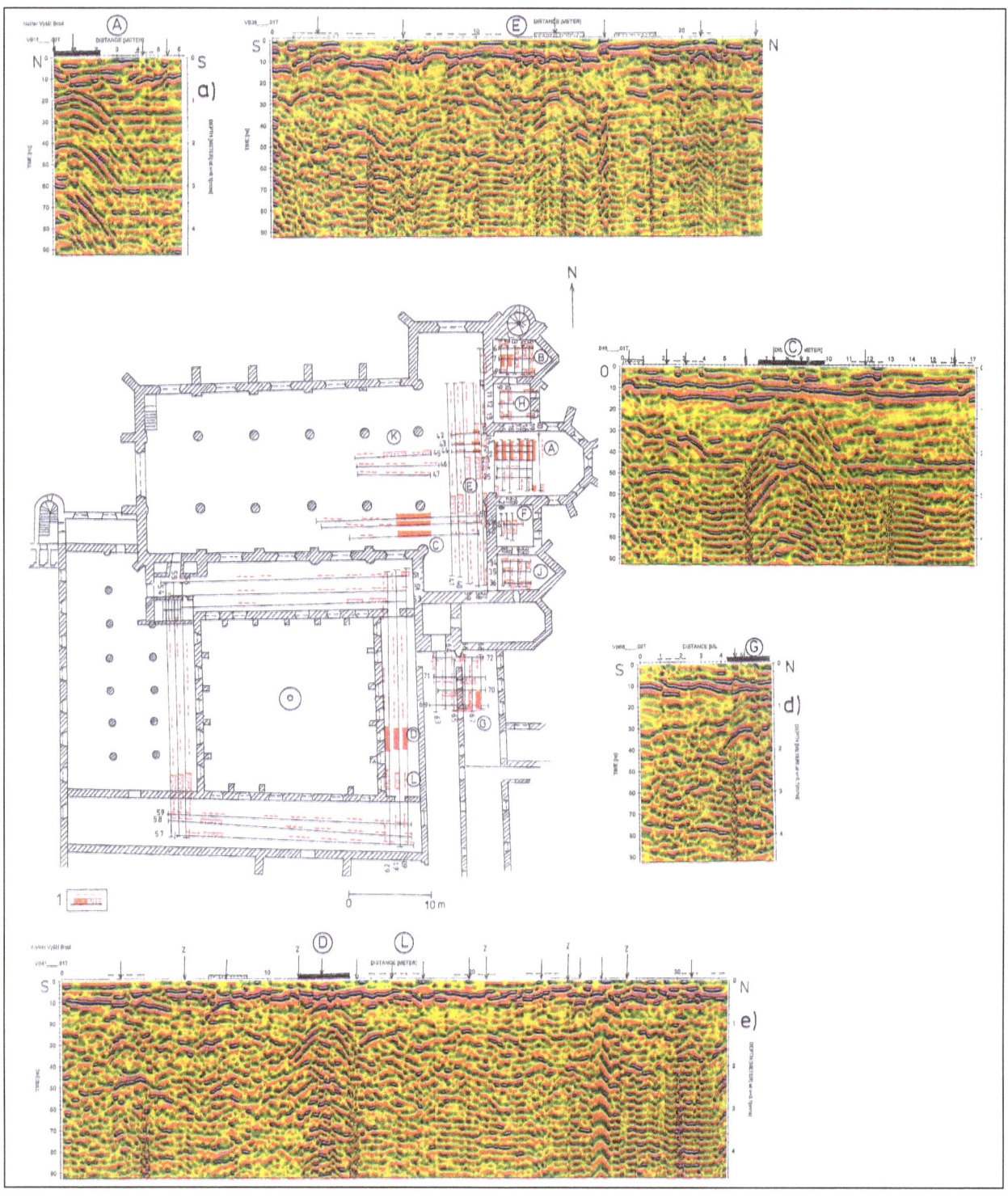

Fig. 23. Vyšší Brod, the Cistercian convent: Correlation scheme of the GPR measuring results, interpreted radarogram from the presbytery area of the Church of the Assumption of the Virgin Mary – indication of the tomb A (a), from the transept – indication of the tomb E (b), from the south side nave – tomb C (c), from the capitular hall – indication of the grave G (d) and from the north-south cloister – graves D, L (e).
1- interpreted near-surface inhomogeneities according to their distinctiveness

A Brief Overview of Geological Situation of the Locality

The monastery area took up the town's name, Vyšší Brod. It is built on a rise on the right bank of Vltava. In the geomorphological structuring the town takes a position in the Czech Moravian Upland, which is a part of the Šumava Foothills (Czudek 1973). The winding Vltava, flowing through the town from the northwest to the southeast, picks up Menší Vltávka from the southwest. Other two small creeks flow in from the south at its south end where Vltava continues towards the east. The whole town including the convent is located on a wide alluvial fan of Menší Vltávka and two nearby creeks that merge into a large dejection cone. It verges the right Vltava bank in the length of ca 1.5 km. These Holocene – Pleistocene sediments form deluvial and deluvial-solifluction stony-loamy and stony-sandy sediments. The south part of the town, however, lies on the Vltava Holocene flood plain formed by fluvial sandy loams, loamy sands or gravels. These young sediments cover underlying medium-grained to fine-grained muscovite-biotite granites of the so-called Eisgarn type which form a part of the moldanubic pluton and are believed today to be Upper Carboniferous. This type of granites meets with an older – Lower Carboniferous type of the so-called Weinsberg granite (coarse-grained to phyric biotite gtanite to granodiorite) or Schlierengranite (amphibolic-biotite granodiorite) along the WSW-ENE boundary. A faulted zone goes through the straight Vltava valley from the Čertova stěna (Devil's Wall) to the southeast. It crosses the Eisgarn type and produces profound thinning of this granite body on the surface at the northeast wing. On the opposite bank of Vltava, migmatitized muscovite-biotite paragneiss with sillimanite and cordierite occurs instead against Vyšší Brod. It is probably a tectonically limited block which is stuck between granites of the Eisgarn and Weinsberg type. Continuation of this significant disturbance towards the southeast of the town and winding of the Vltava valley cannot be proven in the Weinsberg granite. It can be assumed that the rise on which the conventual complex rests will have only small thickness or relic of deluvial sediments under recent athropogenous cover. It is rather a manifestation of shallow granite bedrock.

Geophysical Prospection and Archaeological Interpretation of the Results

The aim and main task of the archaeogeophysical prospection in 2007 in the area of the part of the main nave and transept, presbytery, side chapels, cloister and capitular hall, was to provide more detailed information about existence of a larger Rosenbergs' tomb or smaller tombs and graves from various periods of the monastery existence, also about possible masonry relics and thickness of anthropogenous deposits.

From the GPR data, relatively inhomogeneous environment up to depths of ca 1.6 m to 2.5 m (v_r = 0.10 m/ns), or 1.9 to 3.0 m (v_r = 0.12 m/ns) can be assumed from more or less distinctive reflections of electromagnetic waves at smaller times (t = 32-50 ns) on 72 gauged profiles of total length of 782.4 m. Due to probable rather graded lithological junction between the anthopogeneous cover and Quaternary rock mantle it can be a certain fictive boundary between a layer of recent deposits and surface of weathered rocks of the Moldanubic pluton.

On the basis of the radarograms evaluation we expect a number of local indications of varying depth levels of their upper parts and varying distinctiveness. They can be attributed to (apart from geological causes) manifestation of tombs, possible simple graves, foundation masonry, building and other related elements, such as depression character of underlying structures with various sandy-clayey filling, larger accumulation of stones etc. All these near-surface areal linear inhomogeneities are concentrated into depths of ca 0.4 to 1.0 m (v_r = 0.10 m/ns); their depth oscillates between 0.8 to ca 3.0 m (Fig. 23).

In the interior of the studied building three main kinds of near-surface inhomogeneities can be assumed – tombs, graves, masonry relics, possibly also continuous column foundations (Fig. see 23).

In the area of the convnent, 11 geophysically variably distinctive indications (marked A to L), which occur mainly in the interior of the Church of the Assumption of the Virgin Mary were identified(8), several others are in the cloister (2) and in the capitualr hall (1) (Fig. 23a to e).

The inhomogeneity (A) on the gospel side of the presbytery, sized ca 5 x 3 m can be considered very distinctive. Its top is in the depth of ca 0.8 – 1.0 m (Fig. 24) and in its middle part there is a stone put into the church wall of pink marble with an image of a Rosenberg horse rider. It was found out from available sources that when steps of the church main altar lowered in 1902, sounding works uncovered a vault in this area. Under the masonry there was a space with remains of wooden coffins and two surviving tin coffins. According to literary sources (www.ckrumlov.cz) one of them belonged to Petr Vok. It might be one of possible Rosenbergs' tombs, which are probably more numerous in the church, as ten generations of this family members are claimed to having been buried here.

Another very distinctive but areally smaller inhomogeneity (B) sized ca 2.5 x 1.5 m and 0.5-0.6 m deep was identified in the side chapel of St. Benedict. It is a tomb covered by a tombstone of Jan Zrinský, a Petr Vok's nephew (+1612) (Photo 42).

Variably distinctive inhomogeneities (F, H and J) in chapels od St. Cross, St. Bernard and Virgin Mary are connected, according to tombstones of the abbot Kr. Knoll from 1513 and of other abbots from 1578, 1641, 1668, 1690, 1724 and 1766 placed here, probably with their tombs, maybe partly or totally caved.

The near-surface inhomogeneity (C), oriented by its main axis in the N-S direction, sized more than ca 5 x 3 m (?) is located by the west margin of the transept in the south side nave between the first and the second column (see Fig. 24). Its possible continuation towards the north into the space of media ecclesia (K) is assumed. This is currently not possible to cofirm or deny for insufficient general measuring-in of the abovementioned area.

Less distinctive larger near-surface inhomogeneity, maybe of a tomb character (E) sized ca 4 x 3 m, of top

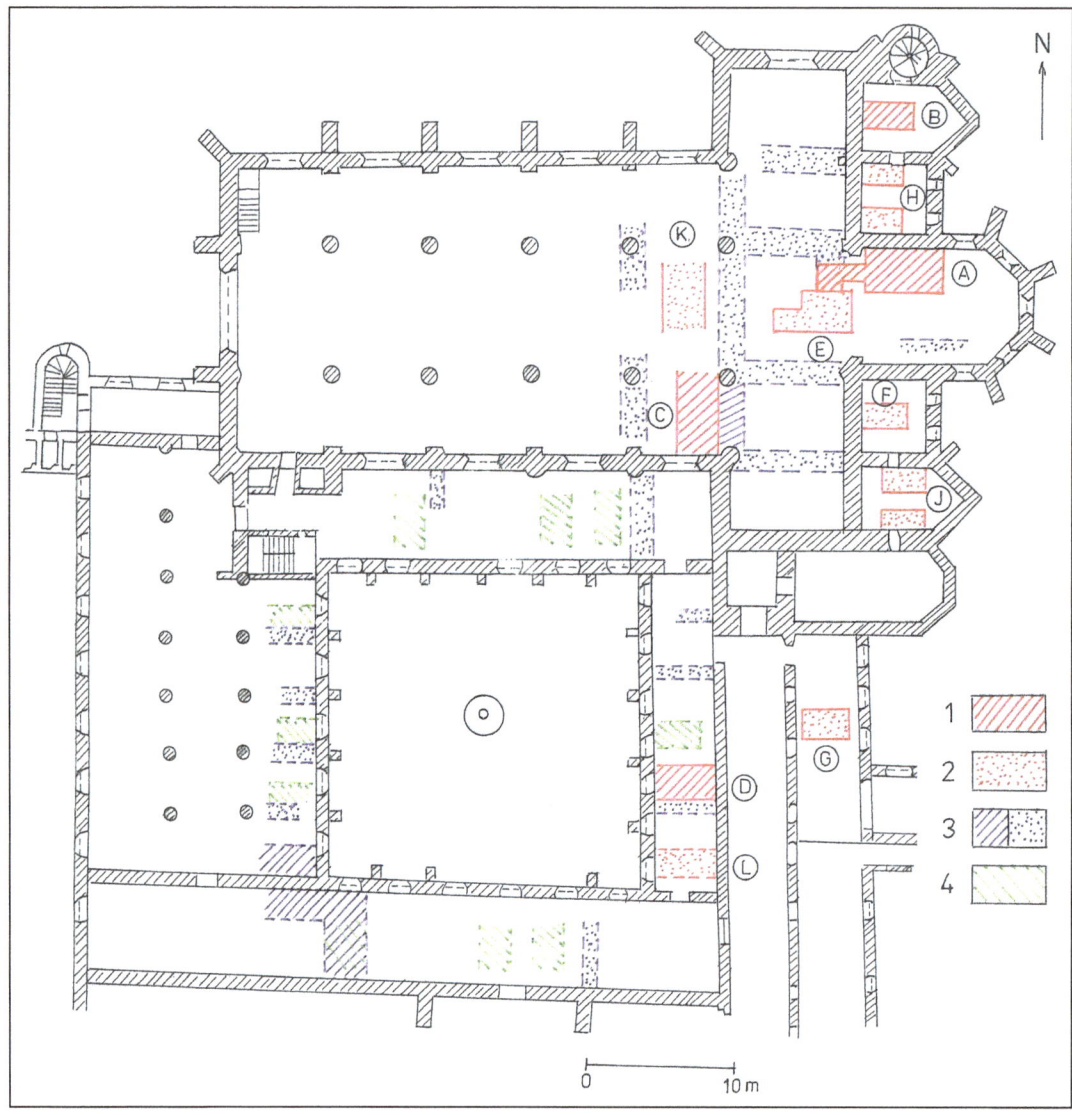

Fig. 24. Vyšší Brod, the Cisterician convent: One of possible variants of interpretation of the prospection results.
1- areal inhomogeneities, very distinctive indications (A, B, C, D)- possible hollow walled-up tombs; 2- areal inhomogeneities, less distinctive indications (E, F, G), indistinct indications (H, J, K, L) – possible half caved-in tombs, graves, lithological changes in backfill of the features etc.; 3- linear inhomogeneities, distinctive and less intense indications – possible masonry relics, accumulations of stones, continuous column foundations, lintels; 4- areal less distinctive inhomogeneities – possible graves, accumulations of stones

depth of ca 1.0 m was indicated in the transept under the triumphal arch (Fig. 24). A possible connection with the structure A cannot be excluded.

A fairly intense indication of a structure sized ca 3.5 x 2.5 m, of top depth of ca 1.0 m (D) was localized in the east part of the cloister, similarly as a less distinctive more southern paraller feature (L) of the same sizes (Fig. see 24). In the first case a half-caved-in smaller tomb or a probable change in lithology of the backfill is assumed, in the second case a simple grave or areal accumulation of stones.

In the capitular hall, an indistinct inhomogeneity (G) sized ca 2.5 x 1.5 m can be expected by the south margin of the outer wall, which could be impact of a grave or a masonry relic (Fig. 24). No other structures of this type were geophysically detected here. In case of consequent positive pedological verification of the inhomogeneities (G or D) it can be presumed that it could be the sought after grave (tomb) of Zavis of Falkenstein (+1290), which was supposed to be buried here, according to newer literary sources (Pangerl 1865).

Apart from the abovementioned structures, manifestations of several simple graves with both E-W and N-S orientation can be presumed especially in the area of the main and side naves. On the basis of the prospection results, altogether 11 of these places (there can be more of them, though) sized ca 2 x 1-1.5 m are identified here. In some cases also larger local accumulations of stone material from various stages of construction and repairs of

Photo 42. Vyšší Brod, the conventual Church of the Assumtion of the Virgin Mary: Relief tombstone of John, Count of Zrin (Photograph by J. Vandělík)

the sacral building are interpreted. When the backfill of simple graves has similar lithological composition or compaction as the surrounding environment, their localization is, due to indistinct changes of physical parameters of soils, very problematic and often even impossible. Masonry relics are documented especially in the transept, in places of columns, where stone continuous foundations for their bases are expected in the main E-W and perpendicular N-S direction, partly also in the space of southern side nave, cloister and capitular hall (Fig. see 24).

Note:
According to an oral report, the geophysical indications on the left side of the presbytery (mkd. A) and in the south side nave (C) (see Fig. 24) were verified currently by two boreholes and documented by camera system.

In the case of interpreted anomalous zone A, a larger tomb sized ca 5 x 3 m was detected with multitude of decomposed wooden coffins and two tin ones. One of them contains an inscription with the name of Petr Vok of Rosenberg (+ 1611). The anomaly C is a manifestation of two parallel thicker stone walls of the N-S direction, representing probably the course of a partition in front of the presbytery.

4.2.3.3. Premonstratensians

The Premonstratensian Order, founded by St. Norbert of Xanten (1080/85-1134) in the beginning of the 12th century, focusing on improving the quality of liturgy, was one of exclusive orders preferrred by bishops, monarchs and feudal lords in the Middle Ages. As for architecture, the scheme of Benedictine and Cistercian monasteries proved satisfactory to the Premonstratensians. At the front of some churches there were sometimes two spires. Support of rulers and feudal lords belonged to Mona-

steries founded in Moravia, such as e.g. royal foundation in Louka u Znojma, or Želiv in Bohemia.

LOUKA u Znojma, the Church of Virgin Mary and St. Wenceslas, District of Znojmo

Conventual Church of Virgin Mary and St. Wenceslas (Photo 43) of the Premonstratensian convent in Louka u Znojma was founded by Czech Prince Conrad Otto and his mother Mary on a river terrace by the left valley slope of the river of Dyje in 1190. However, its construction was prolonged. No sooner than after 1200 a prolate two-nave crypt with a hall was built (Photo 44), whose columns and pillars carry cross vaults without groinings. Approximately double-sized three-nave basilica was built above it. The convent was plundered and destroyed during both the war between Moravian margraves at the beginning of the 15th century and the Hussite wars. It was being reconstructed and rebuilt since the half of the 15th century. Dilapidating buildings were adapted in Renaissance style in the 1570's. Large-scale Baroque reconstruction of the convent began in 1689 but the not yet finished convent was abolished in 1784 and converted into barracks, tobacco manufactory and sapper academy. The building served as barracks until the end of 20th century and its utilization is currently being searched for (Foltýn *et al.* 2005, 795-804).

Photo 43. Znojmo-Louka, the Church of Virgin Mary and St. Wenceslas: Aerial photograph of the former Premonstratensian monastery (Photograph by J. Kovárník)

A Brief Overview of Geological Situation of the Locality

The area of interest belongs orographically to Jevišovice Highland, the subunit Znojmo Highland. The bedrock is

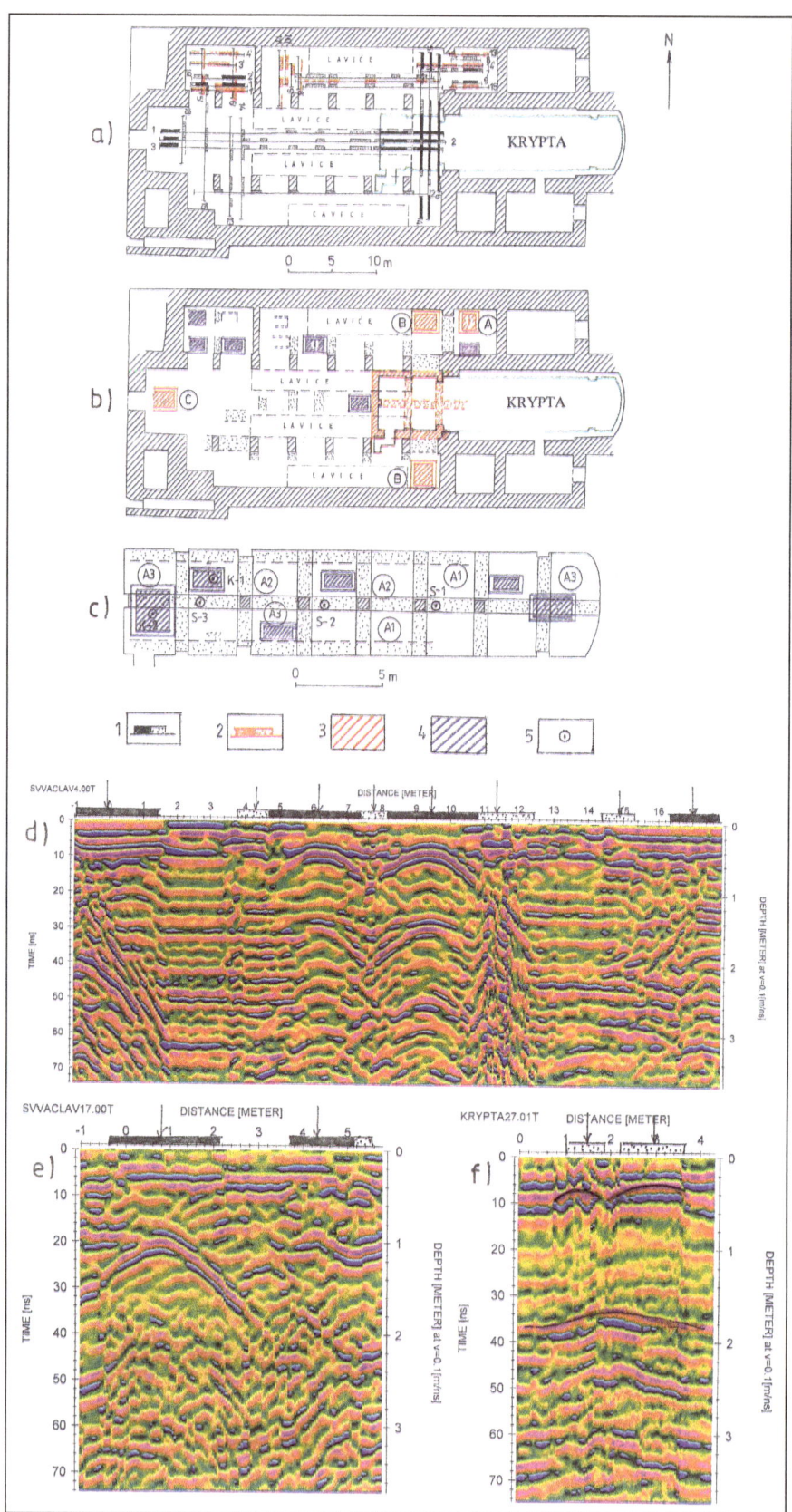

Fig. 25. Znojmo-Louka, the Church of the Virgin Mary and St. Wenceslas: Correlation scheme of results of the geophysical works (a), interpretation of inhomogeneities in the church interior (b) and in the crypt interior (c). Presentation of a crypt in the radarograms (d) and smaller tombs in the side northwest chapel (e) and in the crypt (f). 1- interpreted inhomogeneities according to their distinctiveness (250 MHz antenna), 2- interpreted inhomogeneities according to their distinctiveness (500 MHz antenna), 3- smaller tombs, 4- graves, larger accumulations of stones, 5- pedological proving holes

Photo 44. Znojmo-Louka, the Church of Virgin Mary and St. Wenceslas: Character of floor sagging in the crypt (Photograph by V. Hašek)

formed by biotite granite, which is cataclased towards the west. These plutonites, as a part of the Proterozoic Dyje massif, are in the direct bedrock of most of Znojmo. The rock bottom of the valley is covered by Holocene Fluvial sandy-loamy sediments of higher degree. Quartz gravels and sands, in some places with cardazytic clays (Ottnang-Eggenburg) have survived out of Miocene sediments until the present time on the right bank, high above the valley on the granite base in surface outcroppings. Remains of Pleistocene (Günz) gravely-sandy terrace occur on both sides of the valley. Younger (Riss) sandy-gravely terrace has survived in the base of the convent area. Its surface is recently covered by charges in places.

Geophysical Prospection and Archaeological Interpretation of the Results

The main aim of geophysical works by the GPR method in 2008 (Hašek/Kovárník/Tomešek 2008) was to provide specifying information about locations of various inhomogeneities, i.e. tombs and graves in the interior of the church (or the crypt) for effective focus of possible sounding works.

On the basis of the interpreted radrograms in the church and crypt interior, quite inhomogeneous environment into depths of ca 1.4 m to 1.7 m can be assumed from chaotically arranged reflections on smaller times (t_1 = 24–28 ns, v_r = 0.10 m/ns), due to probable more gradual litholgical transition between antropogenous cover and flood loams in the superincumbent bed of the gravel-sands of the left Dyje terrace (t_2 = 46-48 ns, h = 2.8-2.0 m).

In the main and both side naves of the church, several types (according to their sizes) of inhomogeneities were detected (Fig. 25b). In the first palce, it is a manifestation of an extensive Romanesque crypt (Fig. 25d), of smaller, probably newer tombs (A, B, C) in the middle and west part of the building (depths of tops are ca 0.6 – 0.8 m), several more local simple graves and larger accumulations of stones, situated especially in the space of the north side nave (h = 0.8 – 1.0 m, Fig. 25e). An exception is probably only a grave (?) located in the middle of the main nave in front of the west margin of the crypt (Fig. 25b) and continuous column foundations (h = ca 0.3 m).

In the crypt interior (Fig. 25c) three types of near-surface inhomogeneities, according to their depth (A1, A2, A3), can be identified. The first two types are shallow structures. One leads around the periphery of the building (A1) and it is probably a subsurface circle of stone masonry added to the corona of the foundation wall of the crypt and forming a part of its floor, the other shallow structures are continuous column foundations (A2). Graves and other depressions (Fig. 25f), above which the brick floor could have possibly been collapsing (see Photo 44), are located deeper. Our interpretation hypothesis was confirmed also by verifying pedological research in 1995 (Hašek 1999), whose situation is presented also in the Fig. 25c.

ŽELIV, the Church of the Birth of the Virgin Mary, District of Pelhřimov

The Premonstratensian, originally Benedicine monastery in Želiv was founded at the estate of Prague bishop in 1140's. The monastery tradition connects the act of the foundation with Prince Soběslav I and his wife Adleta. Written records inform of the year 1144, when Vladislav II bestowed the estate of Želiv on Prague bishop Ota and shortly after that a Benedictine monastery came into existence here. In 1148 Benedictines left the monastery. A Premonstratensian convent was called to their place and came to Želiv in 1149. In 1420-1424 the monastery suffered extensive damages due to Hussite commotions. The church with the monasterial buildings were burned down by the Hussites. Monastic life in Želiv was not recovered until 1462, when also construction work began but after five years the monastic products together with the monastery itself were pawned by Burian Trčka of Lípa, who built a castle here. In 1623 the Želiv monastery began to be administered by Strahov and in this period also more profound attempts to reconstruct the dilapidated monastery buildings and the church take place. In 1643 the monastery was recovered as an autonomous convent. In the 17th and following 18th century, the monastery developed rapidly and extensive building activity was done, despite the fact that the monastery was supposed to be liquidated in 1781 due to the Josephine reforms but that did not happen. The monastery was however abolished in 1950, an internment camp for monks and priests was established here, later a mental hospital resided here. Monastic life has been recovered in the monastery since 1991 (Petrů 1898, Wirth 1908, 121-56, Kalista 1970, 32-33, Charouz 1995, Vlček/Sommer/Foltýn 1997, 703-709).

A Brief Overview of Geological Situation of the Locality

The village of Želiv is located in Želiv Highland, which is a part of Křemešnice Upland, in the west part of the Czech-Moravian Upland. It was founded in a deep, even canyon-shaped valley, formed by the Želivka River. The medieval monastery was built on a spur, which formed on the confluence of Želivka and a meandering creek Trnávka. The narrow valley is filled up with Holocene fluvial gravel-sandy and loamy deposits. Both sides of the valley are lined with Holocene – Pleistocene deluvial loams of little importance with fragments of bedrock, which consists of biotite and biotite-sillimanite paragneisses of a motley range, considered as Moldanubic rocks. On the right side of the valley, small-sized lens-shaped bodies of Paleozoic vein biotite and biotite-muscovitic, partly leucocratic granite appear. The complex of the monastery buildings built of the rocks of the above-stated provenience rests on deluvial deposits of variable thicknesses, which line the spur.

Geophysical Prospection and Archaeological Interpretation of the Results

During local survey in the monastic Church of the Birth of the Virgin (Photo 45, 46) in the beginning of 2007 it was found that altogether 5 gravestones (of abbots, brethren, knights Vraždas of Kunvald, Leskovecs of Leskovec and Věžníks of Věžníky) are apparent in the current level of the existing floor and one in the area of the present sacristy. The aim of the geophysical radar measuring in 2007 was to check the positions and sizes of possible tombs in the places of the gravestones, also to provide information about places of other so far unmapped funeral and other objects in the area of the building.

Photo 45. Želiv, the monastic Church of Birth of the Virgin: View from the west (Photograph by V. Hašek)

Photo 46. Želiv, the monastic Church of Birth of the Virgin: Church interior (Photograph by V. Hašek)

Altogether six underground areas located in various places in the building (Photo 47, Fig. 26, 27) were researched by the GPR method and documentation minisystem. They were mostly functional, in the past used tombs where the deceased who were connected with the monastery and the conventual church in some way were laid (Hašek/Maštera/Šindelář/Thomová 2008, 11).

Archaeological Evaluation

The results of the prospection and visual camera research have brought this information:

In the tomb of abbots, sized 2.8 x 2.8 x 1.9 m (A), built in front of the main altar, significant baroque abbots were laid. This crypt was built probably between the years 1682-1684, which is testified by dating with a picture of a cross on the east wall and by dating of the tombstone which covers the entrance to the tomb.

There are several burials in the crypt (Photo 48). Only two are clearly legible, namely the burial in the middle of the crypt and on the right southern side of the crypt area. The last burial laid here belongs to abbot Arnošt Morávek, who was the Želiv abbot in 1752 – 1775. One of the burials is laid into hand-hewn wooden coffin with wooden round turned legs, and most probably is laid on the catafalque without upper covering of the coffin, only the face is covered with a funeral veil. The head is oriented towards the altar, i.e. eastwards. He lies on his back, the arms are folded on the stomach and remains of abbot's gloves are still visible. A metal cross on a necklace, also metal, is around the neck. The funeral by

DISCUSSION OF PRACTICAL RESULTS AND OBSERVATIONS

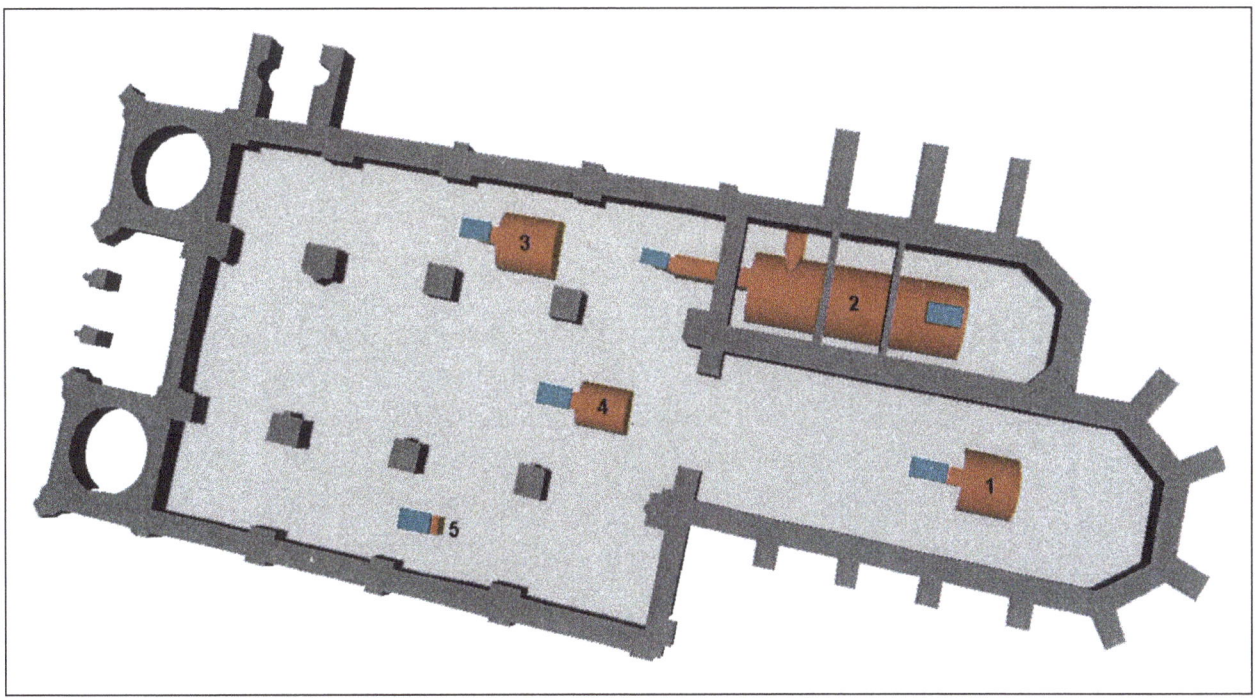

Photo 47. Želiv, the monastic Church of Birth of the Virgin: 3D model of the monastic church with plotting of the tombs (Photograph by J. Vandělík)

Photo 48. Želiv, the monastic Church of Birth of the Virgin: The tomb of abbots (Photograph by J. Vandělík)

the southern wall of the crypt is in much worse condition. The deceased is laid in a wooden coffin, on his back, with his head towards the altar, i.e. eastwards. Remains of a headgear stay on the head. The coffin is filled up with wood shavings. The arms of the deceased are folded on his stomach. A large wooden cross equipped with a copper sheet is placed on his chest. It is perhaps a remnant of funeral equipment. The whole burial is at a high degree of decomposition and is, in contrast to the previous one, less legible. The burials on the left on the northern side are also illegible, it is rather accumulation of wooden boards, mortal remains and palls made of cloth and fillings of coffins from more funerals. Close to the foot of the entrance vaulting on the northern side, other remains are perhaps secondarily put it small wooden chests.

Another tomb – tomb of the brethren (B) – is a pretty extensive bricked vaulted object with large amount of burials that cannot be more closely determined or timed. It can be assumed that they are also burials of brethren of the Baroque age.

The area of the crypt (Photo 49) can be divided into two parts according to placement of the burials. In the front part, the deceased and their torsos are put behind a wooden partition to the southern wall of the crypt. At the northern side, close to an air hole, a certain narrow alley is formed, so approximately in the one third of the crypt area, wooden painted coffins (Photo 50) with the deceased are displayed along the whole width of the crypt. The whole space is simply vaulted and plastered, brickwork shows through the plaster in patches. The masonry is probably stone in the southwest part of the crypt. The coffins are put crosswise in the crypt, so their orientation is north – south but this orientation resulted from later manipulation with the deceased. The mortal remains behind the wooden partition are out of order, rather randomly placed.

Other 3 tombs were explored in the monastic church, they belonged to noble families which were rewarded by confraternity with the Želiv canon for their outstanding service to the monastery, and were buried in the church of Birth of the Virgin Mary. The bricked tomb of the knights Vraždas of Kunvald (C), who belonged to gentry in the

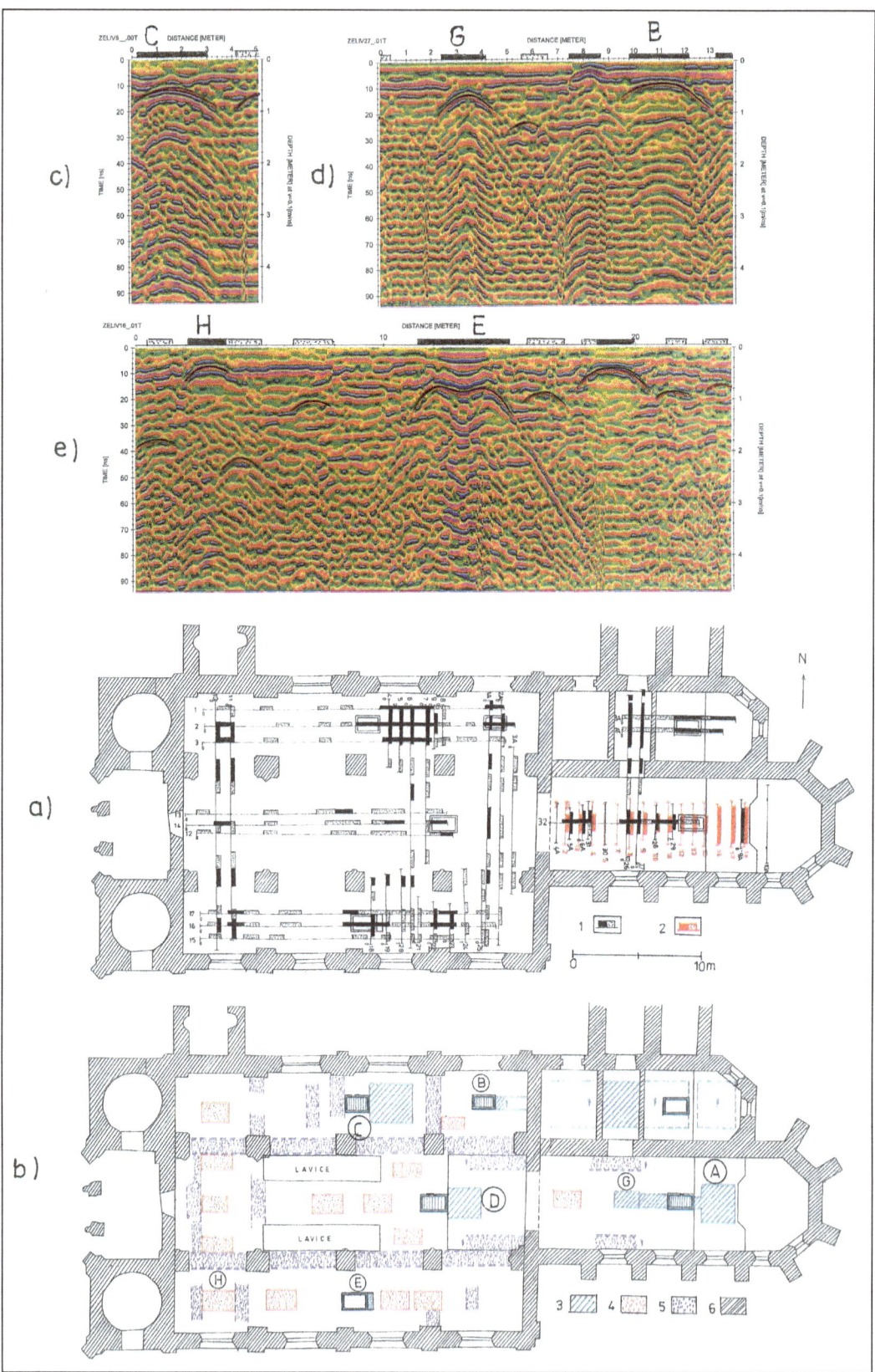

Fig. 26. Želiv, the Church of the Birth of the Virgin: Correlation scheme of the radar measuring results (a), one of the variants of geophysical interpretation (b) and manifestations of tombs and graves (B, C, E, G, H) in radarograms (c, d, e). 1- indications of inhomogeneities from the GPR according to their distinctiveness – 250 MHz antenna; 2- indications of inhomogeneities from the GPR according to their distinctiveness – 500 MHz antenna; 3- tombs with entrances (A- the tomb of abbots; B- the tomb of the brethren; C- the tomb of the knights Vraždas of Kunvald; D- the tomb of the Lískovecs of Leskovec; E- the tomb of the Věžníks of Věžníky; G- the tomb of Siard Falco; 4- the interpreted tombs H- (+ STE PERNER 1752); larger accumulations of stones (?); 5- masonry relics – continuous column foundations; 6- the present masonry

DISCUSSION OF PRACTICAL RESULTS AND OBSERVATIONS

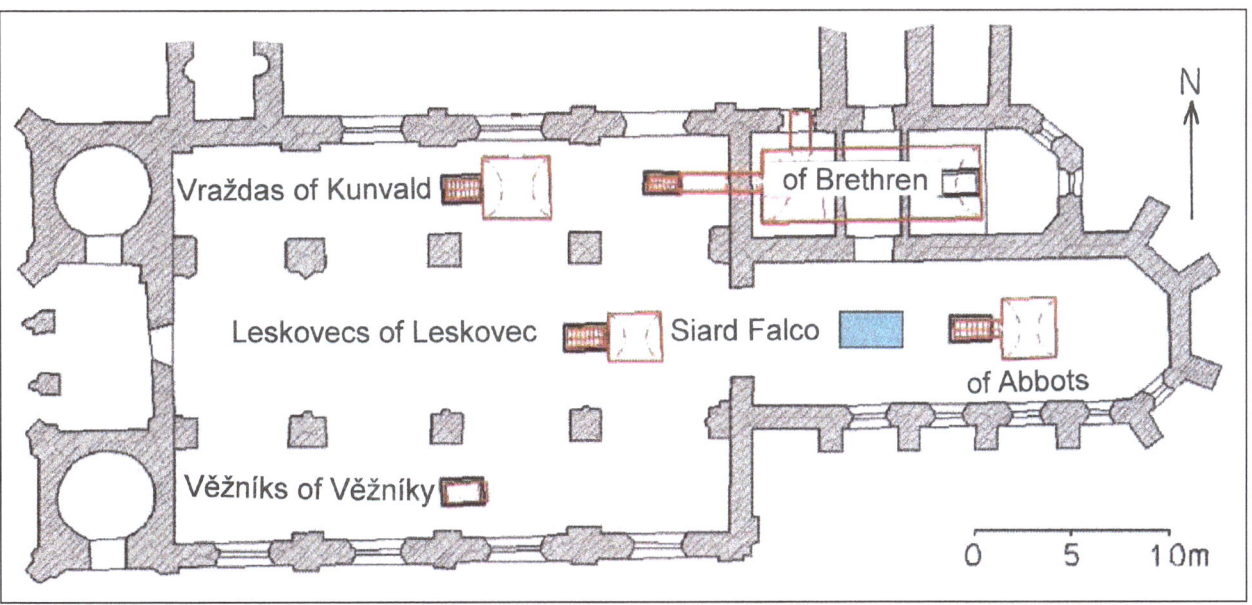

Fig. 27. Želiv, the Church of the Birth of the Virgin: Positions of the localized tombs

Photo 49. Želiv, the monastic Church of Birth of the Virgin: The tomb of the brethern from the east (Photograph by J. Vandělík)

Photo 50. Želiv, the monastic Church of Birth of the Virgin: Decomposed painted coffin in the tomb of the brethren (Photograph by J. Vandělík)

Čáslav region in the 16th century (Janáček/Louda 1988, 336), by the second northern pillar of the baroque quadrature in the northern aisle (3.3 x 3.0 x 1.7 m), was without burials. They were probably relocated in the past.

The least damaged was the tomb of the Lords Leskovecs of Leskovec (D), sized 2.6 x 2.3 x 1.9 m, built in front of the memorial arch of the conventual church. The name of this old noble family is derived from a stronghold called Leskovec by Počátky (Hašek/Maštera/Šindelář/Thomová 2008, 15-17). The area of the crypt itself is simply vaulted space, the plaster is creamy white, coarse. Two massive wooden beams are placed crosswise on the tomb floor in the north – south direction. At most three burials are placed on them, and only the middle one was secondarily manipulated with – it was raised from the beams and put on the burial by the northern wall of the crypt. A dark impression with the outline of a cross-section of the wooden coffin remained on the eastern wall of the crypt after its removal.

Burials in the examined tomb of the counts Věžníks of Věžníky (E) (2.3 x 1.3 x 1.5 m), located by the second southern pillar of the baroque quadrature, were the most damaged and no detailed information about them can be given.

Apart from these abovementioned objects, another, so far unknown smaller crypt was geophysically localized west of the tomb of abbots (see Fig. 26, 27), which belongs to

Abbot Siard Falco (G), as was found out by visual research.

In the area of the nave and the aisles, also existence of graves is assumed besides the discovered tombs. They are probably partly caved, the main axes of the holes are east-west oriented. One of the important indications is that of the grave marked H in the southwest part of the southern side wall (see Fig. 26). In the sector of the grave is the mark + in an original cobblestone and an incomplete inscription STE: PERNER 1752.

In the area of the present columns, strip footings for their bases in the main east-west and perpendicular north-south direction were interpreted. We also do not exclude partial indication of relics of masonry in the presbytery and in the area of the west end of the church.

4.2.3.4. Augustinians

The Order of Augustinians regards St. Augustine (354 – 430) as their spiritual father. It is divided into branches – The Augustinian Canons, having their focus in spiritual administration, and Barefoot Augustinians and Augustinian Recollects aiming to contemplative way of life. Moravian monastic churches in Brno and Šternberk are presented as examples of Augustinian buildings.

BRNO, the Church of St. Thomas, District of Brno

The Church of St. Thomas with the monastery of Augustinians in the Moravia Square (Photo 51) was founded by the Moravian margrave Jan Jindřich around 1350 as a burial ground of Luxembourg secundogeniture. Both him and his son, Margrave Jost, were buried here. Apart from the centre of the church no other significant relic of the medieval buildings survived. The monastery suffered serious damage in 1428 during the Hussite wars and also in 1645 during the siege of Brno by Swedish troops. An extensive new building followed in 1732-52 (Foltýn 2005, 173-180).

A Brief Overview of Geological Situation of the Locality

The Moravian metropolis lies in the Dyje-Svratka Valley. The river Svratka in the west and Svitava in the east flow through the periphery parts of the city. The brook of Ponávka flows through the city centre from the northwest (the village Česká) through the northern city parts. It is a left-side tributary of Svratka in Brno-Komárov. It however left behind a flood plain, fairly wide in places, filled with Holocene fluvial, or even deluviofluvial sandy-loamy sediments. In the base of the Brno glomeration there are eruptive rocks of the Proterozoic Brno massif. Numerous types of granitoids are distinguished there. One of them, a well-known biotite granodiorite "the type of Královo Pole" forms the bedrock of the city centre. Superjacent are Miocene Lower Baden calcareous clays,

Photo 51. Brno, monastic Church of St. Thomas: General view from the southwest (Photograph by V. Hašek)

on which Pleistocene (Mindel) fluvial sandy gravels rest. The centre is covered with Pleistocene loesses and loess loams, which cover intermittently the Brno massif.

Geophysical Prospection and Archaeological Interpretation of the Results

Geophysical prospection focused on the situation in the presbytery, where the tomb of the Margrave Jošt was assumed to be. On the basis of correlation of the data of the accomplished geophysical works by the GPR and DEMP methods performed in 1998 in the church interior, five fairly extensive structures (marked A to E) can be localized in the area of the presbytery and the main nave in loesses, sandy gravels, or calcareous clays. They mostly correspond to positions of tombs or shallower graves. One of the most outstanding structures is the space of the famous Baroque tomb (A) in the axis of the church sized ca 1.7 x 1.2 m, covered with a slab of pink limestone 0.15 – 0.18 m thick, in which remains of son of Jan Jindřich, the Moravian and Brandenburg margrave and Roman king Jošt (+1411) are secondarily laid (Cejnková/Hašek/Loskotová 1999, 425). According to the character of two different types of signals detected by the GPR in this area (Fig. 28 a, b) it was necessary to expect combination of a bricked tomb (Photo 52) with iron poles and a relief of loesses under the backfill. Another grave of a clergyman of a size comparable to the first structure (Fig. 28 a) is attached to the abovementioned tomb (A) on its western side. Manifestations of two larger Baroque tombs of Lichtensteins and Augustinians (B, C), covered with ledgers (Fig. 28 c), were intercepted in the form of multiple reflections on the both gospel and epistle sides of the altar. Their total sizes were not determined successfully by the geophysical prospecting due to various obstacles in the wider area of the main altar. Furthermore, a shallower two-dimensional inhomogeneity sized up to ca 1.2 x 1.6 m (D) was detected near the altar in the axis of the building. It can represent combination of e.g. a smaller half-buried hollow filled with uncompacted material and brick masonry. Indication E located ca 5 m

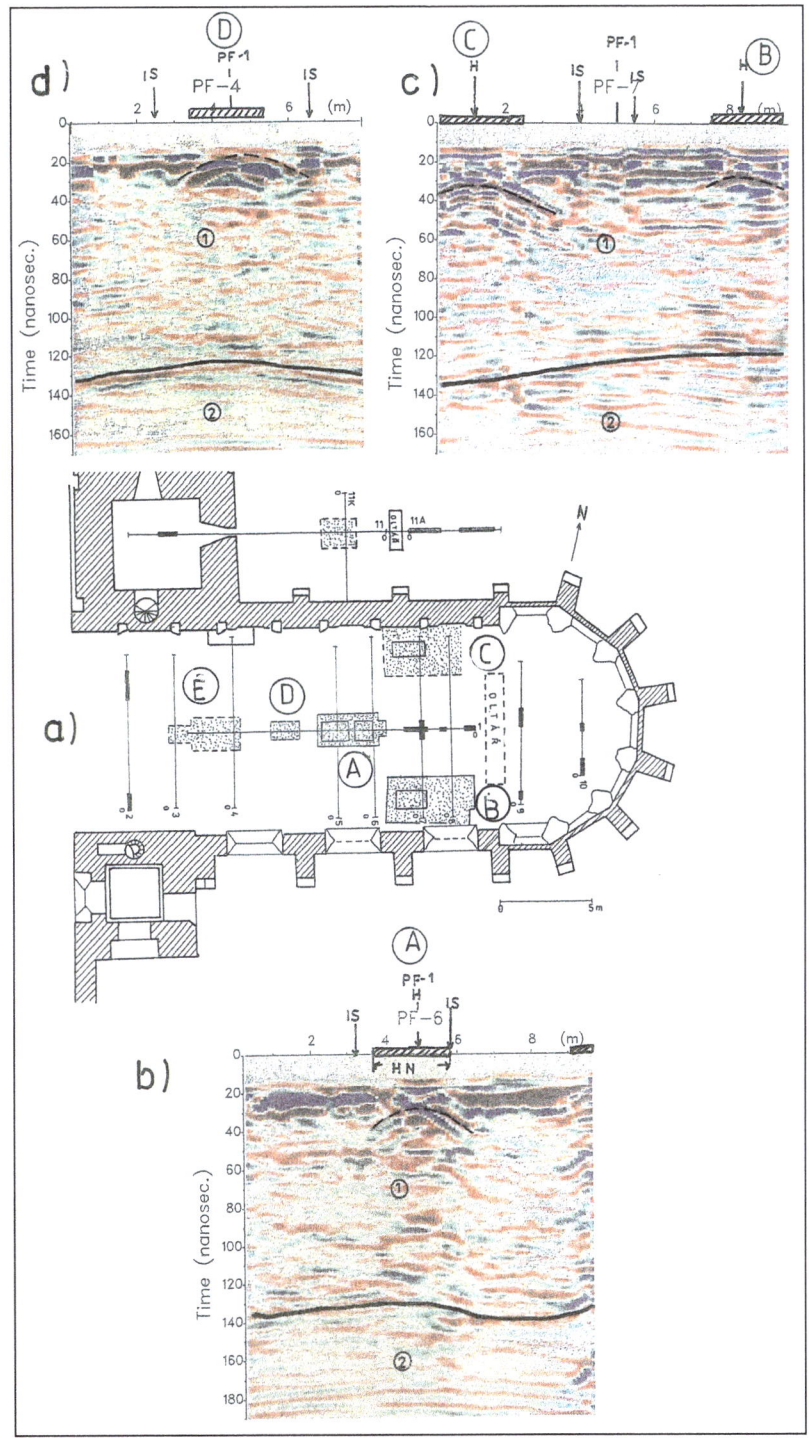

Fig. 28. Brno, the Church of St. Thomas: Correlation scheme of results of the geophysical works and interpreted tombs (a), tomb of Margrave Jošt in the interpreted radarogram (b), manifestation of the Baroque tombs in the GPR (c), interpreted tomb in the church nave (d)

west of the tomb A sized ca 2 × 1.5 m (Fig. 28d) shows similar properties as D. It could be a manifestation of a smaller tomb. Several two-dimensional inhomogeneities were localized on the eastern side of the altar in the closure of the presbytery. They correspond to either possible route of underground services or smaller objects under the stone floor of the building. In the axis of the northern chapel, indications of two structures sized up to ca 1.5 to 2 m were interpreted from the GPR, which could be manifestations of one, or possibly two tombs (Hašek/Peška/Unger 2008, 19).

Archaeological Excavation

The Margrave Jošt's tomb was opened after previous geophysical demarcation at the turn of the years 1998 and

Photo 52. Brno, the monastic Church of St. Thomas: Uncovered tomb of Margrave Jost (Photograph by V. Hašek)

Photo 53. Šternberk, the monastic Church of the Annunciation: View of the front from the west (Photograph by V. Hašek)

1999. The skeleton was subject to anthropological investigation and it was found that the margrave had died at the age of 50 to 55 (according to historical records at the age of 57 years), he was relatively very tall (183 cm), of robust build with well-developed musculature (Cejnková/Loskotová/Maráz 2006).

ŠTERNBERK, the Church of the Annunciation, District of Olomouc

The Augustinian monastery with the Church of the Annunciation (Photo 53) lying near the Šternberk castle in the slope on the walled terrace above the Upper Square, was founded by Magdeburg archbishop Albert of Šternberk in 1371. It is now a lengthwise oriented one-nave building with a two-spired front and circularly closed presbytery, adjacent to the Augustinian monastery and standing approximately in the place of the original Gothic church from the 14th century. The Gothic building was razed and a new church was built on its place according to the plans of F.G. Grimm and under the leadership of the Fulnek builder Thalherr in 1775 – 1783. After abolishing the monastery the church serves as a parish church (Foltýn et al. 2005. 662-668).

A Brief Overview of Geological Situation of the Locality

In the geomorphological structuring of the surface of the Czech Republic, Šternberk occurs exactly on the border line between the Domašov Upland of the Low Jeseník Mountains and the Uničov Plateau of the Upper Moravian Valley. From the geological point of view, the position of the town is fairly difficult. The city is built on the base of the Low Jeseník Mountains, a substantial part of which is built up of Lower Carboniferous sediments in the flysch development, traditionally denoted "the Moravia-Silesia Culm". Still older are basic metavolcanics and metatufs, which are a part of Stínava-Chabičov formation of Devonian age (Ems-Givet). They project in the west (or northwest) vicinity of the town and they also approach this town from the northeast. Apart from the abovementioned volcanics, also probably Devonian quartzose sandstones to quartzites, or possibly silicirudites of the Morava-Beroun formation are folded into the superjacent Lower Carboniferous "Culm" sediments in anticlinal structures. In the intensive fold formation with the axes falling towards the north to northwest, Lower Carboniferous wackes and regularly folded wackes, siltstones and shales of the Andělská hora formation (Lower Visé) appear in the south of the town. In the superincumbent bed of the formation, bassets of Middle Viséan wackes and regularly folded wackes, siltstones and shales of the Horní Benešov formation occur in Šternberk. The morphologically articulate terrain is modeled primarily by the valley of the swift stream Sitka with several left-side tributaries of minor watercourses in deeply recessed beds. Their beds are filled with sandy-loamy to rocky-loamy Holocene fluvial sediments, which e.g. form deluviofluvial alluvial fan on the left side of the church. At the bases of slopes in the town, proluvial sandy-loamy gravels accumulated along the left bank of Sitka in Pleistocene. A substantial part of the town including the square is built on them.

Geophysical Prospection and Archaeological Interpretation of the Results

The aim of the geological measuring in the area of the church in 2000 (Čermák/Hašek/Peška/Vrána 2001, 11)

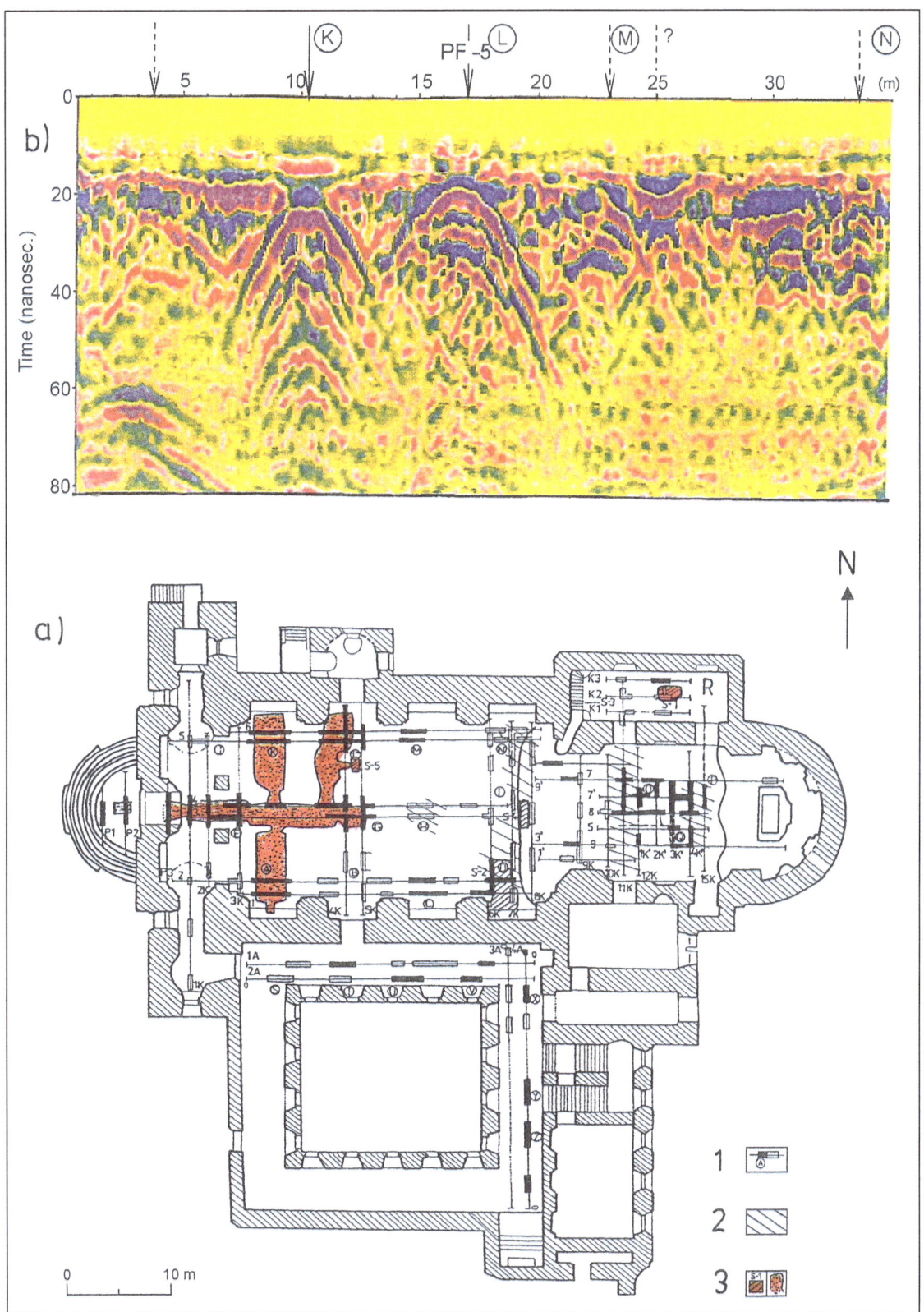

Fig. 29. Šternberk, the Church of the Annunciation: Results of the geophysical prospection and archaeological excavation (a), gauged profile in the north part of the nave and indication of inhomogeneities from the GPR method (b). 1- indication of inhomogeneities according to their distinctiveness; 2- conductivity anomalies from the DEMP method; 3- positions of crypts and the tomb

was to verify possible positions of underground spaces – a crypt and tombs.

From overall correlations of indications of GPR and DEMP methods, a number of fairly extensive structures

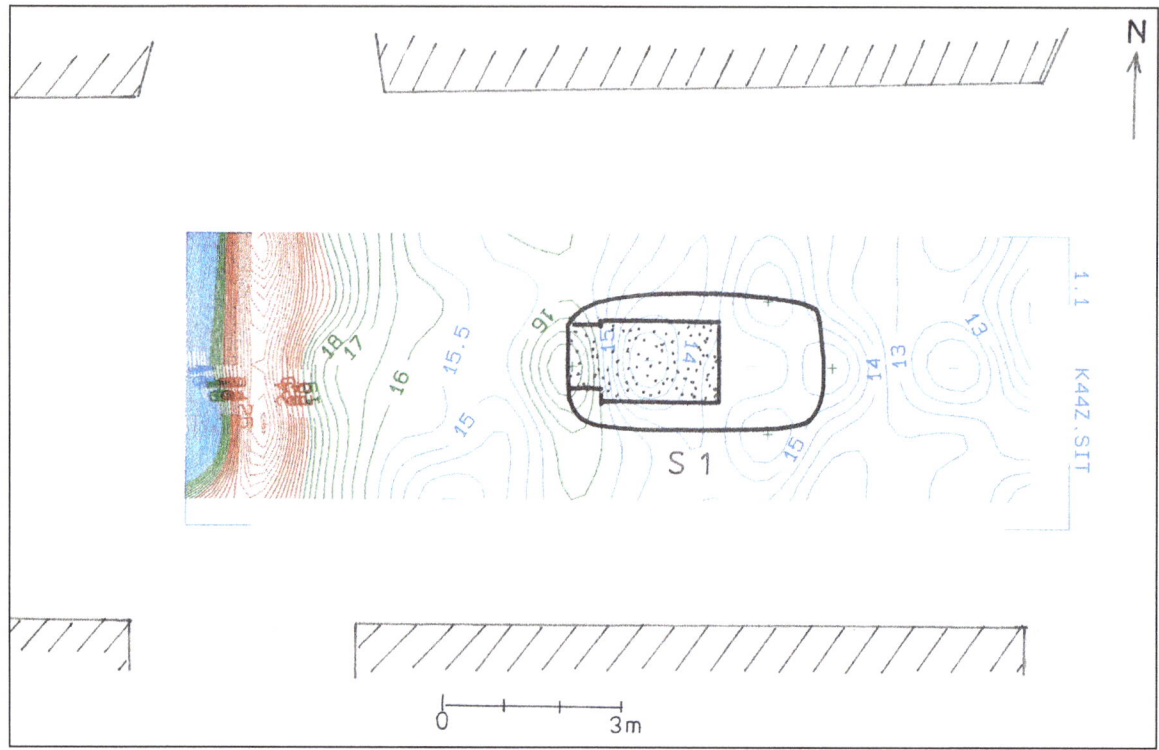

Fig. 30. Šternberk, the Church of the Annunciation: Map of σ_{app} isolines for h = 1.5 m in the area of the Chapel of Virgin Mary the Helper, where a smaller tomb was localized

(A – N), corresponding to various near-surface inhomogeneities, can be localized in the area of the nave. E.g. the zones marked A, E, F, G, K, L (Fig. 29a,b) in the western part of the sacral building are some of the most distinctive reflections of the electromagnetic waves. They represent the summary effect of a larger and more articulate hollow space not very deep under the church floor. We think, and the results also indicate, that a known but not yet fully documented Baroque tomb was intercepted by the measuring.

Also an anomaly area on the SE margin of the researched feature, marked D, is interesting. This inhomogeneity – a combination of a geological cause and foundation walling – could be deeper, possibly under the new mensa. The zone of reduced conductivities ca 8 x 4 m large marked I in the axis of the building by the foot of the presbytery near the triumphal arch can represent probable superposition of manifestation of stone accumulation and two routes of underground services along both its margins. In other cases (zones marked B, C, H, M, A, J in the middle to the NE part of the nave) there can be either so far unknown (half-filled) tombs (e.g. the area B, C, M, A) and shallower graves, or possible relics of the foundation walling from the defunct original building.

In the area of the presbytery, three larger anomalous areas marked O, P, G were identified; they are accompanied by zones of reduced conductivities in some places. We expect impact of basement Culm rocks near the surface and in places the possibility of variable lithology of the backfill from the probable older object cannot be excluded.

Only one anomalous zone (R) was detected by both applied methods by the northern side chapel of Virgin Mary the Helper (Fig. 30); it indicates position of a smaller and shallower bricked tomb with maximum size of 2 x 1.5 m. The entrance into the grave itself, if there is one, cannot be determined from the results of the measuring – there is a manifestation of a deposit of church material.

Distinctive reflections of electromagnetic waves by the western front of the church near the stairs (marked 1) are created by a shallow space – the main entrance into the abovementioned large Baroque tomb.

In the area of the cloister several inhomogeneities were localized (S, P, U, V, X, Y, Z), indicating places of graves with the main axis oriented approximately in the E-W direction (Hašek/Peška/Unger 2008, 20).

Archaeological Excavation

After removing bricks and backfill, a tomb was found in the Chapel of Virgin Mary the Helper (length 1.30 m, width 1.20 m and maximum height 0.94 m) lined with Late Baroque bricks. Two wooden cases were found in it. Remains of Albert II of Šternberk are supposed to be in the larger one (Photo 54). A secondary burial of a man and a woman divided by a partition was in the second one. Remains of Petr of Šternberk and his wife Anna Rebeca are supposed to be here. Skeletal remains of both Petr of Šternberk and his wife Anna Rebeca born of Kravaře were subject to anthropological analysis, during which age of a robust man, about 187 cm tall, managed to be determined; he died in the age of 45 to 55 years and suffered from arthritic changes on his skeleton. The woman, who died at approximately the same age, was about 164 cm tall and also suffered from osteoarthrosis (Drozdová 2001).

Photo 54. Šternberk, the monastic Church of the Annunciation: Tin box with remains of an andult man – perhaps Albert II of Šternberk (Photograph by P. Rozsíval)

In the next stage of the excavation, a Baroque crypt was opened and documented. It adjoins the Gothic crypt under the western part of the building – a corridor and four chambers built of quarry stone and bricks. Their sizes are as follows: 7.90 x 3.30 x 2.20 m (1); 7.90 x 3.10 x 1.90 m (2); 2.80 x 2.9 x 1.8 m (3) and 7.50 x 3.30 x 2.22 m (4). Remains of Augustin Kazimír Herdin (+ 1783) were placed in a very rotten wooden coffin in the first chamber (Čermák/Hašek/Peška/Vrána 2001, 19-20).

4.3. CHURCH BUILDINGS FROM THE 16TH – 18TH CENTURY

Archaeology pays less attention to church monuments from this epoch, nevertheless a number of town and village buildings are known to be investigated. Typical examples of buildings from this time horizon are e.g. Blansko, Brno, Doubravník, Prague, Šumice and Uherské Hradiště.

4.3.1. Village Parish Churches and Chapels

DOUBRAVNÍK, the Church of Finding of the Holy Cross, District of Žďár nad Sázavou

The Church of Finding of the Holy Cross (Photo 55) is located on the north side from the square. It was built in 1535-57 as a burial ground of Lords of Pernštejn in the place of an Early Medieval church connected perhaps with an Augustinian convent founded before 1231 and extinguished in 1543. The new building founded without a sacristy was added to its north side in the beginning of the 1540's. It is a triple-nave hall building built along a NE-SW axis, polygonally closed in the northeast. A prismatic tower is located in front of the west front. The main nave is vaulted by a star-like pattern, the side naves by cross vaults. A new Gothic tomb of the Mitrovskys of Nemyšl was added to the church in 1867 (Samek 1994, 409).

Photo 55. Doubravník, the Church of Finding of the Holy Cross: View from the southwest (Photograph by M. Hotárek)

A Brief Overview of Geological Situation of the Locality

Geomorphologically, the town of Doubravník is located in Nedvědice Upland as a part of the Horní Svratka Upland. The town basically follows the right bank of the Svratka river. The river reaches the width of up to 400 m from Doubravník to Černvír in the north. The valley is filled up by Holocene fluvial sandy-loamy sediments. In this section the course of the river follows the boundary of lithologically variegated Proterozoic Svratka crystalline complex in the west and the Bíteš group of the crystalline complex in the east. In the area of the right-bank tributary of the Rakovec stream, the course of Svratka in the town turns towards the east into a winding narrow valley, which makes its way on towards the southsoutheast through Bíteš crystalline complex to return again to the original straight direction in Borač. Approximately between Doubravník in the north and the spring area of

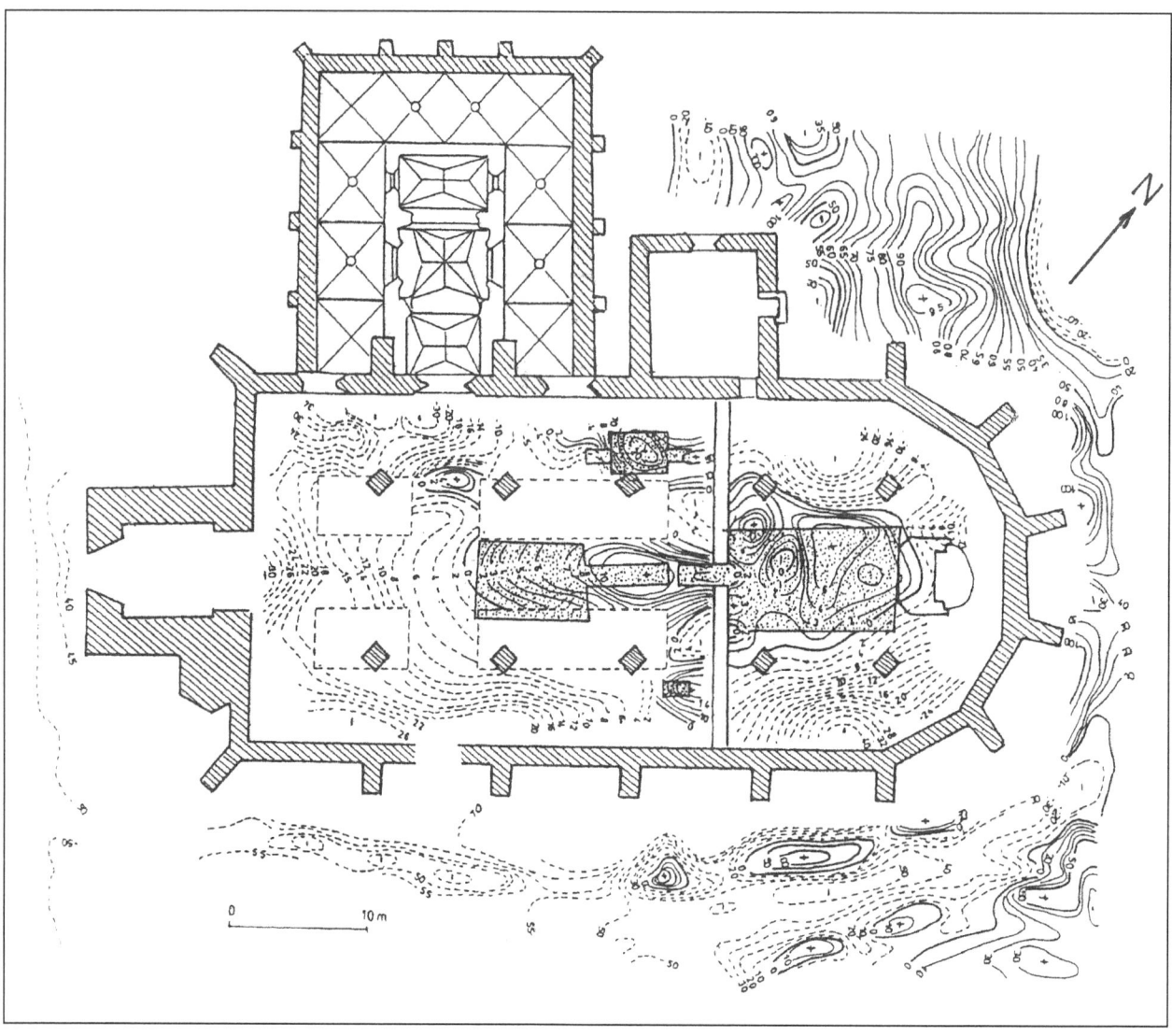

Fig. 31. Doubravník, the Church of Finding of the Holy Cross: Map of ρ_{app}^{anom} isolines in the church area

the stream flowing into Svratka in Borač in the south, a north-south valley filled up with Holocene-Pleistocene deluvial sediments (loamy-sandy and loamy-stony deposits) originated probably in Pliocene-Pleistocene. The bedrock is formed by Bíteš crystalline complex. The sediments are apparently filling of the old and straight Svratka valley. Proterozoic crystalline complex of the Bíteš group is represented by double-mica, often porphyroblastic gneisses with rare occurrences amphibolic gneisses and amphibolites. Much more variegated are north-south rock stripes of proterozoic Svratka crystalline complex, which are represented by double-mica garnetic mica schists, double-mica migmatites and "orthogneisses", and stripes of Letovice crystalline complex, represented by fine-grained biotite-muscovite garnatic paragneisses, double-mica garnatic mica schists and crystalline limestones. The prevailing part of the town with the church is built on deluvial sediments, and the part in the slope above the road is founded on eluvium of porphyroblastic gneisses of the Bíteš group.

Geophysical Prospection and Archaeological Interpretation of the Results

The aim of the geophysical works conducted in the interior of the Late Gothic Church of Finding of the Holly Cross in 1993 was to search for possible existence of the foundation wall from the original church that stood in this place probably as soon as in the 13th century and a convent was attached to it (Oharek 1923, Doležel 1998). In the current building there are, apart from tombs of Pernsteins and Lichtensteins, situated in its axis, also smaller tombstones from the 15th and 16th century (Hašek/Unger 1994, 32-33, Hašek/Unger 2001, 98). Complex processing of the DEMP method with apparatuses of two different depth ranges (h = 1.5 m and 3÷5 m) indicated, according to identfied linear zones of increased resistivities, the course of the foundation wall relics, probably from the original church, lining the walls of the tomb of the Pernsteins in the presbytery and partly continuing to the area of the main nave near the supporting columns of the building (Fig. 31), consisting

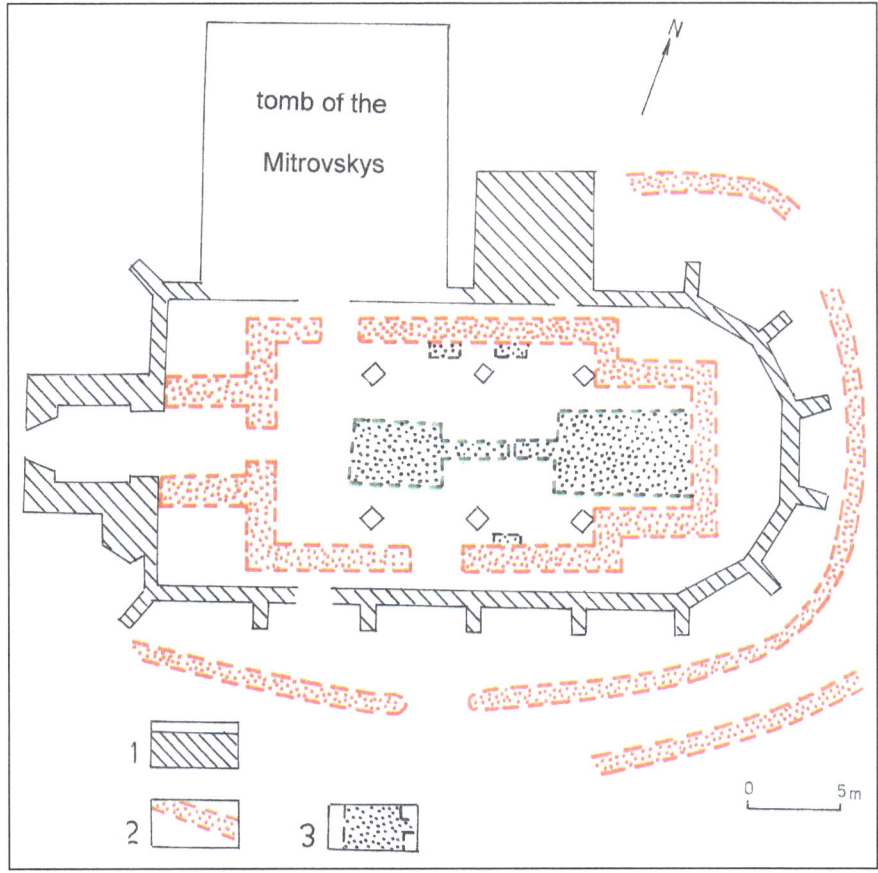

Fig. 32. Doubravník, the Church of Finding of the Holy Cross: Correlation scheme of results of the geophysical works. 1- the current built-up area; 2- relics of the interpreted masonry; 3- positions of tombs and graves

of a presbytery of probably a square ground plan, an oblong nave sized ca 16 x 10 m and a prismatic tower at the west front (Fig. 32).

Three-dimensional anomalous values ρ_{app} localize the position of the tomb of the Pernsteins under the presbytery and of the Lichtensteins in the main nave, also places of shallower tombs by both outer walls of the original sacral building. The church walling can be observed outside the building (Fig. 32) and in the NNE section an indication of foundation wall of a former family church of the Augustinian nuns, founded by Stephen of Medlov before 1231 and extinguished in 1534, serving as a family burial ground of the founding manorial nobility (Samek 1994, 408).

ŠUMICE, the Church of Birth of the Virgin, District of Uherské Hradiště

The single-nave Church of Birth of the Virgin, located in the east part of the village (Photo 56) was built in 1863-64. It is situated in an area where a medieval to early modern religious building was localized by research. Total reconstruction of the church was done in 1896 but this building was removed in 1997 and replaced by a new church in 2000.

Photo 56. Šumice, the new Church of Birth of the Virgin: View from the southwest (Photograph by J. Pavelčík)

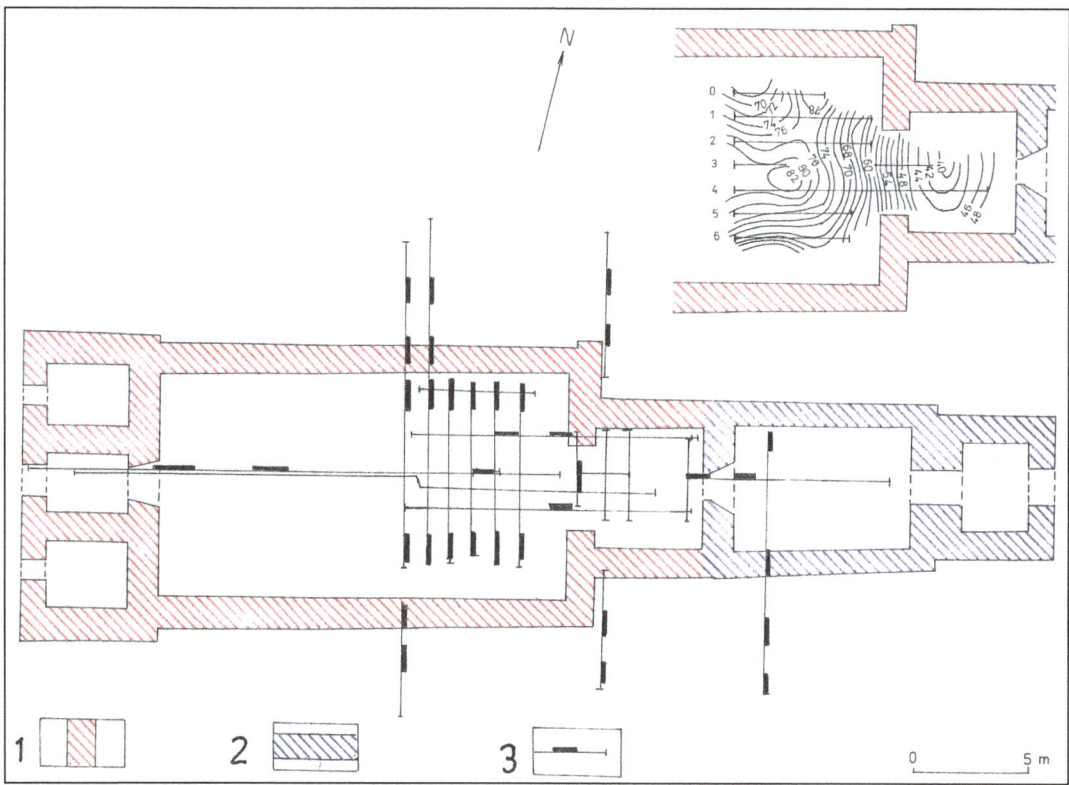

Fig. 33. Šumice, the Church of Birth of the Virgin: Correlation scheme of results of the geophysical works and map of DEMp ρ_{app} isolines for h = 3-5 m. 1- building from the 19th century; 2- Gothic building from the 14th century; 3- identified inhomogeneities

A Brief Overview of Geological Situation of the Locality

The village is located in Hluk Highland as a part of the Vizovice Upland. Its main part lies on a west-east flood plain of Olše and in the wide estuary of Ovčírka. Their sediments consist of Holocene fluvial sandy loams. A thrust plane in the southwest – northeast direction passes through the east margin of the village. The Bílé Karpaty subunit of the flysch West Carpathians has thrusted itself on its top towards the northwest across the Račany subunit, which is represented here by Vsetín Layers of the Zlín formation consisting of coarsely rhythmic flysch, which is consisting of glauconitic sandstones and calcareous claystones of middle Eocene age. The Bílé Karpaty unit, southeast of Šumice, is represented by fine rhythmical flysch lithofacies of the Nivnice formation of Paleocene age with the characteristic motley calcareous claystones, containing laminated calcareous sandstones. The base of Šumice, except for the Holocene deposits, is formed by Vsetín layers covered with Holocene to Pleistocene deluvial sandy loams.

Geophysical Prospection and Archaeological Interpretation of the Results

The purpose of the geophysical works in the interior of the parish Church of Birth of the Virgin in 1993 (Hašek/Unger/Záhora 1997; Hašek 1999, 81) was to find possible relics of the foudation wall of the older pulled-down building and localize possible position of a tomb or graves in the place of the original building. Total thickness of anthopogenous deposits up to ca 1.9 m and of clayey loams to clays up to 3.4 m in the superincumbent bed of the gravel sand was determined by the GPR method (Fig. 33). The identified local inhomogeneities are concentrated into depths of mostly 0.8 – 1.9 m, i.e. in the anthropogeneous layer. Their interpreted width is ca 0.8 – 2 m. Foundation wall of the pulled-down building can be the source of shallower "anomalies", in deeper positions the anomalies are probably manifestations of graves. In the church interior, it is possible to interpret, according to organization of the graves by the inner side of the outer wall of the current building (see Fig. 33), position of an older sacral feature sized ca 5.5 x 11 m with a possible tower by the west front. Sizes of the presbytery roughly agree with the present object (ca 5 x 3 m) from the 19th century. Some anomalous elements indicating places of e.g. graves were detected by measuring (GPR, DEMP) in the area of the nave of the abovementioned building. Situation is different in the area of the original identified presbytery, where area of decreased resistivities can be localized; they are accompanied by rather extensive inhomogeneities on the GPR profiles (see Fig. 32). We assumed a smaller tomb to be here with foundation wall from the original or another maybe older building, or an altar mensa covered by a larger stone slab.

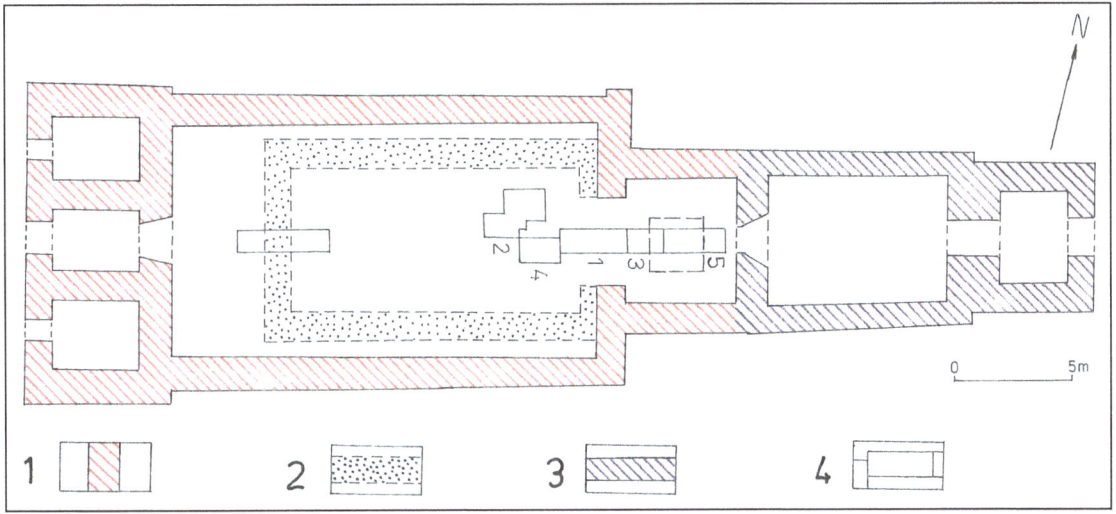

Fig. 34. Šumice, the Church of Birth of the Virgin: Performed archaeological research in the area of the building.
1- building from the 19th century, 2- interpreted masonry relics from the 17th – 18th century; 3- Gothic builing from the 14th century; 4- positions of the verifying probes

Archaeological Excavation

According to research of the South Moravian Museum in Uherské Hradiště (Pavelčík 2003, 107, 109), the oldest single-nave Gothic church with a tower was built of sandstone ashlars (Fig. 34) in the 14th century. A triumphal arch separated the presbytery from the rectangular nave, narrower and shorter than the building from the 19th century. The older mensa was probably connected with this building. The newer building originated towards the end of the 17th or in the 18th century. Another rebuilding was done in 1825. The existing presbytery was kept and a new mensa was built. The nave of the old little church was used as a sacristy and the sacristy and the presbytery as a tower.

In the area of the church 5 probes S-1 to S-5 (A –E) were done in the places of the GPR indications by 1997 (see Fig. 34) that detected 15 graves and a foundation of the altar mensa from the older church. All the detected graves had W-E orientation. It ensued from the abovementioned facts that the original sacral building from the 14th century was surrounded by a cemetery. The church covered part of the graves as it was expanded later (Pavelčík 2003, 105-106).

UHERSKÉ HRADIŠTĚ, the Chapel of St. Roch, District of Uherské Hradiště

According to a historical source (Fišer 1920) and a report about a standard non-destructive constructional-historical research (Komendová 2008), the Chapel of St. Roch in Uherské Hradiště (cadastral district of Jarošov) was founded under the top of the Černá hora (Black Mountain) in 1680 and it was not finished before 1687. It ensues from these data that the original building was more extensive than its present version. It consisted of a tower, a choir, a nave, a presbytery and a sacristy. This feature was abolished during the reign of Emperor Joseph II in 1786 and it was sold to the city of Uherské Hradiště, which had the tower and the galilee removed. Subsequently a powder house for the local garrison was established here in 1807. The chapel was restored and consecrated in 1931 and subsequently also in 1968 (Photo 57).

Photo 57. Uherské Hradiště, the Chapel of St. Roch: View from the west (Photograph by V. Hašek)

A Brief Overview of Geological Situation of the Locality

The wider area of Uherské Hradiště is located at a boundary of the Lower Moravian Valley and Hluk Highland, more broadly Vizovice Highland. Most of the city extends on the east side of the ca 2.5 km wide river

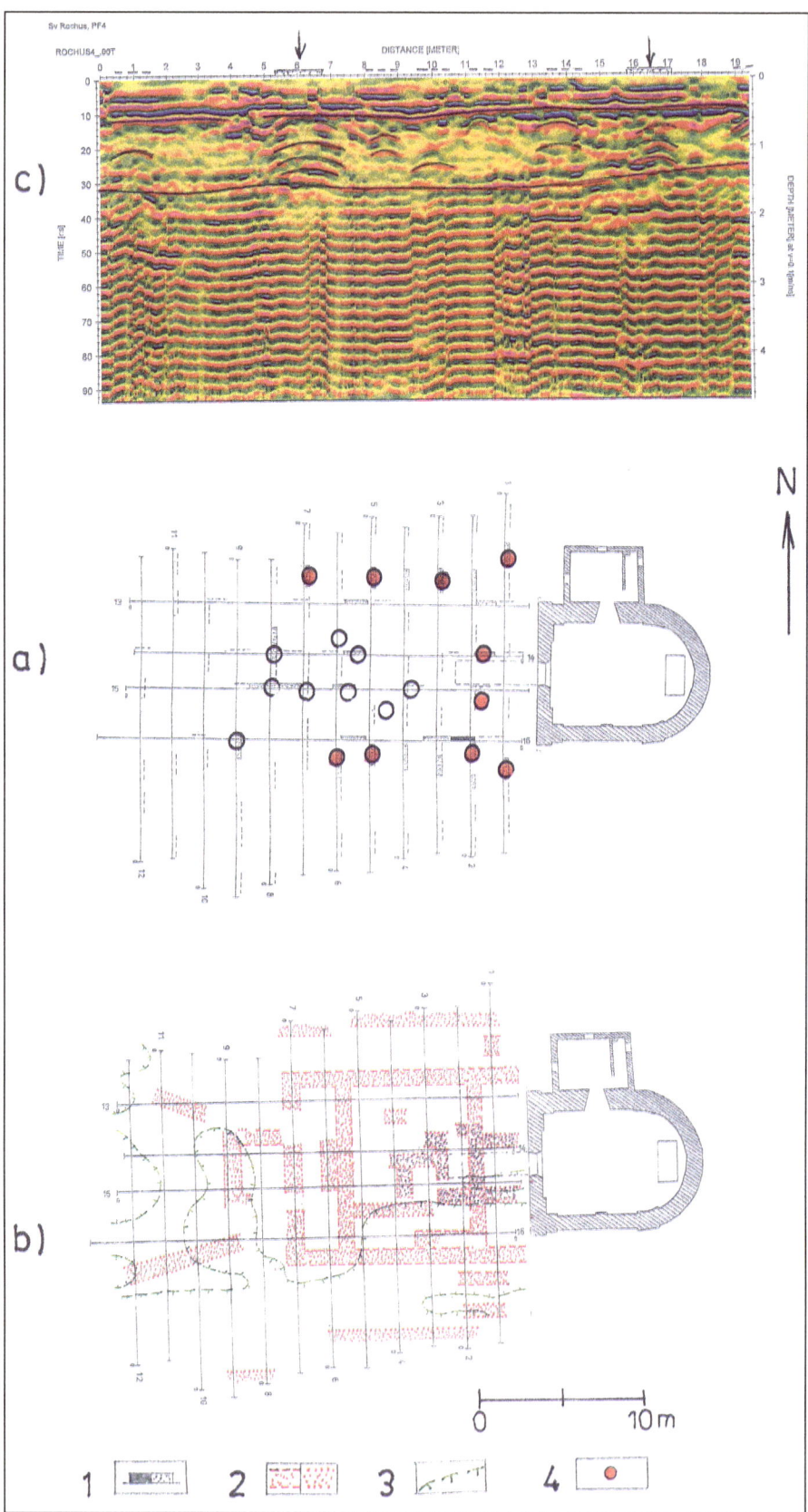

Fig. 35. Uherské Hradiště, the Chapel of St. Roch: Correlation scheme of results of GPR measuring with marking of positions of verifying GPR measurings with marking of positions of verifying pedological probes (a), one of possible variants of the prospection interpretation (b) and interpreted radarogram with manifestation of brick masonry relics (c). 1- identified inhomogeneities according to their distinctiveness; 2- interpreted masonry from the pulled-down building; zones of increased conductivities; 4- pedological probes with brick material

of Morava. A substantial part of Staré Město lies on the west side of the flood plain, on a flat bank. The river Morava winds its course between both towns. The flood plain of Olšava flows into it about 1 km south of Uherské Hradiště in Kunovice. A tectonic disturbance in the northeast-southwest direction passes through the east part of Uherské Hradiště. It demarcates sharply the boundary of the wide flood plain, formed by Holocene sandy-clayey loams with sands, and the east bank of Morava. The highland here is covered by Upper Pleistocene loesses and loess loams. Surface outcroppings of sediments of the Paleogene Magura group of nappes emerge under them in the east part. Rocks of Paleocene to Middle Eocene Zlín formation occur in places on the surface of the terrain From the Račany unit of the Magura group. It is flysch alternation of glauconitic sandstones and calcareous claystones. Upper Miocene clays and sands have stayed in small amount on the top.

Geophysical Prospection and Archaeological Interpretation of the Results

The main task of the soil radar method complemented by DEMP in 2008 was to localize possible places of the foundation wall of no longer existing parts of the current building, or places of other inhomogeneities connected with this building, characterized probably only by little different physical parameters (flysch sandstone etc.) from the surrounding environment built up mostly by sandy-clayey soils (destruction layer).

By complex processing and interpretation of all the measured geophysical data (GPR, DEMP) in the form of correlation scheme (Fig. 35) with consideration also of results of the 1st Josephian military mapping in 1764-1768 and 1780-1783, increased number of indications on inhomogeneities (Fig. 35a) was localized in the examined sector; some of them were recommended for verification by archaeological sounding.

From the GPR data, two more distinctive boundaries of reflected electromagnetic waves were detected on most profiles of the area. They are located on times $t_1 = 8–12$ ns and $t_2 = 30–42$ ns. After introducing constant speeds $v_r = 0.10$ m /ns, the first case may be more sandy inhomoheneous humous anthropogenic layer (maybe arable land) of fictive thickness of $h_1 = 0.4–0.6$ m in the superincumbent bed of thicker and lithologically variable complex of quaternary loamy-sandy loess loams and loesses, lying above the complex of rock sof the Račany unit of the Magura Flysch. Relatively less articulate reliéf of the base horizon without near-surface weathering is located very approximately in depths of 1.5 to 2.1 m.

By interpretation of the map σ_{app} (see Fig. 35) a rather extensive zone of increased conductivities can be identified on the whole south and southwest margin of the interest area; it indicates probably position of a thicker pelitic layer of loesses and loess loams in this area, which, however, in the SSW – NW direction passes gradually into an areal zone of decreased conductivities corresponding lithologically to base sandy-clayey rocks of the Magura Flysch, or their near-surface disturbance (weathering). Route of underground services may be the cause of narrower zone of more intensive higher σ_{app} in the southwest part of the area; in the other parts, the indication of local conductivity anomalies represents recent issues or possibly also manifestations of masonry relics also in negative imprint.

In the studied area (Fig. 35a), several areal, maybe less extensive anomalous zones can be expected, only having geophysically smaller differentiation ability due to lower differentiation of their geophysical properties, with their tops in depths of ca 0.3 to 1.3 m and ca 0.8 – 1.0 m wide, corresponding, according to their size and linear configuration, probably to indications of masonry relics (also in negative imprint), larger accumulations of stone material, lithology of Quaternary cover.

Indication of manifestation of linear building elements of variable sizes can be expected west of the chapel on the basis of correlation of individual inhomogeneities (Fig. 35b).

The interpreted object is assumed to be a larger and inside more articulate structure sized ca 16 x 10 m. They can be relics of the church nave foundation wall situated right in front of the entrance into the current chapel.

Photo 58. Uherské Hradiště, the Chapel of St. Roch: Aerial phototgraph of the archaeology excavation (Photograph by M. Vaškových)

Archaeological Excavation

Sounding and uncovering works (Photo 58) performed on the basis of results of geophysics and 15 pedological

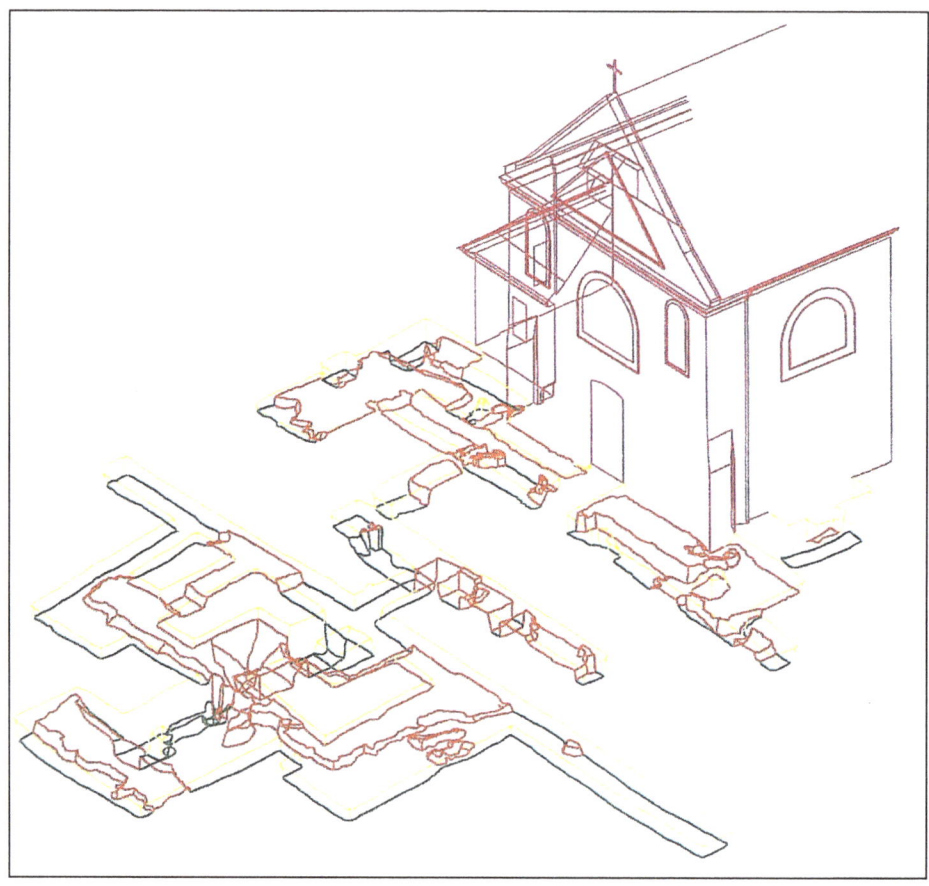

Photo 59. Uherské Hradiště, the Chapel of St. Roch: 3D model of the archaeology excavation (Photograph by M. Vaškových)

proving holes (Fig. 35a) proved the existence of relics of brick masonry of a rather extensive building, probably a church nave, belonging to the present chapel (Photo 59). It ensued from the results obtained that a larger church stood in this place at the end of the 17th century and the current chapel is only its eastern (presbytery).

BLANSKO, the Church of St. Martin, District of Blansko

The building mentioned as soon as in 1136 and totally rebuilt in the 18th century is located by the SW part of the town by the right bank of Svitava. It is an oblong single-nave feature (Photo 60) with a set-off semicircularly terminated presbytery (Photo 61). The original church was being adapted in the half of the 15th century and perhaps also in the 2nd half of the 17th century and a a tower was added to it in 1707. The current rebuilt church contains the southwest quoin of the nave and the whole west wall built of ashlar stones probably from the half of the 13th century (Samek 1994, 64).

Photo 60. Blansko, the Church of St. Martin: View from the south (Photograph by M. Hotárek)

A Brief Overview of Geological Situation of the Locality

The city extends on both steep slopes of the north-south valley of the Svitava river. Orographically, it belongs to the Adamov Upland, which is a part of the Drahany Upland. Svitava takes in a larger amount os streams from both sides, the most water-bearing one being the left-side tributary from the Moravian Karst area. A well-known

DISCUSSION OF PRACTICAL RESULTS AND OBSERVATIONS

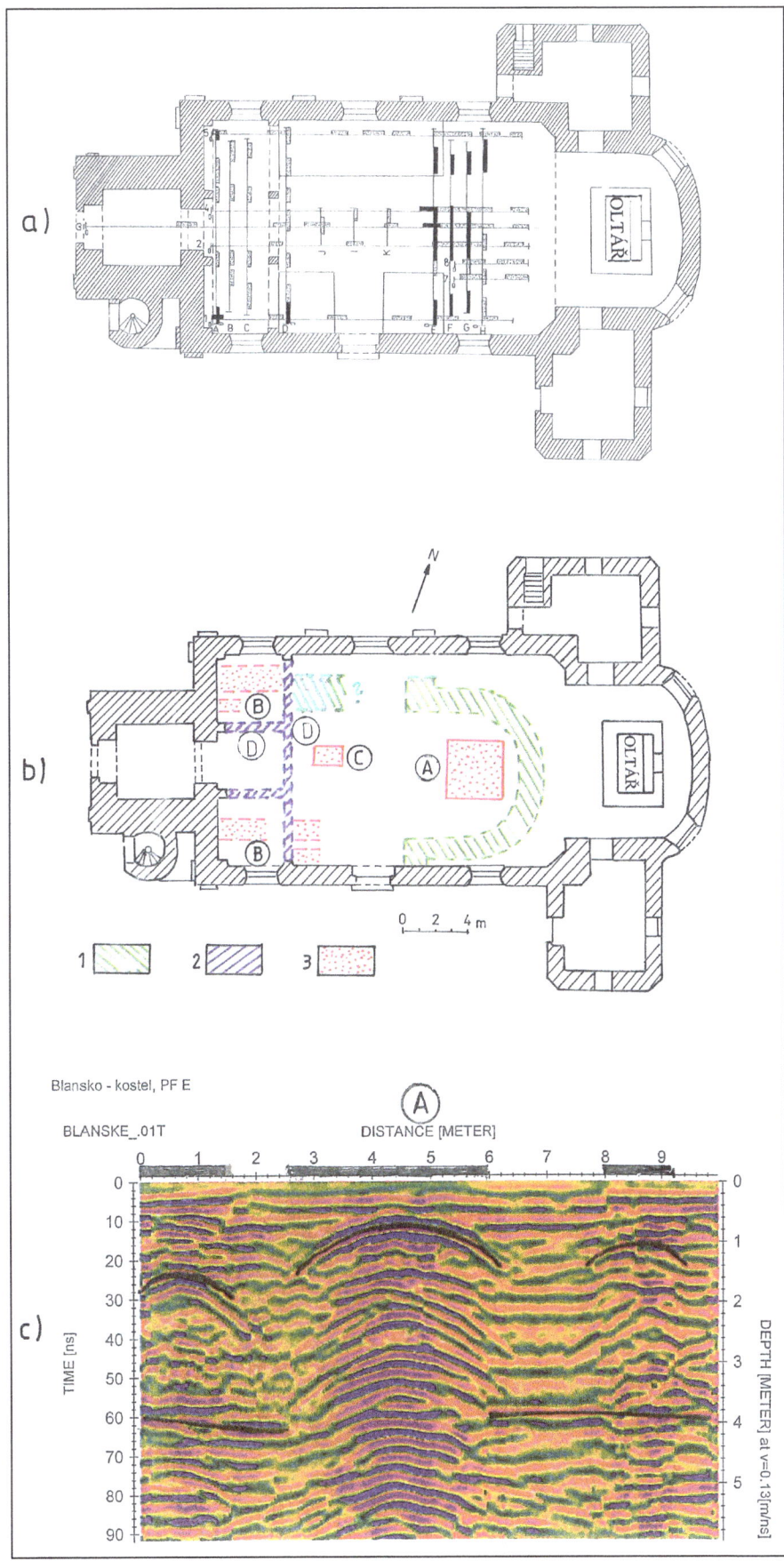

Fig. 36. Blansko, the Church of St. Martin: Correlation scheme of the results from the GPR method (a), presumed position of the older building (b), image of the newer tomb (c). 1- part of the interpreted ground plan of the Romanesque church and other building elements – masonry, 2- continuous column foundations under the gallery, 3- tomb, graves

Photo 61. Blansko, the Church of St. Martin: Interior from the West (Photograph by M. Hotárek)

karst river Punkva flows into Svitava at the south end of the city. The prevailing part of the city is concentrated on the east slopes. The centre is located at their toe, which is covered by thick Holocene-Pleistocene loamy-sandy to stony deluvial sediments. The bottom of the Svitava bed is filled by Holocene sandy-loamy sediments. Granitoids of the Brno Massif represent rock massif in the slopes and under the toe sediments. The Brno Massif is formed by a number of petrographically diverse types. In Blansko and its vicinity it is the Blansko type, which is biotite and biotite-amphibolite granodiorite, exploited abundantly in the past not only as building stone but also for highly demanding stonemason's work. The church occurs north of the nearby main square and it is founded in deluvial sediments, probably also on bedrock.

Geophysical Prospection and Archaeological Interpretation of the Results

The task of the geophysical measuring by the GPR method in the church interior was to find out possible relics of the foundation wall of the original Romanesque building from the half of the 12th century, possibly also places of tombs and graves from various stages of its building process (Hašek/Tomešek/Unger 2006).

From the overall correlation of inhomogeneities identified by prospection (Fig. 36a) a number of anomalous zones can be interpreted in the space of the nave of the current church. They are mostly linear and represent relics of foundation wall of an older, pulled-down, probably Romanesque building of inner sizes of 13 x 9 m and terminated on the east side near the triumphal arch by a semicircular apse with the diameter of ca 6.5 m (Fig. 36b). The total size of this feature with unclear west limitation is ca 16 x 11 m. The stone wall thickness is ca 1.2 – 1.4 m. In the second, east third of the current nave a larger tomb (A, Fig. 36c) sized 3.5 x 3 m can be expected. It is apparently related to the present church. Also new church builders can be buried here, i.e. Rozmitals, Gelhorns, maybe even the priest P. Mader. Other discovered near-surface building elements are either part of the original building (or continuation of continuous column foundations) (D) or represent possible positions of newer simple graves (B). The inhomogeneity in the church axis by its west segment (marked C) may represent a smaller tomb or a grave sized ca 2 x 1 m.

Archaeological Excavation

For partial verification of the interpreted situation a test pit was placed in the northwest corner of the church nave. It managed to be determined by this research that the north part of the west wall of the church nave is built on a loamy layer (Photo 62) containing human remains from the cemetery and was therefore built at the time when burials were already performed here, probably around already existing church. According to the character of the wall, it is younger than the surviving and visible wall in the south part of the church nave. Because overburnt stones from the older building are used also in this masonry, the building history of the church appears to be very difficult and indicating at least three building stages. None of the detected graves or grave pits was disturbed by the standing wall, which however does not exclude the possibility of some graves being older that this walling. Geophysical anomalies were not verified in the church nave.

Photo 62. Blansko, the Church of St. Martin: Test pit in the northwest part with uncovered wall (Photograph by M. Hotárek)

BRNO, the Church of St. Joseph, District of Brno

The Church of St. Joseph in Joseph Street was built in 1651-53 as a substitute for the church in front of the city walls, founded in 1617 and pulled down in 1643. The new church (Photo 63) is an oblong single-nave building with slightly set-off presbytery of a square ground plan with a

A Brief Overview of Geological Situation of the Locality

The church is located at the SE margin of the historic part of the town in close proximity of the extinct city fortification. The pre-Quaternary base is formed here by eruptive rocks of the Brno Massif. In the interest area it is biotite granodiorite of the "Královo Pole" type and its equivalents. The superjacent sediments are Miocene Lower Baden calcareous clays, Pleistocene (Mindel) fluvial sandy gravels, loesses, loess loams and anthropogenic recent deposits.

Geophysical Prospection and Archaeological Interpretation of the Results

The purpose of the archaeological excavation and the constructional-historical research conducted in the space of the early Baroque Church of St. Joseph in 1995 was determinimg possible causes of emergency conditions of the building that came to destruction in connection with gradual appearing of cracks in the wall, vaults and portals of the church (Hašek/Měřínský/ 1997, 430). Also detailed geophysical measuring performed in the interior of the building itself and its closest vicinity became a part of these works. Microgravimetry (Mrlina 1994), DEMP and georadar (Hašek/Unger 2001, 95) were used for solving the task. Two rather extensive areas of increased resistivities were determined by prospection by the DEMP method (Fig. 37) in the area of the main nave and

Photo 63. Brno, the Church of St. Joseph: Vew from the west (Photograph by V. Hašek)

rectangular nave and a prismatic tower by its north wall. The presbytery vaulted crosswise in the nave is a barrel vault. Buildings of the Franciscan convent altered by modern construction work adjoin the north side of the church (Samek 1994, 207).

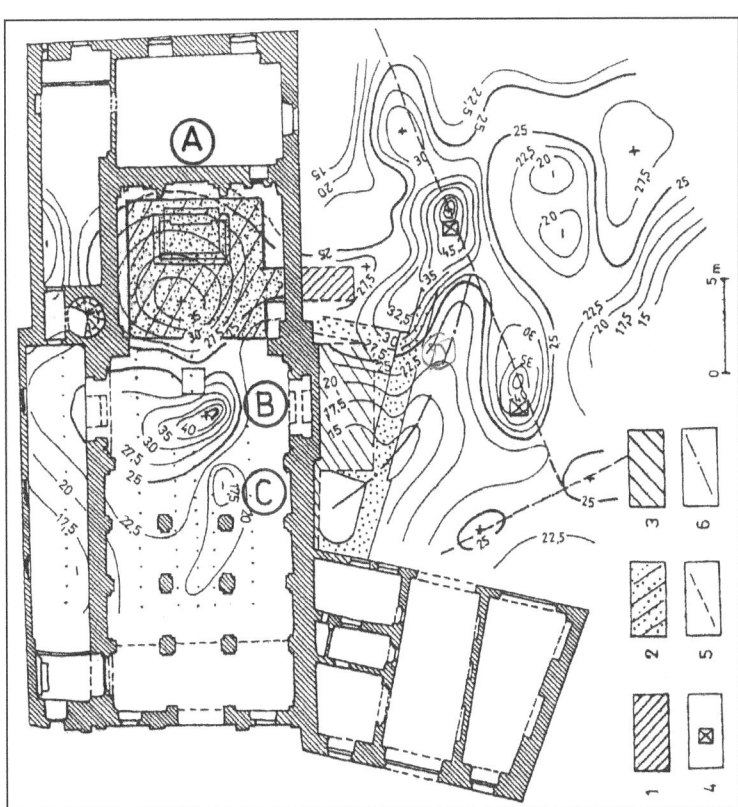

Fig. 37. Brno, the Church of St. Joseph: Map of DEMP ρ_{app} isolines for h = 3-5 m and correlation scheme of results of the geophysical works. 1- side entrance and the known tomb; 2- masonry relics; 3- area of the archeology excavation; 4- sewer; 5- route of the sewers; 6- axis of the conducting zone

the presbytery. The first of them, observed west of the main altar (A), is a manifestation of a larger known crypt of the Franciscan (Ursuline) convent with a southern side entrance; it is obvious also from the results of gravity measurings and the GPR. The second one between the altars of St. John of Nepomuk and St. Augustine with the axis approximately in the north-south direction could be caused probably by some larger inhomogeneity, e.g. lithological change in near-surface layers, i.e. by varying character of the landfill, its greater thickness and compaction, decreased humidity of the filling material against the surrounding environment (B). More local maximum of values of resistivities in the west part of the building, continuing to the west section of the court, will be related probably to a change of consistence and properties of the anthropogenous deposits (C). In the researched area of the courtyard, a less distinctive zone of increased resistivities was detected apart from the route of waste water disposal system in the northeast – southwest (or northnorthwest-southsouthwest) direction continuing the drainage ditches (see Fig. 37). The zone of increased resistivities corresponds, according to archaeological probing (Himmelová 1993), to position of relics of combined foundation wall of the older extinct building (D).

UHERSKÉ HRADIŠTĚ, the Church of St. Francis Xavier, District of Uherské Hradiště

The Baroque Church of St. Francis Xavier with a former Jesuitical college is located at the south section of the Masaryk Square in Uherské Hradiště (Photo 64). Foundations of its outer walls were founded in 1673 on oak piles whose upper parts are disturbed by constant changing of ground water surface level. The bearing walls of the current crypt and smaller tombs were not underlaid by piles, therefore they are not stabilized and when the surface level rised the clay component in the underlying sediments segregated. The statics of underground objects is thus disturbed, e.g. by their general subsidence, therefore also floors in the church nave are breaking etc. Also an extensive flood caused large deformation of floors in 1997. Apart from a larger crypt in front of the altar, entrances to other assumed smaller tombs covered by tombtones are not apparent on the current tile floor (Pavelčík 2000, 258).

A Brief Overview of Geological Situation of the Locality

The area of the city of Uherské Hradiště is located at the boundary of the Lower Moravian Valley and the Hluk Highland, more widely Vizovice Highland. Most of the town extends on the east side of ca 2.5 km wide Morava flood plain formed by Holocene sandy-clayey loams and sands. The base of the building consists of less appropriate river alluvium with the character of flood clayey-sandy loams, their superincumbent bed is formed by landfills ca 2 m thick.

Photo 64. Uherské Hradiště, the Church of St. Francis Xavier: View from the west (Photograph by www.uherskehradiste.cz)

Geophysical Prospection and Archaeological Interpretation of the Results

Geophysical research in the area of the Church of St. Francis Xavier focused on determining possible causes of static disturbances of the building originated probably as a result of floods (Hašek/Unger 2001, 106). The main goal of the realized measuring by the GPR method in 1998 was to determine positions of tombs and graves in the whole inner area of the sacral building. Indications of the georadar (Fig. 38) pointed to existence of several Jesuitical crypts covered by tombstones – some of a more complicated ground plan (those near the main altar and two smaller ones in the north and south chapel – B, C), also several shallower graves in the main nave (D, E) and relics of the foundation wall from pulled-down houses (Fig. 39). Causes of static disturbance of the sacral building especially in the area of the presbytery are connected with compression of surface uncompacted layers of soils in the area of shallowly founded underground objects (tombs, masonry), with transforming compressible layers reaching to larger depths, sinking foundation soils and their bearing power in connection with oscillating of the ground water surface level.

Archaeological Excavation

Works conducted by the South Moravian Museum in Uherské Hradiště in 1999 found out that the crypt at the boundary of the main nave and the presbytery in front of the main altar (A, see Fig. 39) consists of four to five rooms, four of which were proved by research. All parts of this feature are closed by barrel brick vault (Photo 65, 66). Interpreted east wing of the structure, according to the GPR of the same sizes as the west one, was not archeologically studied. Only space filled up with loam and debris was found out by pedological probe. Originally 23 individuals were laid in the west wing of the tomb (Pavelčík 2000, 259-260).

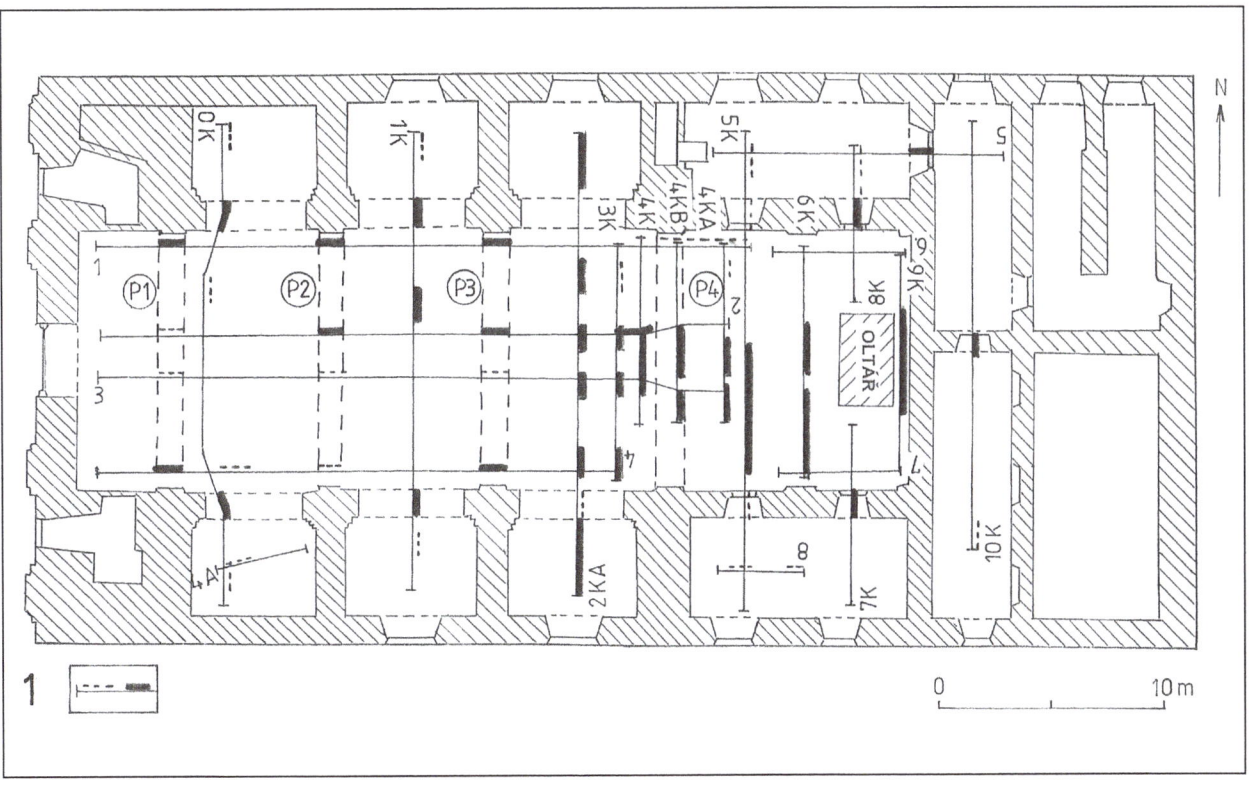

Fig. 38. Uherské Hradiště, the Church of St. Francis Xavier:
Correlation scheme of results of the geophysical works.
1- identified inhomogeneities according to their distinctiveness

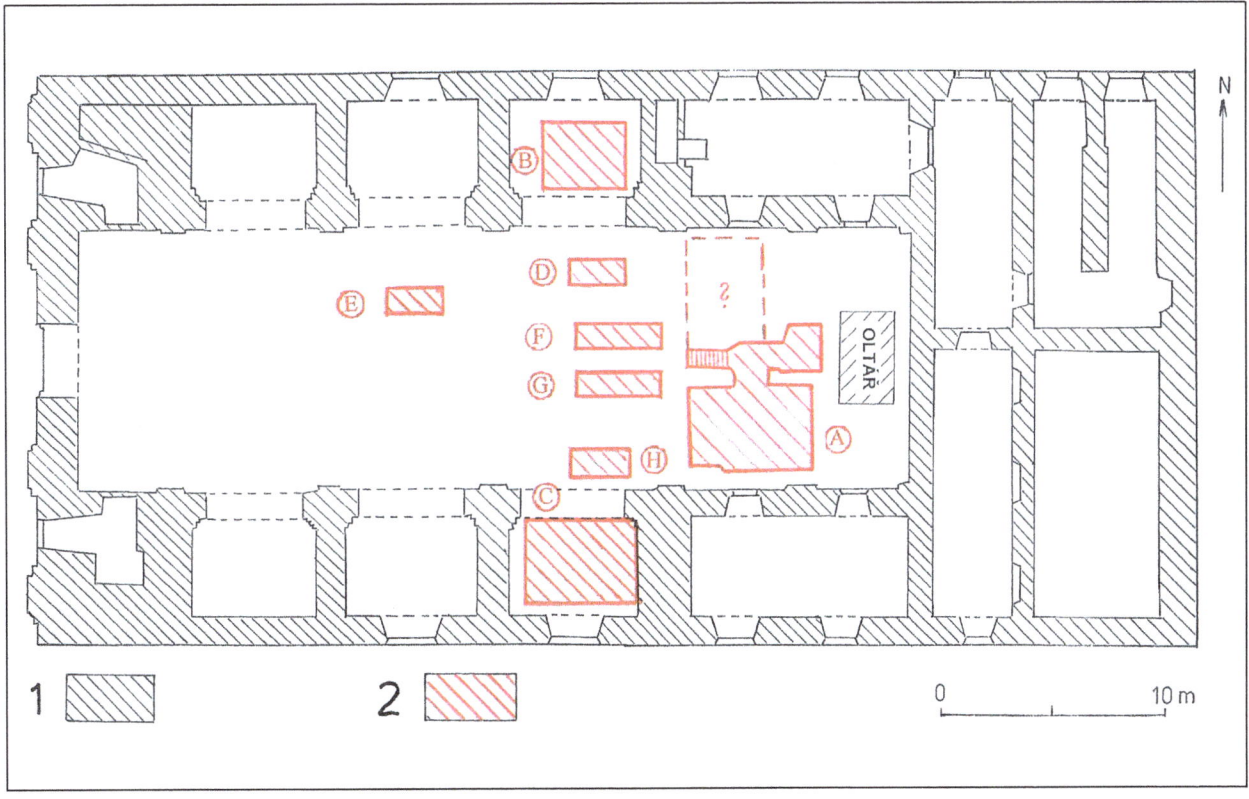

Fig. 39. Uherské Hradiště, the Church of St. Francis Xavier: Interpretation of inhomogeneities
from the GPR method, some of which were verified by archaeological excavation.
1- the present masonry; 2- positions of crypts and tombs

Photo 65. Uherské Hradiště, the Church of St. Francis Xavier: Barrel Vault of the west wing of the tomb, vaults and chambers on the left (Photograph by J. Pavelčík)

Photo 66. Uherské Hradiště, the Church of St. Francis Xavier: View of the northwest corner of the tomb C. Positions of the skeletons and remains of coffins after lowering of the flood waters (Photograph by J. Pavelčík)

4.4. JEWISH MONUMENTS CONNECTED WITH RELIGION

A synagogue, ritual bath (mikvah) and a cemetery are the most important parts of a Jewish religious community. The main parts of a synagogue is a niche for placing the Torah and a place from where the Torah is read. Geophysical and archaeological researches were so far performed in the areas of two synagogues in Tábor and Jihlava, where features from the 19th century were detected in both cases.

JIHLAVA

The wrecked Jewish synagogue from 1863, built in the Romanesque-Moresque style and burnt down by the Nazis in 1939 (Photo 67) was located by the WNW margin of the city historic centre, at the place of the present market and car park at Benešova street, by the outer side of the city walls (Photo 68).

A Brief Overview of Geological Situation of the Locality

The interest area of the geophysical prospection belongs to the Czech–Moravian Upland, the subunit of the Jihlava-Sázava Furrow. The geological composition of the pre-Quaternary base of the main part of the district-town is relatively easy. The base of the bedrock are cordierite-biotite migmatites – gneisses, showing a high degree of regional metamorphosis. The precambric substrate was strongly influenced by central Moldanubic pluton that has gotten through, which caused origination of cordierite and strong penetrations of metatect in the

Photo 67. Jihlava: The studied area of the extinct synagogue near the city fortifications (Photograph by V. Hašek)

Photo 68. Jihlava: The building of the synagogue in 1920 (Photograph by the State District Archive in Jihlava)

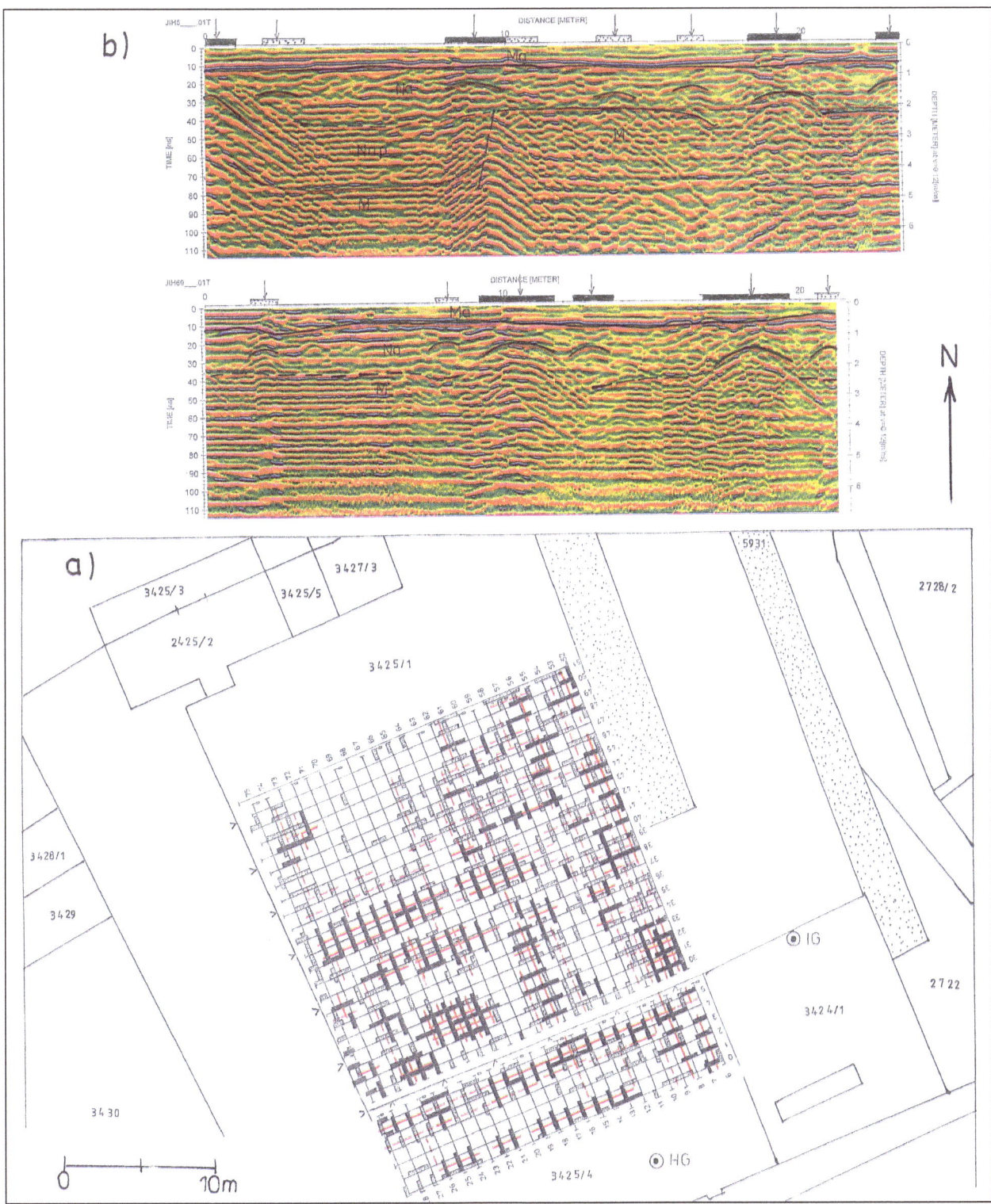

Fig. 40. Jihlava, the synagogue: Correlation scheme of geophysical works (a) and an example of interpreted radarograms with manifestation of identified inhomogeneities (b)

gneiss mantle, which changed the original gneisses to distinctive migmatites. Easily diggable dense Pliocene sands with clays and sandy gravels represent the cover of the bedrock in the place of the car park, market and in close vicinity of the city walls and the moat. In the neighbourhood of the cark park and the market, a number of parallel faulted linear structures in the NNE-SSW direction were verified in the bedrock by an old geological research. They demarcate ca 500 m wide zone in which fine-grained biotite-muscovite gneisses come up towards the surface. They represent the basic plutonic rock type that builds up the abovementioned central

Moldanubic massif. Perhaps this faulted structure limited the rising of the granitoid stripe from lower levels and its penetration into superjacent migmatites.

In the west-east geological section, migmatites build up the base of the studied area including the surviving fortification. The abovementioned granites that form e.g. the base of the nearby Masaryk Square and the Church of St. James emerge in close proximity towards the east. Pliocene sediments represent rare relics of extensive Neogéne transgression. They leveled certainly highly articulate relief of the bedrock and they are several metres thick. The highest layer is formed by not very thick Quaternary deposits of sandy loams with building remains (anthopogenous deposits).

Geophysical Prospection and Archaeological Interpretation of the Results

The aim of the realized measuring by the GPR and DEMP methods on the area of total size of 672 m² in 2007 was to provide detailed information about the position of the foundation wall of the redeveloped building of the synagogue and also about other building elements. Two (three in some places) distinctive boundaries of reflected electromagnetic waves were identified from the GPR. They occur at times $t_1 = 8–12$ ns and $t_2 = 20–46$ ns, also $t'_2 = 52–92$ ns. After introducing constant speed $v_r = 0.1$ m/ns, the first case may be macadam of fictive thickness $h_1 = 0.4–0.6$ m in the superincumbent bed of prevailingly inhomogenous anthropogenous stony-sandy layer lying probably above homogenous Miocene sandy-clayey sediments, whose articulate relief occurs approximately in the depths of $h_2 = 1.0–2.3$ m (landfill of varying lithological composition outside the moat) or $h'_2 = 2.6-4.6$ m. Larger thicknesses of both unorganized and more homogenous landfills are assumed to be in the area of the moat by the NE margin of the studied area. The width of this fairly extensive depression structure, probably walled-up on both sides, with the axis oriented in the NNW-SSE direction, is expected to be ca 8-9 m (Fig. 40).

Five main, both linearly and areally extensive inhomogeneities (A to E) can be identified on the basis of overall interpretation of the GPR and DEMP in the interest area. They indicate position of the synagogue, torn down in the past (A) and its other building elements (B, C), also some close buildings (D) by the north section of the Jewish sanctuary, but also a linear formation (E) by the WNW margin of the bailey rampart in the same direction as the city fortification. The formation is accompanied by concrete pillars, apparent also on the surface of the asphalt terrain (Fig. 40, 41).

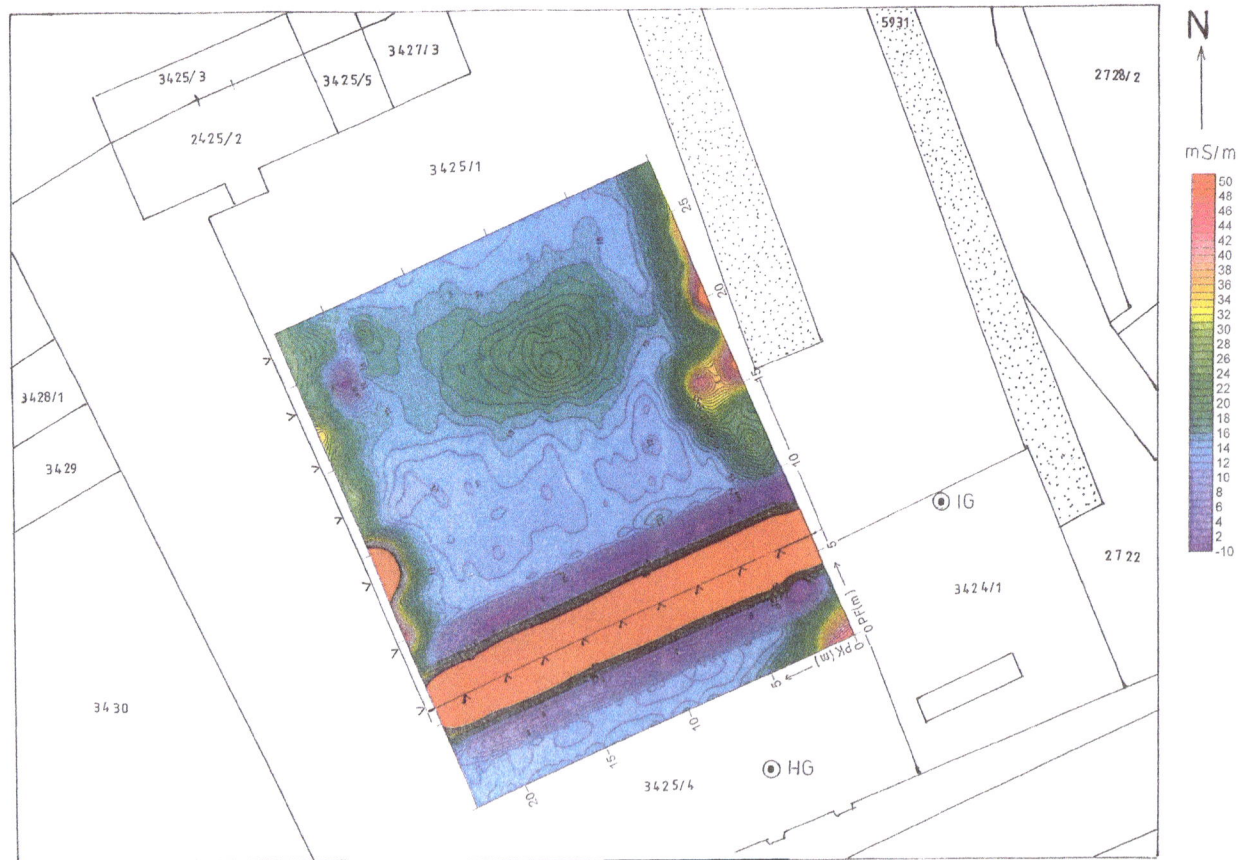

Fig. 41. Jihlava, the synagogue: Map of σ_{app} isolines from the DEMP method

DISCUSSION OF PRACTICAL RESULTS AND OBSERVATIONS

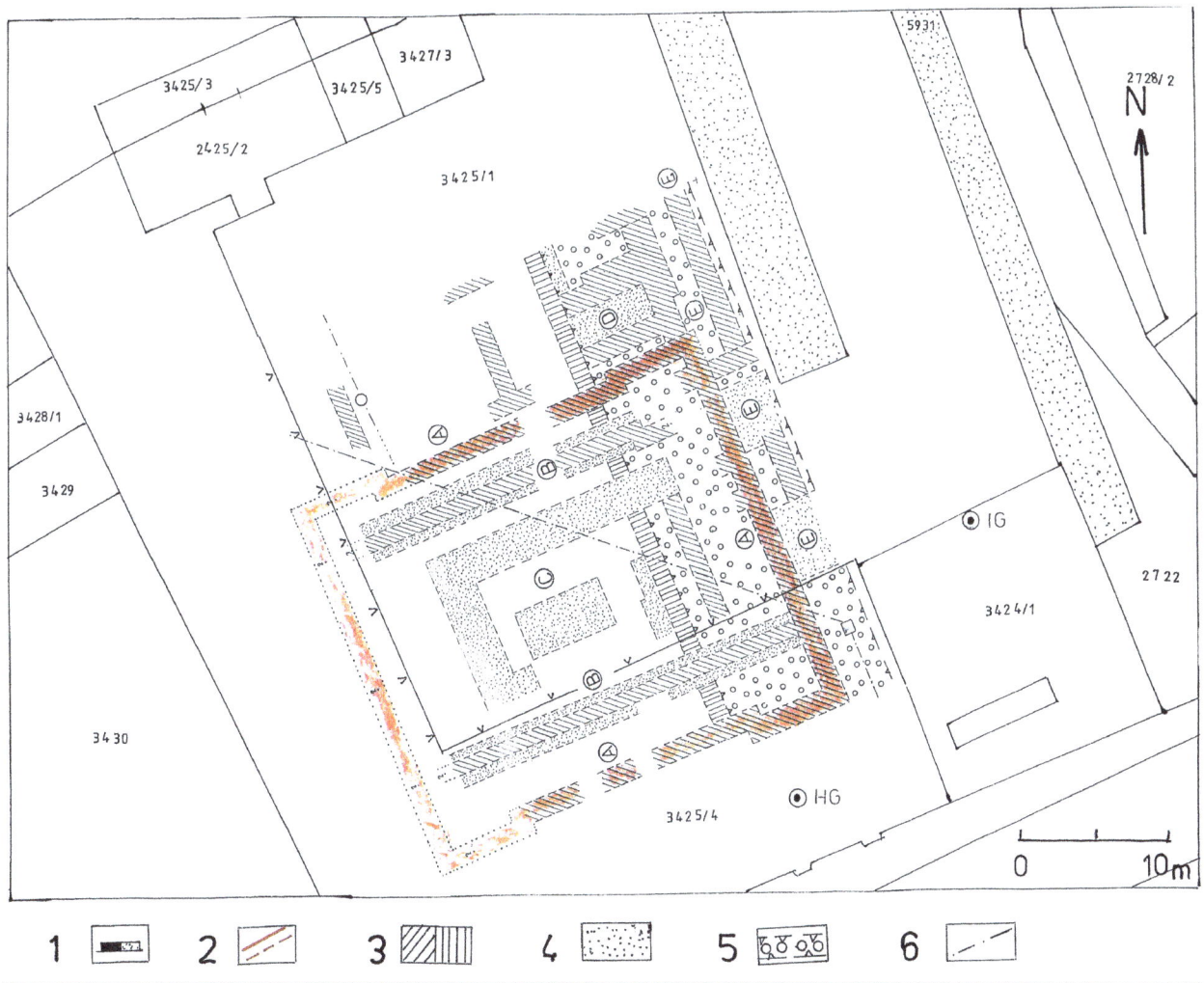

Fig. 42. Jihlava, the synagogue: Probable situation of the synagogue. 1- identified inhomogeneities according to thein distinctiveness; 2- axes of interpreted inhomogeneities; 3- masonry relics; 4- probable accumulations of stones; 5- anthopogenous backfill of the most of the city walls; 6- route of the underground services

The dominant inhomogeneity (A) sized ca 18 x 23-24 m (Fig. 42) corresponds, in combination with decreased conductivities from the DEMP method (Fig. see 41), to the course of the wall of the Jewish synagogue, ca 1 m thick, possibly with smaller destruction of the stone material in close proximity, where it is not possible to find out its WNW limitation due to the route of the wire fence in this area. Inside this identified structure, two wider parallel indications of linear character (ca 2.0-2.5 m), not further than 3 m from the outer wall (B) were also found. They correspond to position of two nearby narrower walls. Also larger accumulations of parallel stone destructions in the ENE-WSW direction cannot be excluded. Anomalies located approximately in the middle part of the building (C) are of similar character. Possible localization of underground cavities – cellars, larger accumulations of stones, berms etc. is not excluded there.

Outside of the sanctuary, an areal anomalous zone (D) was interpreted from the GPR by its north side. It indicates position of an object of increased conductivity in places, corresponding to some larger extinct building founded on more conductive landfill in the moat sized ca 7-8 x 6 m.

The linear anomaly (E) can be caused by either inhomogeneities from the pulled-down feature in close proximity of the bailey fortification (cellar, stone destructions), or by a charge of building material from the pulled-down city fortification.

In case of other indications of more local importance we assume that they are mostly caused by a route of underground services (waste water disposal system etc.), or possibly also by larger isolated stone blocks.

Archaeological Excavation

Uncovering research works conducted in 2007 by the Horácké Museum in Jihlava and aimed only to mapping the outer wall of the synagogue with the main goal of determining its ground plan for subsequent park arrangement of the area confirmed fully the results of the geophysical prospection. Relics of the abovementioned wall were determined under the asphalt topping with macadam in the depth of ca 0.5-0.6 m.

TÁBOR

The car park in the historic centre of the city of Tábor (Photo 69), adjacent to the area of the former castle and brewery, is located at the south periphery of the historical town reserve between the streets Na Parkánech and Hradební. It ensued from the written cartographical and iconographical sources that relics of medieval city fortification wall, remains of two destroyed houses and of a Jewish synagogue can be assumed to be in the abovementioned area (Photo 70, 71). They were built here in 1885 and destroyed, similarly as both the abovementioned houses adjacent in the east, in 1977. It cannot be excluded that even the original medieval economic background of the Tábor castle was partly at the area of the present car park (Hašek/Krajíc 2007, 75).

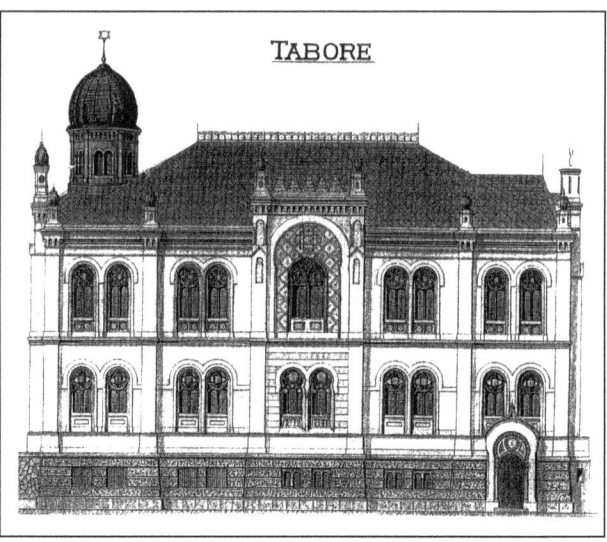

Photo 70. Tábor: The south side of the Tábor synagogue according to the planned documentation of J.V. Staněk from 1883

Photo 69. Tábor: The studied area of the extinct synagogue in the area of the lower car park (Photograph by V. Hašek)

A Brief Overview of Geological Situation of the Locality

The historical part of Tábor lies at the contact of biotite-pyroxenic Tábor syenitic massif and biotite paragneisses of the motley series of the Czech branch of the Moldanubic. The contact proceeds approximately from the gate to the yard of the castle of Kotnov and further in the NE direction to the Žižka Square. The explored area is, according to the existing data and exposures, formed only by syenite. It is a medium to coarse-grained dark blue-grey rock with confining structure, largely fissured and irregularly weathered or even mouldered (eluvium). This body is interveined by aplite and aplite granites by its margin. The surface of the terrain was modified and leveled by landfill of very variable thickness and

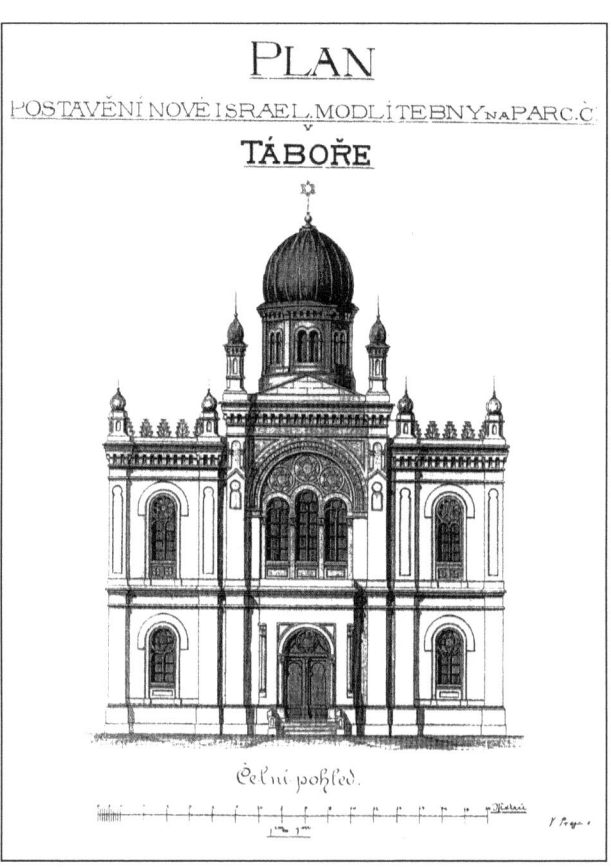

Photo 71. Tábor: The west side of the Tábor synagogue according to the planned documentation of J.V. Staněk from 1883

composition. It can be said to illustrate the situation that the asphalt topping and its rock bed is ca 0.4-0.5m thick at the car park; relief of the weathered syenite ranges in depths from ca 1 m to ca 3.5-4.0 m in places.

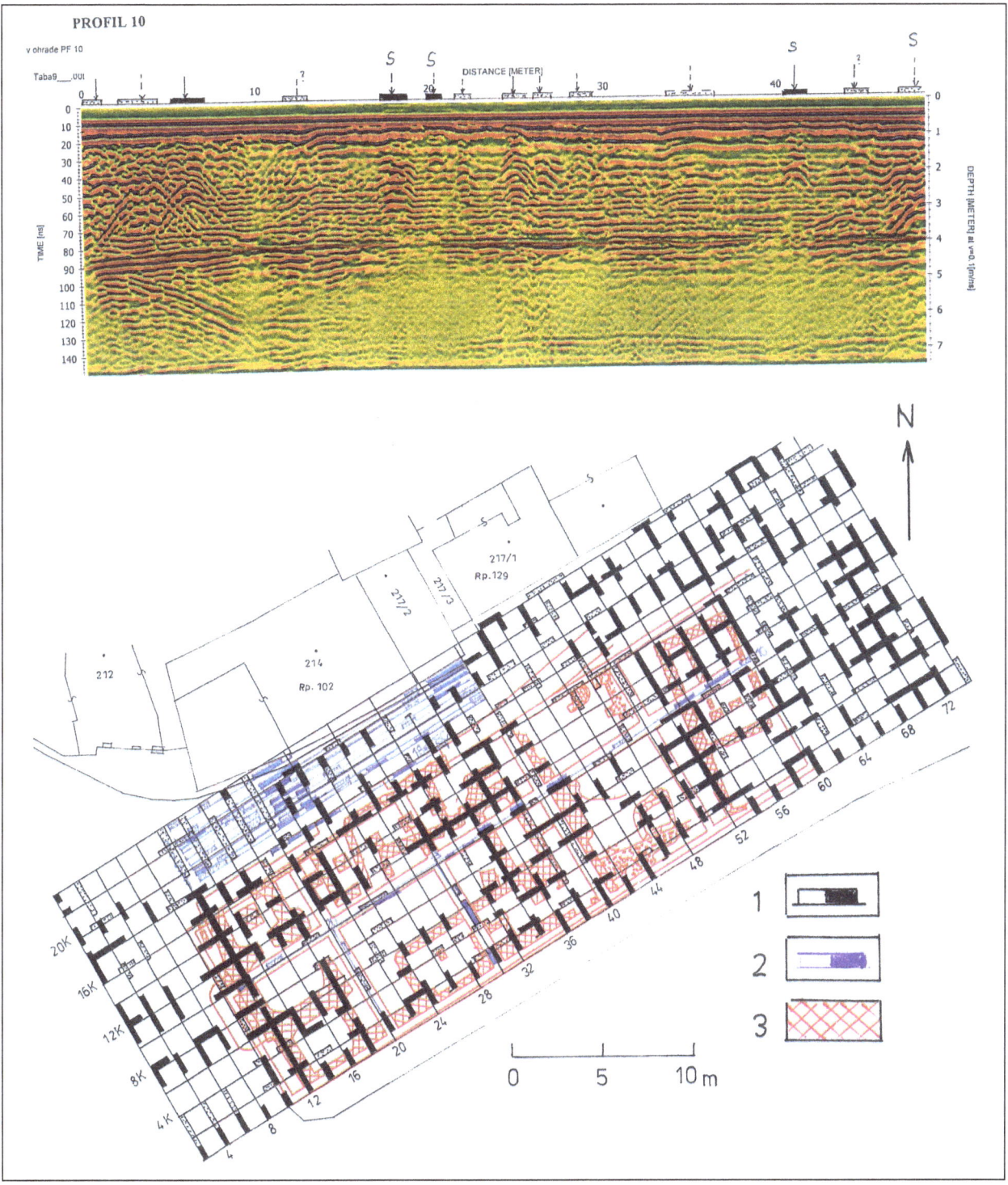

Fig. 43. Tábor, the synagogue: Correlation scheme of results of the geophysical works (a) and interpretation of radarograms on the profile 10 – 250 MHz antenna. 1- near-surface inhomogeneities according to their distinctiveness from the 1st stage of the prospection – black; 2- near-surface inhomogeneities according to their distinctiveness from the 2nd stage of the prospection – blue; 3 – relics of the uncovered masonry – red

Geophysical Prospection and Archaeological Interpretation of the Results

In the whole interest area of the lower and upper car park, two areas of total sizes of 2330 m² were geophysically measured in the 2004 stage. Also machine boreholes were done in order to determine the depth and angle of repose of the base, samples of soils and rocks were taken and analysed by both terrain and laboratory methods.

During the stage II, i.e. complementary geophysical prospection in 2005, several sub-areas sized 333 m² were

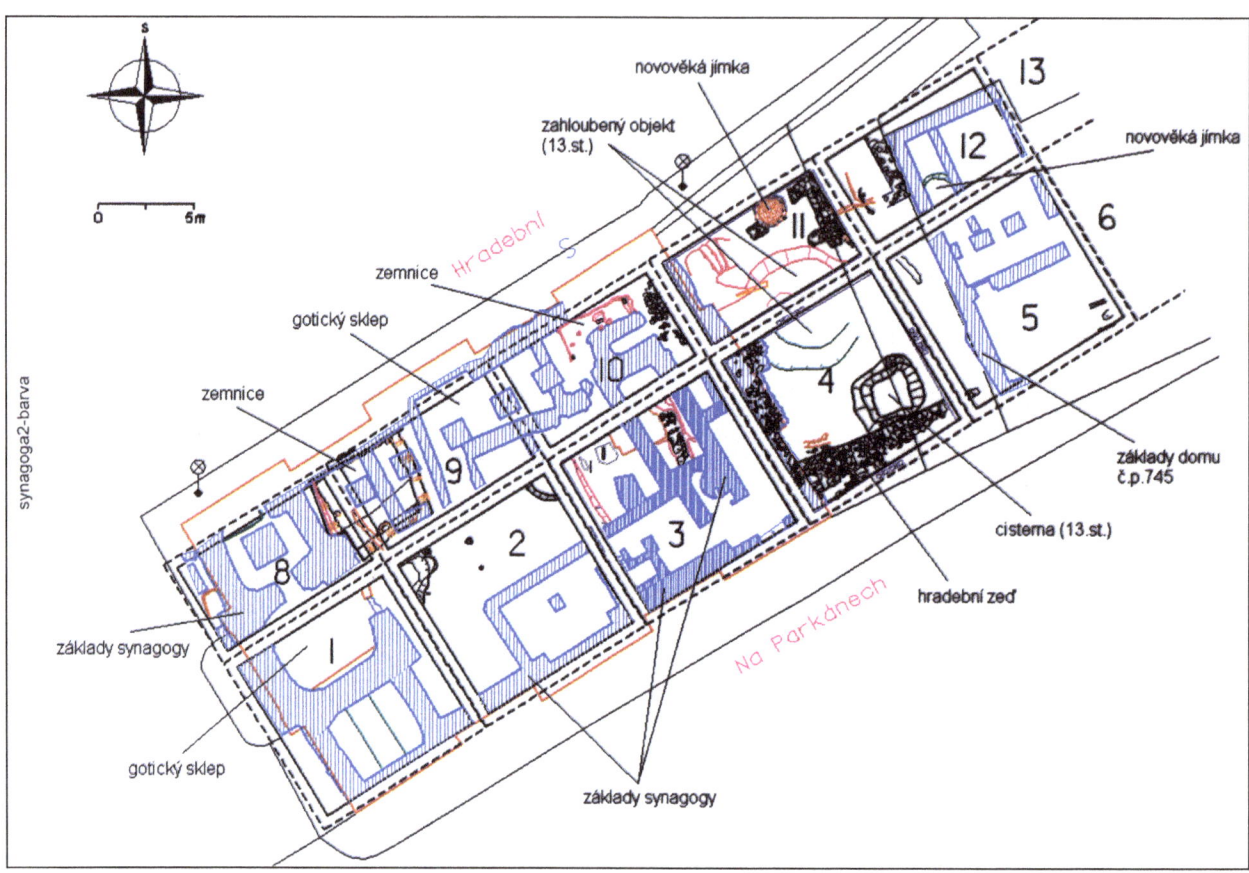

Fig. 44. Tábor, the synagogue: generally archaeologically excavated area (probes I-V and VIII-XII) with marking of the most significant objects

surveyed (with limited terrain possibilities) in the area of the synagogue uncovered by the excavation. It ensued from the general processing of the GPR and DEMP in 2004 that masonry relics or positions oh half caved-in cellars of extinct buildings are characterized by indications of the georadar (illustration in Fig. 43b) accompanied by mostly decreased quantities σ_{app} which probably indicate also combinations with larger accumulations of stony-sandy anthopogenous layer in these places.

The position of the destroyed synagogue sized ca 30 x 18 m in the SW part of the area is dominant on the area of the lower car park. It is characterized by a thicker outer wall which runs around the whole circumference of the building and also by a number of fractional walls and pertitions in the interior. On the basis of the interpretation, a position of a cellar by the NW margin part of the building cannot be excluded (Fig. 43).The SSE bearing wall of the synagogue could have been built also on relics of the city fortification. Indications of inhomogeneities of linear character were detected in this locality along the whole margin of the road "Na Parkánech".

Areal anomalies in the east and northeast section of the studied space sized ca 10 x 6 m and 10 x 7 m outside the sacral building itself, correspond proably to positions of both extinct houses – relics of masonry also in combination with insunk objects covered with thicker sandy-clayey superjacent layer. Comparison of results of geophysical works with uncovered situation of the synagogue and remains of settlement (stone, brick) built already from the 13th century, is presented as a whole in the Fig. 44.

Only one anomalous zone with linear orientation was identified by the GPR measuring on a smaller area of the upper car park. We assume manifestation of underground services here and we cannot exclude superposition with some other linear building structure, possibly also with parallel position of a nearby extinct building.

The fictive relief of a relatively articulate syenite weathered massif is located on both areas under the anthropogenous layer in the depth of ca 1.0-> 2.0 m (Fig. 43b).

Even in spite of complicated morphological conditions for complementary geophysical measuring in 2005 due to complicated stratigraphy and increased share of relics of uncovered masonry, shielding possible impact of other archaeological structures, four anomalous GPR zones marked A, B, C, D (see Fig. 44) indicate (with other indices like cavities) the most distinctive manifestations of narrower underground spaces – cellars, holes. In case

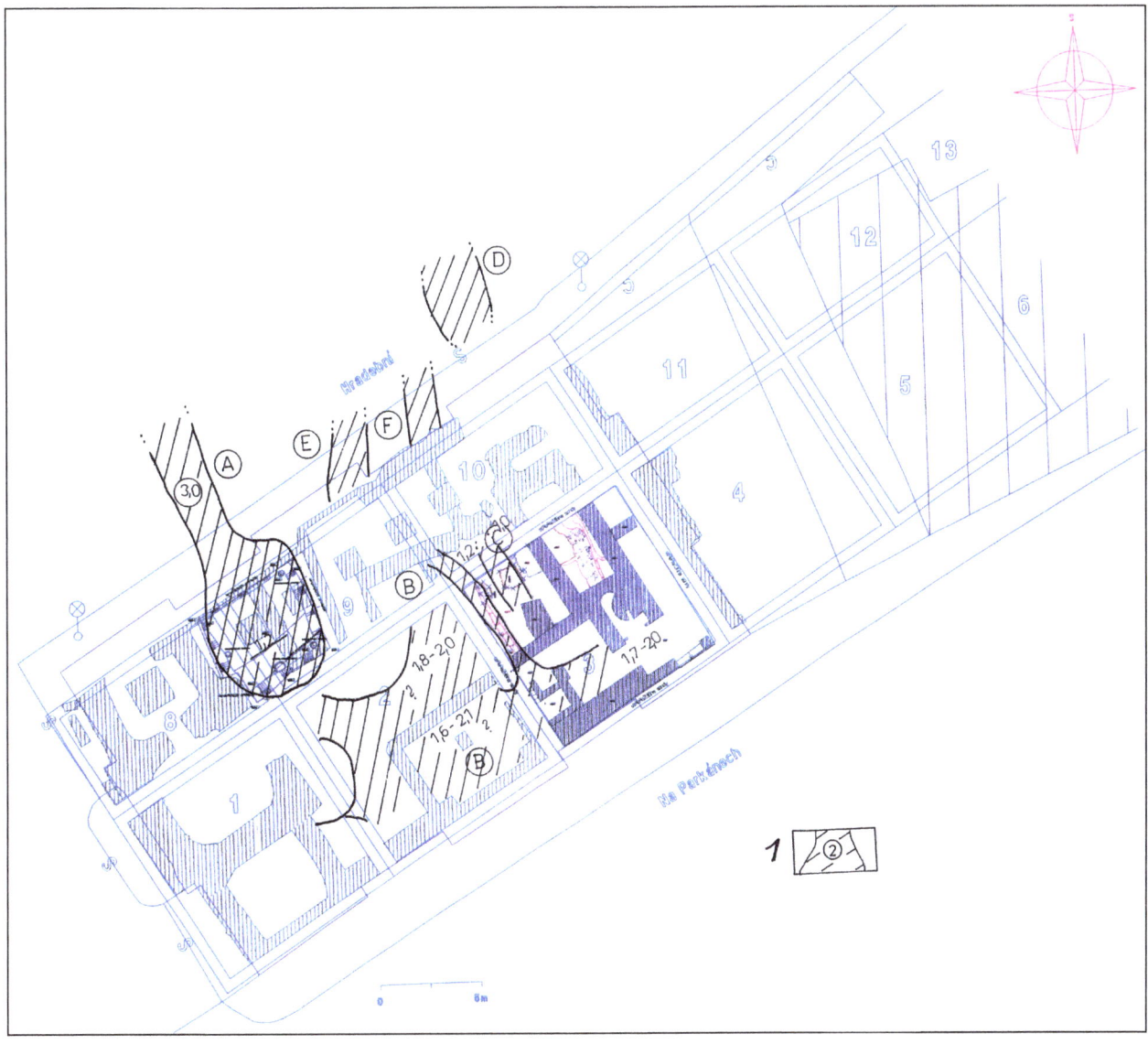

Fig. 45. Tábor, the synagogue: Results of the geophysical research of the Tábor syenite massif under archaeological probes, in which hollows were discovered in several places (probes III and IV) in otherwise compact firm base.
1- presumed underground spaces, or also lithological changes in the underlying syenite rocks
(depths of ceilings or of rock surfaces)

of other indications only inhomogeneities of rather local character are assumed – morphology of rocks, accumulations of stones, masonry relics etc.

Archaeological Excavation

Archaeology excavation of the Hussite Museum in Tábor (Hašek/Krajíc 2007, 88-89) at the studied area of the former car park, which is divided into a regular net 10 x 10 m (areas I – VI and VIII-XIII, Fig. 45) is one of the most significant terrain project performed on Tábor during the last decade. Some of the main results are e.g. localization of the Jewish synagogue from 1885, whose relics (outer stone wall, interior spaces, inner dividing wall, pillars etc. were detected by the probes I – IV and VIII-XI (Photo 72, 73). In the wider area of the building and its base, the research in 2005 brought also other information, e.g. not only about the double-layered settlement of the Tábor spur in the 13th century but it also enabled to determine these two settlement horizons more precisely as for their content and age.

The older medieval settlement on the Tábor spur is from the age that preceded the Premyslid development of the town of Hradiště and apparently can be identified with property interests and settlement activities of the Vítkovci. Its settlement demonstrations on the researched area are surprisingly intense. They include a dugout, tank and a large insunk feature with a staircase entrance. All the above mentioned objects disappeared by fire. It can be assumed that this situation reflects local dramatic events, when the Vítkovci did not want to give out the settlement to King Premysl Otakar II around the third quarter of the 13th century.

Photo 72. Tábor: Foundation walling of the extinct synagogue in probes I-III and VIII-X. View from the northeast (Photograph by R. Krajíc)

Photo 73. Tábor: Detailed view of the extinct synagogue masonry relics (Photograph by V. Hašek)

The "second" settlement of the Tábor spur in the 13th century followed probably after the end of the settlement of the Vítkovci, when the king started to build a city here in the 1270's, called Hradiště. He let built a castle in the southwest corner, and he let the locality enclosed by a city bailey. Traces have stayed after this activity in the form of buried older buildings and thick leveling courses of a characteristic structure (dark gray unctuous clay).

After the death of Premysl Otakar II, the city apparently did not further develop and disappeared for the most part. The city was newly founded after as much as 150 years from the initiative of the Hussites in 1420, when the city got the name Hradiště hory Tábor. Evidence of beginnings of the Hussite settlement at the studied area are not only in the form of movable finds (e.g. cultural layers in larger areas above the exinct tank) but also in settlement relics (see Fig. 45).

Evidence of house-building from the 15th century testify to change of the city after the Hussite wars, especially after its status improvement (it became one of royal cities in 1437). Especially insunk parts of houses have survived (cellars, sometimes with entrances into holes and a with brick arches from the Gothic-Renaissance period, apparently also parts of surface walls). It seems according to backfill of cellars that houses in this part of town disappeared during the 17th century, perhaps in connection with events of the the Thirty Year War.

Modern settlement on the studied area is further documented by economical-functional objects such as pits and sumps.

5. CONCLUSION

The monograph aims to show that efficiently chosen complex of nondestructive methods has became already an integral part of complexly interpreted archaeology excavation in the Czech Republic during several last years, despite certain complications. These methods are also bound with constructional-historical research, when solving various issues concerning localizing tombs, graves, crypts and masonry relics from older pulled-down features in interiors of both medieval and modern sacral buildings in the Czech Republic. In connection of geophysical methods and visual research and subsequent archaeological probing, or areal exposure situated into interest areas, which are identified according to the data obtained out of the abovementioned disciplines, this approach ensures the optimum solution of the required tasks, from the aspect of acquiring large amount of information (e.g. about the position, character, sizes and contents of individual objects), from the aspect of time and, last but not least, also from the economic aspect.

From the results of prospecting at individual sites up to now, the optimum method for localizing tombs and graves in interiors of churches appears to be the method of soil radar, or DEMP if necessary, with subsequent survey and documentation by camera system.

Determining of tombs and graves in interiors of churches by georadar and DEMP depends, according to the existing results, on the lithological character of the inhomogeneity, i.e. whether the object is walled-up or if it is just a simple grave, whether it is empty, caved etc. In the optimum case the tomb is walled up, hollow and of a larger size. In such case the reflections of electromagnetic waves are most distinctive and the object is very well detectable. When caved, the interpretation can be multivalent; it can be assigned, among others, to larger areal accumulations of stones, lithological changes in the backfill of the anthropogenous layer, relics of masonry from an older pulled-down building etc. Therefore other complementary information about the building is very useful here, such as possible positions of tombstones, location of these structures in the sacral building, routes of underground services etc.

The abovementioned complexity of geophysical conditions of the anthropogeneous layer, Quaternary cover or soil mantle and bedrock, with respect to their great lithofacial variability (clays, sands, loesses, stones, eluvium of basement rocks) and consequent variable characteristics of physical parameters of studied objects and the surrounding environment, often complexity of hydrogeological, or technical conditions – causes the necessity of wider choice of not only appropriate complex of prospecting methods, but also of processing and interpreting the measured data when solving a concrete task concerning both the overall localization of areal and linear structures and their subelements. When backfills of simple graves are of similar lithological composition (or compaction) as the surrounding environment, their interpretation is very problematic and localization often even impossible due to indistinct changes of physical parameters of soils.

We mentioned here only some most important results and possibilities of nondestructive methods in localizing various structures in sacral buildings in the Czech Republic. A number of partial tasks, which will have to be solved, lie ahead, such as detecting caved tombs and simple graves in interiors of churches etc.

It can be stated that the abovementioned nondestructive geophysical and visual archaeological research contributes to further, more detailed, learning about history of important church areas in the whole territory of the Czech Republic.

References

BARTH, V. et al. (1971): Geologické exkurse do Hornomoravského úvalu.- PřF UP Olomouc.

BEDNÁŘ, J., NOVOTNÝ, A., ŠVANCARA, J. (1980): Mikrogravimetrie a její uplatnění v archeologii.- Sborník referátů 1. celostátní konference "Aplikace geofyzikálních metod v archeologii a moderní metody terénního výzkumu a dokumentace". Petrov nad Desnou, 21-40.

BELCREDI, L. (1993): Archeologický výzkum kaple svaté Kateřiny a areálu kláštera Porta coeli v Předklášteří u Tišnova.- Archaeologia historica 18, 315-343.

BERNAT, J., HAŠEK, V. (1973): Příspěvek k průzkumu podzemních dutin v okolí hradu Veveří.- Zprávy ČSSA při ČSAV XV, seš. 1-3., 8-14.

BUKOVSKÝ, J. (1994): Královopolský kartouz.- Blok Brno.

CEJNKOVÁ, D., HAŠEK, V., LOSKOTOVÁ, I. (1999): Archeogeofyzikální prospekce kostela sv. Tomáše v Brně.- PV AÚB 40 (1997-1998), 422-428.

CEJNKOVÁ, D., LOSKOTOVÁ, I., MARÁZ, K. (2006): Die Erforschung der Grablegen der mährischen Luxemburger Jobst und Prokop in Brünn.- Publications de la Section Historique de l'Institut G.-D. de Luxembourg CXVIII, 591-611.

CHADRABA, R. et al. (1984): Dějiny českého výtvarného umění I, 1, I, 2.- Academia Praha.

CHAROUZ, J. (1995): Oživené dědictví. Premonstrátský Želiv včera a dnes.- Želiv.

CZUDEK, T. (1973): Geomorfologické členění ČR.- Stud. Geographica 23- NČSAV Praha.

ČERMÁK, M., HAŠEK, V., PEŠKA, J., VRÁNA, J. (2001): Geofyzikální prospekce a archeologický výzkum v kostele Zvěstování P. Marie ve Šternberku.- Ve službách archeologie 2, 11-24.

DOLEŽAL, J. (1998): Ante aream monasterii Sante Crencis-klášter v Doubravníku ve světle dosavadních výzkumů.- Pravěk NŘ 8, 321-349.

DOMANSKÝ, J. (1983): Ověření polohy krypty v základech kostela Nejsvětější Trojice v Praze.- Geofyzika a archeologie 1982, 129-131.

DOSTÁL, P., HAŠEK, V., TOMEŠEK, J. (2006): Zpráva o archeogeofyzikální prospekci na akci Třebíč-bazilika sv. Prokopa.- MS Geopek, spol. s r.o. Brno.

DROBILKOVÁ, P., HAŠEK, V., HLOBIL, I., ZAPLETAL, J., ZATLOUKAL, R. (2004): Nález sakrální stavby na Malém dvoře u dómu sv. Václava v Olomouci.- Ve službách archeologie V, 67-76.

DROZDOVÁ E. (2001): Antropologický rozbor kosterních pozůstatků připisovaných biskupovi Albertu I ze Šternberka, jeho synovci Petrovi ze Šternberka a jeho ženě Anně Rebece, rozené z Kravař.- Ve službách archeologie 2, 37-70.

DVORSKÝ, J. red. (1989): Dějiny českého výtvarného umění II, 1, II, 2.- Academia Praha.

FIŠER, B. (1920): Paměti Hradišťské.- Valašské Meziříčí.

FOLTÝN, D. et al. (2005): Encyklopedie moravských a slezských klášterů.- Libri Praha.

GRUNA, B., GRUNOVÁ, E. (2008): Topanov, Moravskokrumlovsko.- Urbania s.r.o.

HAŠEK, V. (1999): Methodology of Geophysical Research in Archaeology.- BAR Intern. Series 769. Oxford.

HAŠEK, V., KOVÁRNÍK, J. (1996): Geofyzika v moravské středověké archeologii.- Muzejní a vlastivědná práce 104, 2, 65-88.

HAŠEK, V., KOVÁRNÍK, J., TOMEŠEK, J. (2007): Zpráva o archeogeofyzikální prospekci na akci Znojmo, rotunda sv. Kateřiny.- MS Geopek, spol. s r.o. Brno.

HAŠEK, V., KOVÁRNÍK, J., TOMEŠEK, J.(2008): Zpráva o archeogeofyzikální prospekci na akci Znojmo, Louka- kostel Panny Marie a sv. Václava.- MS Geopek, spol. s r.o. Brno.

HAŠEK, V., KRAJÍC, R. (2007): Geofyzikální prospekce a archeologický výzkum prostoru bývalé židovské synagogy v Táboře.- Ve službách archeologie 1, 07, 75-99.

HAŠEK, V., MAŠTERA, L., TOMEŠEK, J. (2007): Zpráva o archeogeofyzikální prospekci na akci Olomouc – farní kostel sv. Mořice.- MS Geopek, spol. s.r.o. Brno.

HAŠEK, V., MAŠTERA, L., TOMEŠEK, J., UNGER, J. (2007): Zpráva o archeogeofyzikální prospekci na akci Tasov u Velkého Meziříčí – farní kostel sv. Petra a Pavla.- MS Geopek, s.r.o. Brno.

HAŠEK, V., MAŠTERA, L., ŠINDELÁŘ, J. and THOMOVÁ, Z. (2008): Non- destructive research of the church of Birth of the Virgin in Želiv by Humpolec.- Študijné zvesti AÚ SAV, 43, 5-22.

HAŠEK, V., MĚŘÍNSKÝ, Z. (1991): Geofyzikální metody v archeologii na Moravě.- MVS Brno.

HAŠEK, V., PEŠKA, J., UNGER, J. (2008): The contribution of nondestructive prospecting methods to the archaeological excavation of burial grounds in Moravia.- Študijné zvesti AUSAV 44, 5-49.

HAŠEK, V., PETERA, J. (2001): Geofyzikální prospekce a ověřovací sondáž podzemní chodby v Přepychách, okr. Rychnov nad Kněžnou.- Přehled výzkumů 43, 317-322.

HAŠEK, V., ŠINDELÁŘ, J., THOMOVÁ, Z., TOMEŠEK, J. (2008): Nedestruktivní průzkum kostela sv. Víta v Českém Krumlově.- Ve službách archeologie 1, 08, 55-63.

HAŠEK, V., ŠINDELÁŘ, J., UNGER, J., VAŠKOVÝCH, M. (v tisku): Nondestructive Methods od Research of Historic Sacral Buildings in the Czech Republic.- Archaeological Prospecting, Bradford.

HAŠEK, V., TOMEŠEK, J. (1999): Zpráva o archeogeofyzikální prospekci na akci Bruntálsko-kostely.- MS AÚ AV ČR Brno.

HAŠEK, V., TOMEŠEK, J. (1999a): Zpráva o geofyzikálním průzkumu na akci Přepychy – kostel, okr. Rychnov nad Kněžnou.- MS AÚ AVČR Brno.

HAŠEK, V., TOMEŠEK, J. (2001): Geofyzikální prospekce při archeologickém výzkumu hrobek a krypt.- Ve službách archeologie 2, 87-112.

HAŠEK, V., TOMEŠEK, J. (2001a): Zpráva o geofyzikální prospekci na akci Přepychy, okr. Rychnov nad Kněžnou – farní kostel, II. etapa.- MS AÚ AVČR Brno.

HAŠEK, V., TOMEŠEK, J. (2009): Zpráva o geofyzikální prospekci na akci Topanov, k. ú. Rybníky u Moravského Krumlova.- MS Geodrill, spol. s r.o. Brno.

HAŠEK, V., TOMEŠEK, J., UNGER, J. (2002): Zpráva o archeogeofyzikální prospekci na akci Tišnov II – Předklášteří, okr. Brno-venkov, Klášterní kostel.- MS AÚ AV ČR Brno.

HAŠEK, V., TOMEŠEK, J., UNGER, J. (2006): Zpráva o archeogeofyzikální prospekci na akci Blansko – kostel sv. Martina.- MS Geopek spol. s r.o. Brno.

HAŠEK, V., TOMEŠEK, J., ZATLOUKAL, R. (2003): Zpráva o archeogeofyzikální prospekci na akci Olomouc-Václavské náměstí a Dóm sv. Václava.- MS AÚ AV ČR Brno.

HAŠEK, V., UNGER, J. (1994): Archäogeophysikalische Prospektion der historischen unterirdischer Räume in der Tschechischen Republik.- Der Erdstall 20, 30-43.

HAŠEK, V., UNGER, J. (2001): Geofyzikální prospekce při archeologickém výzkumu hrobek a krypt.- Ve službách archeologie II, 87-111.

HAŠEK, V., UNGER, J. ZÁHORA, R. (1997): Archäologische Prospektion mit Georadar in Mähren.- Beiträge zur Mittelalterarchäologie in Österreich 13, 23-39.

HEROUT, J. (1961): Staletí kolem nás.- Orbis Praha.

HIMMELOVÁ, Z. (1993): Brno, bývalý klášter Voršilek, sonda na jižní straně kostela sv. Josefa. Popis archeologické situace.- MS ÚAPP Brno.

HLOBIL, I., TONER, M., HYHLÍK, V. (1992): Proboštský farní kostel sv. Mořice.- Velehrad.

HÖSCHL, V., PUFFR, M., BÍLÝ, M., KOVÁRNÍK, J. (1996): Geofyzikální průzkum románské rotundy sv. Kateřiny ve Znojmě.- Vesmír 75, No 8, 436-441.

JANÁČEK, J., LOUDA, J. (1988): České erby.- Praha.

KALISTA, Z. (1970): Česká barokní gotika a její žďárské ohnisko.- Brno.

KLÍMA, B. (1995): Znojemská rotunda ve světle archeologických výzkumů.- Brno.

KOMENDOVÁ, N. (2008): Kaple sv. Rocha 1680 Uherské Hradiště, k. ú. Jarošov. Standardní nedestruktivní stavebně-historický průzkum.- MS NPÚ Kroměříž.

KONEČNÝ, L. (2005): Románská rotunda ve Znojmě.- Brno.

KRSEK, I. et al. (1996): Umění baroka na Moravě a ve Slezsku.- Academia Praha.

KUDĚLKA, Z., KALINOVÁ, A., KONEČNÝ, L., SAMEK, B. (1982-83): Výzkum románské architektury na Moravě III.- Sborník prací Filosofické fakulty Brněnské university, F 26-27, 79-87.

KUTHAN, J. (1994): Česká architektura v době posledních Přemyslovců.- Tina Vimperk.

MERHAUTOVÁ, A., TŘEŠTÍK, D.(1984): Románské umění v Čechách a na Moravě.- Odeon.

MICHNA, P., POJSL, M. (1988): Románský palác na olomouckém hradě.- MVS Brno.

MOJŽÍŠ, V., PTÁČKOVÁ, M., BARTH, L. (2004): Nebovidy 1104.- Břeclav.

MRLINA, J. (1994): Brno – kostel sv. Josefa. Mikrogravimetrický průzkum I. etapa.- MS GÚ AV ČR Praha.

MRLINA, J. (2007): Mikrogravimetrický výzkum ve znojemské rotundě. Etapová zpráva-měření a zpracování dat.- MS GFÚ Praha.

OHAREK, V. (1923): Vlastivěda moravská. Tišnovský okres.- Brno.

PANGERL, M. (1865): Urkundenbuch des Cistercienserstiftes BMV zu Hohenfurth in Böhmen.- Fontes rerum austriacarum II, 23. Wien.

PAVELČÍK, J. (2000): Geofyzikální a archeologický průzkum kostela sv. Františka Xaverského v Uherském Hradišti.- Přehled výzkumů 41, 257-262.

PAVELČÍK, J. (2002): Výzkum v kostele Narození P. Marie v Šumicích u Uherského Brodu.- Ve službách archeologie IV, 101-110.

PETRŮ, V. (1898): Klášter Želiv.- Praha.

POCHE, E. et al. (1977): Umělecké památky Čech 1. A, T.- Academia Praha.

POCHE, E. et al. (1980): Umělecké památky Čech 3, P, Š.- Academia Praha.

RICHTER, V. (1959): Raněstředověká Olomouc. Stavební dějiny vzniku města.- Spisy FF Brněnské University.

SAMEK, B. (1994): Umělecké památky Moravy a Slezska A, I.- Academia Praha.

SAMEK, B. (1999): Umělecké památky Moravy a Slezska J, V.- Academia Praha.

ŠEBELA, L. et al. (1991): Objev hrobky opata Kryštofa Jiřího Malušky ve Křtinách.- Blansko.

UNGER, J. (1991): Předstihový archeologický výzkum pozůstatků kostela sv. Václava v Hustopečích, okr. Břeclav.- Informační a odborně metodický bulletin. Památkový ústav v Brně 62, 68.

UNGER, J. (2006): Pohřební ritus 1. až 20. století v Evropě z antropologicko-archeologické perspektivy.- Brno.

UNGER, J. (2008): Archeologie církevních památek na Moravě a ve Slezsku.- Slezská univerzita v Opavě.

VLČEK, P., SOMMER, P., FOLTÝN, D. (1997): Encyklopedie českých klášterů.- Libri Praha.

WIRTH, Z. (1908): Barokní gotika v Čechách v XVIII. a 1. polovici XIX. století.- Památky archeologické XXIII, 121-156.

WOZNICA, L. (1993): Zhodnocení průzkumných prací v jihovýchodním sektoru od rotundy sv. Kateřiny ve Znojmě.- MS Klubu přátel znojemské rotundy, pobočka Brno.

ZEZULA, M. (2001): Bohušov, okr. Bruntál.- Přehled výzkumů 42, 197-198.

www.ingramcontent.com/pod-product-compliance
Lightning Source LLC
Chambersburg PA
CBHW061545010526
44113CB00023B/2804